# CONTEMPORARY ISSUES
# IN BUSINESS ETHICS

---

*The Callista Wicklander Lectures*
*DePaul University*
*1991-2005*

---

Edited by

## Keith W. Krasemann
## Patricia H. Werhane

University Press of America,® Inc.
Lanham · Boulder · New York · Toronto · Oxford

**Copyright © 2006 by**
**University Press of America,® Inc.**
4501 Forbes Boulevard
Suite 200
Lanham, Maryland 20706
UPA Acquisitions Department (301) 459-3366

PO Box 317
Oxford
OX2 9RU, UK

Library of Congress Control Number: 2006921602
ISBN-13: 978-0-7618-3436-6 (paperback : alk. paper)
ISBN-10: 0-7618-3436-2 (paperback : alk. paper)

# Contents

# CONTEMPORARY ISSUES IN BUSINESS ETHICS

## THE CALLISTA WICKLANDER LECTURES

### FORWARD AND DEDICATION

Some years ago Callista P. Wicklander, a visionary and forthright Chicago resident, endowed the Wicklander Chair in Business Ethics at DePaul University. This was a one–year rotating chair given on a competitive basis to worthy scholars at DePaul. One of the requirements of the chair holder was to present a public lecture, and this collection represents in written form the content of those lectures.

Callista Pfeiffer Wicklander was born in Chicago to George Philip Pfeiffer and Mary C. Reynolds. Her father was a grandson of a Civil War veteran and, because of that heritage, Mrs. Wicklander became a member of the Daughters of Union Veterans.

Mrs. Wicklander attended Senn High School and later worked at Rotary International, where she met her husband, Raymond Wicklander, Sr, who was beginning his printer business, Wicklander Printing Corporation. They were married in 1935 and had six sons–Raymond Jr., Philip, Dale (deceased as an infant), Robert, James, and Douglas.

The family first settled in Oak Park in 1944 where Mrs. Wicklander became active in Alter & Rosary Society. Later they moved to Riverside Illinois where she lived until 1991. Mr. Wicklander died in 1985 and Mrs. Wicklander moved to the Bethlehem Woods Retirement Center until she died on May 4, 2005.

Mrs. Wicklander served as Secretary and Treasurer of the Wicklander Printing Corporation for many years. With her husband they established the Wicklander Foundation and Mrs. Wicklander served as its president for 20 years. She also served as a Trustee at Fenwick High School and was the first woman to be named to Fenwick's Hall of Fame in 1995. She is Lady Grand Cross of the Equestrian Order of the Holy Sepulchre of Jerusalem and was awarded the Palm of Jerusalem for her distinctive contributions to the Order. She was also Dame Grand Cross of the Equestrian Order of St. Lazarus of Jerusalem. She was a Life member of the Art Institute of Chicago, and served as a founding member and President of the DePaul University Women's Board until 1987. Still, despite that fact that Mrs. Wicklander was active in the Wicklander business, her community, and in the Church, her family was always her primary focus.

Callista Wicklander's dedication to her family, her community, and to deeply held religious values evidences her clear sense of right and wrong and her commitment to improve our society. Today because of her vision, her strong values orientation, and her generosity the Wicklander Chair is a permanent funded position at DePaul University. We dedicate this volume to her wisdom and to her memory.

# ACKNOWLEDGEMENTS

This volume was made possible by the generous support of the Wicklander family and the Institute for Business and Professional Ethics which funded part of the publication. We especially want to thank the Board of the Institute for their continuing support and encouragement of this series, and DePaul's College of Liberal Arts and Sciences and the College of Commerce for their financial underwriting of the Institute and its projects.

The substance of the volume, the essays, are the result of work by the Wicklander Chairs whose contributions make up the volume. We want to thank all of them for writing and revising these important and timely essays for this particular collection.

We also want to thank Michele Hoffman, the administrative assistant of the Institute for Business and Professional Ethics, and Karyin Boulom for her help in preparing the book.

# Introductory Essay:
# Promoting Business and Professional Ethics to New Generations of Civic and Business Leaders

## Keith W. Krasemann

> *The fundamental issues in today's world are ethical. Leadership in this world requires courage, commitment, and a fierce realism to address these challenges head on. Furthermore, we need vision–the capacity to have dreams. Authentic leadership is to repeat the story of creation: to create meaning out of chaos.*
>
> *– Peter Koestenbaum*

The 21st century has brought unprecedented global change. Radical, rapid and revolutionary change now structures the environment within which leadership, ethics, values and human creativity will dynamically interact. Such a world will be characterized by increased complexity, confusion and chaos, uncertainty and novelty. Already this change has given rise to a host of new challenges with which businesses and corporations must deal: international competition, multicultural perspectives, new technologies, demands for higher quality products and services, employee motivation, a diverse knowledge-based workforce and ethical issues. How corporations respond to these new challenges will determine, on the one hand, their success and, on the other hand, their survival.

But such change also grants numerous opportunities to make business better. New challenges for leadership provide possibilities to re-think and reconceptualize the ways in which business is conducted. Given the new global reality of rapid change and the increasingly dynamic human condition the task of promoting business and professional ethics to new generations of civic and business leaders must be visionary–not reactive. How will ethical opportunities be managed? What, for example, will it mean to be an ethical organization and what will the good corporation of the 21st century look like? What will it mean to be a 21st century professional? What ethical challenges might reasonably be anticipated? What ethical skills will be needed by succeeding generations of professionals? How might individuals responsibly participate in the creation of an ethical world and an ethical corporate culture? How, in short, can we equip future civic and business leaders with both the moral understanding and skillful means to meet the ethical challenges of the 21st century?

The Wicklander Chair for Business and Professional Ethics was established in 1991 by Callista P. Wicklander. The purpose of the Wicklander Chair is to promote and further the teaching of business and professional ethics to new generations of civic and business leaders. For a decade the Chair rotated among faculty members in various departments and schools–philosophy, religious studies, business and management, the College of Law, and the School for New Learning. Rotating the Chair annually allowed for a concentration on ethics in different fields and each year the outgoing chair–holder is the featured presenter at the Wicklander Colloquium.

The Colloquium provides a forum for reflection and dialogue about the study and practice of business and professional ethics. In 2003, Patricia H. Werhane accepted the position as full–time Chair and Director of the Institute for Business Ethics. The dual appointment linked the Wicklander Chair to a group of ethically committed leaders within the greater Chicagoland business community. The next year, as a result of Mrs. Wicklander's generous giving, Wicklander Fellows were added to continue the research and teaching of business and professional ethics. This volume is an edited collection of the presentations from the Wicklander Colloquiums. The essays in this volume are arranged in the order that the Wicklander Lectures were delivered and many of the selections retain the spirit, force and freshness of the original live presentation. This thoughtful collection of essays by experienced professors from six different fields opens a dialogue that will be of tremendous importance to the teaching and practice of business and professional ethics in the 21st century.

On the subject of teaching professional ethics Paul Camenisch begins with questions about where, why and how such courses are to be taught. However, these questions lead to further questions concerning who will teach said courses and what will be taught. In "Teaching Professional Ethics: Where, Why and How?" Camenisch identifies three varied settings in which three quite different groups teach and write about professional ethics–the university or academic setting; the church/parish/congregation or religious setting; and the business or professional group or association–the practitioners setting. Camenisch invites the reader to consider whether the teaching of professional ethics is setting–dependent in contrast to mathematics, for example, which would be setting independent. If one assumes that the teaching of professional ethics is setting–dependent, then the setting has profound implications with respect to the purpose, the methods, the teachers and the content of such courses.

In all three settings the teaching of ethics will employ a normative/descriptive distinction–a distinction that separates values and facts. Furthermore, promoting business and professional ethics to new generations of civic and business leaders is a goal found in all three settings and, in that sense, each setting has a normative component to its teaching. Achieving optimal effectiveness in the teaching of professional ethics, for Camenisch, is a function of the extent that each setting is willing to stretch towards the descriptive end of the spectrum.

The university has been entrusted to communicate a particular cultural heritage to future generations. Some universities such as DePaul publically declare a commitment to fundamental values that provides both a particular identity and proclaims a distinctive mission. For the unique setting of the university Camenisch offers two key insights: First, in transmitting a cultural heritage that includes both moral values and facts the university must employ teaching that retains a critical edge that respects the autonomy of the student. Second, that the explicit value commitment of the university not be urged upon students in the classroom. Camenisch believes that universities will be most effective and students will be better served when institutional values and commitments are embodied in campus life or in special classes designated and advertised for that purpose.

The religious setting, by definition, will be normative. Various religious settings will be concerned to promote their own worldviews and values by imparting these values to and within their particular moral communities. But, in an increasingly diverse, multi–cultural and rapidly changing world a religious community that speaks solely from its own internal normative position and does not venture towards the descriptive end of the spectrum will, according to Camenisch, "condemn itself to irrelevance." Such traditions, Camenisch says, must engage a larger world and in so doing, engage their own tradition in order to be effective.

In the business corporation/professional association setting it has become standard practice to include core values as a part of corporate mission statements and to produce codes of business/professional conduct. These declarations allow (and, in some cases, require) its members to be knowledgeable about the kind of conduct that will be encouraged or expected. Furthermore, such open declarations encourage moral conversations in the workplace and should not, therefore, be seen as an imposition of values. However, Camenisch warns of conflicts of interest that often occur in this setting because of competing interests of profit and economic gain.

However, Dennis McCann cites difficulties with Camenisch's view and insists that if the undergraduate teaching of business ethics courses is to be effective, then such courses must be oriented to the lived experience of managers within the corporate settings and not to the needs of academicians wishing to demonstrate the applicability of their own scholarly disciplines. In "Can Business Ethics Be Taught?" McCann, in the tradition of Socrates, answers the above question negatively, if such teaching implies imparting moral knowledge or communicating a moral sensibility where none existed before. But, if it means provoking a recollection of one's moral sensibilities or clarifying moral values that exist in the organizational structure in a way that the force of that insight contributes to mastering new social situations, then his answer is "Yes." If a course on business ethics is to be effective, its "truths" must be appropriate to the realities of the moral environment that one is about to enter.

McCann takes the position that the primary setting for learning and teaching business ethics is the modern corporation itself. He notes that leading corporations have made enormous strides in internalizing business ethics in their organizations and that good ethics is understood to go hand–in–hand with good business. Thus, the organizational structure of modern corporations already embodies certain moral values that contribute to the common good. Viewed in this light, goals of teaching business ethics include a clarification of the values already embedded within the organization and challenges to reach higher standards and to strive for continuous improvement based on core values. If managers are to be educators, then, McCann suggests, educators should structure the learning environment as if they were managers.

In "Corporate Social Responsibility in a Global Economy," Brother Leo Ryan draws from his life's work in management and business ethics and shares the six pillars of his management philosophy. For Brother Leo, business is a public trust, a "morally serious calling," a true vocation. As both an economic and social enterprise business presumes moral conduct. As a human organization business is governed by accepted standards of common morality that include: truthfulness, honesty, promise keeping, mutual aid, non–malevolence, and respect for both persons and property. Management, Brother Leo tells us, is an art and using increasingly codified principles and practices seeks the status as a profession. Decision–making will involve making moral choices and all corporate boards must make moral choices. Business renewal in a global economy will require inspired leadership, adaptability innovation and ethical insights.

Brother Leo addresses the current moral condition of global business by combining his six management pillars with four religious virtues and four secular virtues. Sound management principles combined with deep values, he believes, will result in responsible moral decisions in business. Always an optimist, Brother Leo reverses the classic phrase of Charles Dickens as follows: "It was the worst times; it was the best of times." The high profile corporate moral missteps that "taint and tarnish" all business give us new opportunities to re–examine accounting practices, management decision–making and corporate governance in ways that will promote ethics and corporate social responsibility in our national and global economy.

In both ethics and law impartiality has long been seen as a key to making good judgments. But as human beings with points of view and preferences, likes and dislikes, feelings, beliefs and varying degrees of knowledge one wonders how it is possible to responsibly and effectively approach the ideal of impartiality. Jeffrey Shaman takes up the question of impartiality as it relates to judges in a way that critically challenges long standing assumptions about judicial impartiality and lays out criteria that will help judges to be faithful to the law and maintain professional competence in it. His essay "The Impartial Judge: Detachment or Passion?" utilizes principles and precedents from law, standards of professional conduct, biography and personal anecdotes and observations to produce an "embodied criteria" for making good judgments.

The Code of Judicial Conduct sets up ideals and specifies rules of conduct for judges and applies both to off–the–bench and on–the–bench conduct.   Thus, judges extrajudicial activities should be restricted.   However, some believe that the Code goes too far in the direction of isolating judges from the rest of society and feel that improved laws and a better society are directly related to the participation of judges in public discourse.   The embodiment of the disinterested and detached judge is Oliver Wendell Holmes, Jr. and Justice Benjamin Cardozo represents the ideal of judicial passion.   Navigating between the extremes of the above embodied ideals, Shaman moves across the legal landscape critically balancing the obligation to follow the law and need to keep an open mind but avoid bias and prejudice.   Judgment cannot be reduced to a detached mechanical process but must issue forth from one who is knowledgeable of the law and legal precedent, equipped with refined interpretative skills and is both intellectually and emotional engaged.

In "How to Read a Contract: From Self–Interest to Fairness and Decency" Kenneth Alpern reminds us that the "aim of the Wicklander Chair is to promote excellence in the teaching of ethics in the professions." To that end professor Alpern provides a framework and a rationale for structuring a course in professional ethics that incorporates Liberal Studies Program skills such as reading, writing, and speaking, skills of cogency, analysis, interpretation, critical reflection, imagination, and judgment. And, as a philosophy course, it should include an understanding of moral theory and moral concepts. Since the concern of such a course is business practice, the said course should illuminate the ethical dimensions of business practice in areas including finance accounting, marketing, and advertising. Broader social contexts and considerations of justice will be part of understanding applied ethics.

Alpern also points out the importance of an expanded vision, that is, "to take them out of Chicago." Because of the rapidly expanding realities of a global economy it is imperative that courses address the international context of business. But, he also sees the purpose of an expanded vision to foster "a frame of mind that probes beyond clichés, slogans, and platitudes, that probes beyond what is normally taken for granted..." Finally, Alpern holds an aim of a course in business ethics is "to make them moral" in that students have increased moral sensitivity to important issues and a more ethical and informed view about their lives.

Although he is convinced of the intrinsic value of abstract conceptual study in ethics, nevertheless, Alpern employs active and critical learning that starts from particular problems and concrete situations.

He begins his teaching demonstration by having students read an apartment lease and proceeds to lead them to a consideration of principles of fairness and justice. In addition, he shows the inevitability of areas of critical indeterminacy where the exercise of judgment, practical wisdom and decency are necessary in order to live well.

Evil has long been a fundamental concern for ethics. Traditionally evil has been linked with the deep structures of human freedom and becomes manifest as a result of certain choices. How do we think about evil in the workplace? In our civic institutions? In multinational corporations?

Many people, it seems, are uncomfortable using the term. Although there is no paucity of examples of wrongdoing, illegal practices and harmful acts that occur in business, these behaviors are described in ways that fall short of being termed "evil." Is the term itself is too hard or is the reality toward which it points too difficult to face or accept? Perhaps others feel that they do not understand its meaning or depth sufficiently to apply the term.

Nevertheless there seem to be clear examples of evil that cannot be ignored. Is not poverty evil? Is it not evil to control, manipulate, debase and abuse other human beings? And is it not evil to destroy people morally and to break people physically, emotionally and financially? Does not evil deny the value of another's inwardness? Is it not evil to crush the dignity of another or to prevent a man or woman from reaching their full potential? Ethically evil must be taken seriously.

In "What is Evil?", Ms Daryl Koehn cautiously and critically returns the concept of evil to the workplace. First, Koehn looks at one variant of the criminological model that is commonly used in analyzing evil in the workplace. According to this model, the acts of vicious individuals take the form of betrayal. Evil, on this view, lies within the individual and arises because of low self–control and a defective self–narrative. Koehn points out that the criminological model is one–dimensional and rests on three uncritically held assumptions; namely, that evil is resident primarily in the individual, that evil acts are those that deviate from the norm and that the problem of evil is a problem of self–control. Because it is one–dimensional and since it rests on problematic assumptions, the criminological view of evil is not, in itself, adequate to account for evil in the workplace. In order to open our understanding of the concept of evil Koehn turns to other disciplines to gain deeper, better and more comprehensive insights. Specifically she explores understandings of evil drawn from novelists Henry James and Jim Thompson. In addition, Koehn examines insights on evil from the writings of theologian Martin Buber.

1

8        Keith W. Krasemann

Henry James does not define evil–he shows us evil at work. In his novella, *The Turn of the Screw*, evil is disclosed as "dreadful portentousness." It resides in both the individual and the social environment. In the work of Jim Thompson, evil emerges as labeling that impedes development. Consider cases where labeling annihilates personhood by reducing individuals to stereotypes, caricatures, or things or where language locks people into modes of self–definition that does not permit their soul to grow. And for Buber, evil is loosing one's soul in omni–possibility such that it no longer takes its bearings from reality. In the ocean of imagined omni–possibility, evil "stems primarily from indecision."

Finally, with respect to the question concerning the nature of evil Koehn identifies three common threads: evil is a human phenomenon, evil resides in the mode of representation more than in the act or the action's effects and evil resides in both individuals and the community at large when they hold a false self–image to be a certain truth.

In "Technology and Ethics: Privacy in the Workplace," Laura Hartman addresses the ethics of workplace privacy in relation to technological advancement that is driven by the desire for information and the relative ease of its collection. In the light of new technologies the ethical balance between an employee's right to privacy and an employer's need for information with which to manage the workplace must be reassessed. For example, should the technological ability to find something out make it relevant? Should the employer find out information about employees just because he or she can? In what ways do the dynamics of faceless communication impact workplace relationships and decision–making? What are the implications of excessive technological controls on employees? How does controlling information about persons effect their autonomy?

In the 21st century the line between personal and professional lives is blurred. Personal business is and, at times, must be carried out in the workplace and work is often done at home. Furthermore, technology has changed the ways people work and is reshaping our understanding about what the whole idea of workplace means. And, new technologies make it easier for employers to monitor employees every act. Given that both employees and employers have legitimate rights: the right to privacy, on the one hand, and the right to manage the workplace, how in the light of awesome technological advancement are these rights to be balanced?

Hartman is passionate about striking the morally appropriate balance of legitimate interests in the workplace and she is thorough in her analysis of the ethical issues. She provides the reader with a clear framework for ethical decision–making, raises important questions, cites relevant facts, accesses the limitations of legal remedies and reaffirms our deepest hopes that resolution to these vital questions will be disclosed in a call for ethics. Hartman believes resolution is possible if one follows an integrity/accountability approach. Such an approach respects the interests of the employee in ways that insure individual autonomy and personal space and, at the same time, protects the interest of the employer to effectively but ethically supervise employees work.

We all lead storied lives. By way of storytelling, we enter into a communally articulated narrative and a shared humanity. Through the hearing and telling of stories, we are able to tell our own uniquely personal story; and, in fact, become the story we tell. In the telling and recounting of autobiographical stories key themes that shape and guide our lives emerge. Critical reflection on these stories and their themes leads to self–understanding, personal transformation, and an increased vision concerning human possibilities.

In "The Ethics of Everyday Life: Social Class and Moral Character in Woman's Narrative," Frieda Kerner Furman draws from the rich and varied experiences of three women separated by ethnicity, religion, sexual orientation and nationality to tap the potential of storytelling for transversing boundaries, building bridges, making inroads, and closing the gaps between seemingly disparate communities and cultures. By way of reflection on the continuing in–depth conversations between the three women, Furman is able to locate profound commonality, while at the same time respecting differences that are conditioned by diverse backgrounds. Moreover, in the concrete embodied experiences of these women, expressed in autobiographical narrative, the moral dimensions of their lived experiences, what professor Furman calls the "ethics of everyday life," emerges. It is through the narratives that organize lived experience that one is able to locate, not ethical abstractions, but the "living and breathing sources of moral character, moral predisposition and moral action."

In "Lying and Lawyering: An Honest Perspective," Steven Resnicoff tells us that lying pervasively affects the practice of law. To address the problem of "lying and lawyering" Resnicoff structures his remarks by discussing the following propositions and questions:

1. As a general rule, lying is morally wrong.
2. Nevertheless, there are times when lying may not only be morally correct but may be morally mandated.

3. Some legal ethics rules seem morally wrong. They allow some deceptions that are arguably NOT justified while forbidding others that ARE justified.
4. The actual practices of attorneys are in many ways even worse than those prescribed by the rules.
5. What explains the nature of the rules and actual attorney practices?
6. What, if anything ought to be done?

Professor Resnicoff calls attention to the seriousness of lying, brings clarity to issues within the legal profession and proposes possible ways to address the problems of lying in the law school and in the legal profession.

According to Resnicoff's expansive definition, lying "includes any verbal action, or inaction, that is intended either to make it more likely that someone *believe* something that is *not* true or more likely that someone *disbelieve* something that *is* true." In other words, the practice of lying is always an assault on the truth and truth is the central notion that governs both the personal and communal life of individuals. He further points out that lying is the like stealing from the mind of another and the practice of lying has a "morally corrosive effect on the soul of the liar himself." Resnicoff's moral insights on lying have important implications for business and civic leaders and, thus, the applicability of his work extends beyond the legal profession.

There are deep spiritual traditions that link spirituality and work. Additionally, there is a rapidly growing popular interest in workplace spirituality. In "Spirituality in the Workplace: Individuals and Organizational Transformation," Michael Skelley attempts to draw out key features concerning the relationship between spirituality and the workplace that will promote individual, organizational, and societal transformation. Moreover, Skelley believes that the technological, organizational, economic, and social structures in which work is now carried out create a crisis in meaning and perpetuate disparate new levels of injustice, violence, and environmental destruction. Beginning with a definition of spirituality and then looking at spiritualities of the workplace, spiritualities for the workplace and spiritualities in the workplace, Skelley explores ways in which authentic spirituality can address the present crisis of work.

There are countless instances of ethical failure and moral missteps that can be attributed to business leaders and managers. Recent examples of ethical wrongdoing in corporate settings can be seen in the highly publicized scandals that occurred at Enron, Arthur Anderson, Tyco, Worldcom, Imclone and Adelphia, to name a few. A disillusioned public asks what kind of person would do something like that and quickly attribute such actions to arrogance, selfishness and greed on the part of corporate leaders. Undoubtedly the popular conclusion is true in some cases, but there are other factors that help us better understand moral mistakes committed by business leaders.

In many cases bad things have been done by good people. How is this possible? How is it that people who consider themselves ethical, care for their families, display a sense of fairness to their friends, and contribute to their communities, behave unethically in their business affairs? In "Why Do Good People Do Bad Things? The Challenge of Business Ethics and Corporate Leadership" Patricia Werhane undertakes a comprehensive analysis of a problem that people have been debating since the time of Aristotle: "Why is it that good people engage in questionable behavior and even repeat their mistakes?" In constructing this analysis Werhane, in effect, outlines, a framework for creating a strategic moral vision for organizations. Werhane's view is strategic because it incorporates comprehensive, long–term systems–thinking and her analysis is visionary because it creatively taps the insights of the moral imagination. Among the factors that contribute to moral mistakes Werhane includes self–interested greed, retarded moral development, confusion of legal and moral demands, possible conflicts of interest between professional and institutional commitments, conflicts of role responsibilities, and/or the identification of moral responsibility with role responsibility. She concludes that a careful analysis of the above factors are helpful in pinpointing moral weakness in corporate decision–making. However, such analysis does not successfully account for the problem of repeated moral errors.

The Chinese have a saying that speaks to the need for an alternative vantage point: "I cannot see the true face of Mount Lu because I am standing on top of it." Likewise, we do not really see our own culture or morality because we are too close to it. In order to see ourselves clearly and better evaluate both the strengths and weaknesses of our own point of view an experience with the life–world of "the Other" provides a mirror. In "'It's Business; We're Soldiers' *The Sopranos*, Liberal Business Ethics and this American Thing of Ours" H. Peter Steeves draws examples from a successful T.V. series about a fictional mafia family, the Soprano's, to look at the distinction between liberalism and communitarianism and to consider differences between rights–bearing individuals and role–bearing persons.

According to Steeves, Tony Soprano's identity and, hence, sense of self and values are created within the community in which he was raised. His identity is constituted by many narrative threads. As a relational–self "[h]e *is* his roles and relationships–father, husband, lover, Don, friend, and executioner." He is a part of a particular group and understands himself only in relation to Others. Thus, his choices will always be tied to the community and, in this sense, Tony is a communitarian.

Liberalism, in contrast, is a philosophy based on the radical isolation of the individual. Societies are made up of atomistic, rights–bearing individuals coordinated by way of objective impersonal principles and laws. This particular concept of an individual and view of self lies at the foundation of capitalism, contemporary democracy, the U.S. Bill of Rights, and Western systems of justice and education. Liberal models structure business ethics in America and in Liberal Democratic States. It also underlies the notion of universal human rights.

Steeves guides us through narrative episodes in the life of Tony Soprano in a way that illuminates moral situations that occur in liberal business ethics. From a liberal point of view Tony stands condemned for the personal violence he perpetrates and the pain he causes others. Yet, the liberal point of view fails to see the many ways in which it impersonally and bureaucratically perpetuates violence and causes pain in similar situations. Hence, Liberalism and Communitarianism are metaphorical mirrors that allow each perspective to see itself. Furthermore, both points of view have strengths that complement the weaknesses of the other.

In "Tissue Banking: Disclosure, Informed Consent, and the Rule of Law" Michele Goodwin critically examines a host of ethical, legal, moral and political issues that are emerging as a result of the accelerated growth in biotechnology and medical science with respect to new uses for human tissue and the commercial enterprise of body trading. Science insists that the utilization of human bodies for research and reprocessing for transplants is necessary for the advancement of biotechnology and saving lives. But, the rapid progress in biotechnology continues to outpace regulation and the public lacks both awareness and understanding about a global industry of body trading: body part buying, selling, re–trading and transplanting. Altruistic donors are often exploited due to ignorance and relatives are dumbfounded and outraged to learn that their loved ones are now products in the highly profitable global business of tissue commerce.

Professor Goodwin "scrutinizes the clandestine nature of the commercial body part trading industry, including the surreptitious nature of body part procurement and the risks associated with their products." She concludes that there is a need for better regulation and public disclosure about body trading. To do this a common lexicon must be developed to better understand both the legal and social issues involved in determining the status of cadaveric body parts. Finally, Goodwin holds that tissue manufacturers have a moral responsibility to place healthy tissues on the market and that strict liability is an appropriate remedy for patients injured because of manufacturer negligence.

For over three decades much has been done to promote good business and professional ethics. The academy has developed a new field of academic teaching, research, publications, associations and conferences to address important issues in the area of business and professional ethics. Corporations have spent huge sums of money to develop legal guidelines, hire compliance officers, draft ethics codes and initiate ethics training programs. Core values have become an important part of corporate mission statements. Ethical investing is an emerging financial trend. Despite the highly publicized ethical problems in business, it is generally recognized that good ethics translates into good business.

However, past and current attempts to address ethical issues that arise in business and the professions do not go for enough because they concentrate primarily on traditional or conventional morality. There is, of course, much to be said in favor of traditional or conventional morality. In the first place, it stands in opposition to a pre–conventional morality where self–interest and power are the primary considerations in decision–making. In the second place, conventional morality offers reliable guidance in moral decision–making in a wide–range of instances. Furthermore, it articulates basic rights and responsibilities and provides moral frameworks within which both individual ethics and the ethics of the group are understood. But, the world is becoming increasingly non–traditional and more non–conventional.

Radical, rapid change, new technologies and globalization have created novel circumstances and produced more complex situations in which moral decision–making occurs. Although most ethical principles are clear, the application of these principles to new and complicated cases is often far from clear. Traditional conceptions of morality alone do not provide adequate guidelines for decision–makers in a variety of situations that require choice. 21st century professionals and business and civic leaders will find themselves in increasingly complex and confusing situations that impose conflicting demands upon them. In order to effectually engage ethical reasoning in dynamic business contexts, well–intentioned individuals must be equipped with the appropriate intellectual "tools" needed for reasoning about difficult moral dilemmas in a responsible and insightful manner.

Finally, ethical leadership in business and civic organizations will be a priority for successful organizations in the rapidly changing, dynamic New Economy. Such leadership will be more inclusive and will require expanded skill sets in order to properly balance two imperatives of the new century: business results and human values. A critical mass of ethically savvy leaders will be the key to creating a meaningful, sustainable and effective culture of integrity within organizations. The Wicklander Lectures have opened a dialogue that will help articulate a coherent moral vision for the 21st century and help future business and civic leaders meet the difficult ethical challenges ahead.

# 1

# Teaching Professional Ethics: Where, Why and How?

## Paul F. Camenisch

If one is honor bound to undertake all that a title suggests, then [Dennis]* McCann and I are rash indeed to travel under this banner. But for an occasion such as this, titles often indicate a territory in which we will tarry a while together, without suggesting that we will exhaust it during our sojourn. For clearly there is no way to exhaust this topic this afternoon. But perhaps a decent beginning will be enough, for this chair in professional ethics is also at its beginning, and the generosity of the Wicklanders in endowing it promises DePaul and future chair holders an indefinite future for pursuing this important business.

* Editor's note: Paul Camenisch and Dennis McCann delivered their Wicklander Lectures at the same Wicklander Colloquium. Camenisch was the first speaker.

Many people in the field of applied ethics move with considerable ease among three quite different settings or address three quite different groups as they teach and write about business and professional ethics–the university or academic setting; the church/parish/congregation or religious setting; and the business or professional group or association–the practitioners' setting. They often move or change audiences not only with ease, but with eagerness once they discover how much better the corporation or professional association usually pays.

But the differences among these three as settings for professional ethics need to be taken seriously. Math or English taught in any of these three settings would seem to be untouched by the setting itself. Good computation and punctuation would seem not to be setting–dependent. 'Two' and 'four' and 'square root' have certain meanings, and semi–colons and question marks have certain uses that might change in different mathematical or linguistic systems. But those changes are not dictated by the institutional settings in which we speak about them.

But what about professional ethics? Is it also setting independent? In order to see why the situation is not so simple with professional ethics, we need to add another question to our already too large agenda, the 'what' of professional ethics. To begin with the 'where,' 'why,' and 'how' of teaching professional ethics assumes that we all agree on the 'what' of professional ethics. But it is not at all self–evident that we do. Thus we need to take a moment to look at that 'what.'

Now part of our reason for including the 'where' in the title was our awareness that the business and professional ethics taught in our three different settings may vary, may in fact, quite *legitimately* vary in its content and motivation.

So while acknowledging the possibility of such setting–dependent variation, let me begin by looking at the 'what' of business and professional ethics in the academic setting. That is, after all, where we and this chair are located. Furthermore, if time permitted, I think I could offer more substantive reasons for taking this as the appropriate starting point, some of which should become evident in the following comments.

So what, from the perspective of the academic setting, should we teach when we teach professional ethics? Many seem to assume that just as studying piano is intended to produce piano players, so studying professional ethics is intended to produce ethical professionals. Sometimes this expectation, or its disappointment, is expressed quite bluntly. Arjay Miller, former dean of the Stanford Business School, was cited some time back as having observed that "There are a lot of people in jail today who have passed ethics courses" [PFC, *JHE*, 8, p.6].

In a similar vein, in 1976 an issue of the *CPA Letter* told of a certified public accountant disciplined by his professional association, the AICPA, for "soliciting engagements by letter and . . . conduct[ing] a practice under a 'fictitious name'". His 'sentence' was "to take a course in professional ethics" [PFC, *JHE*, 5, p. 274].

Now we teachers of such courses often become uneasy when such expectations surface, at least when they are stated as explicitly as this. Our responses often move along some of the following lines:

"We're in the business of education and learning, not of moral formation, or of altering future conduct."

Or, "We don't even know how to change future conduct, nor how to measure any changes we might cause." Or we might respond in light of our understanding of the nature of moral agency and of moral convictions along the following lines: "Even if we did know how to change conduct, we have too much respect for the autonomy of the moral agent, and are too aware of the necessity for authentic moral positions to be rooted in the agent's own moral being, for us to impose some set of supposedly 'authoritative' answers on our students."

Or we might respond in light of our understanding of the university: "The university is a place of free inquiry, a place for testing ideas and values through close examination and analysis, through bringing them into conversation with competing ideas or values. It is a place, especially in the area of values and conduct, for opening up the conversation on issues, and for hearing all defensible perspectives without distorting the conversation and its outcome with some pre–established and mandatory set of answers."

The grounds and implications of each of these responses could occupy us far beyond the time we have available. So for the sake of our current concern, permit me to assume that such protests do provide some quite strong arguments–whether conclusive is another matter–that in the University classroom we should not undertake as a central goal of such courses the direct shaping of students' future conduct, the production of ethical professionals. What then do we do 'in professional ethics? What is to be taught there? A look at textbooks and journal articles, at course syllabuses and curriculum reports makes clear that several different kinds of things are taught in such courses. They include:

1.    Clearly factual material–historical materials on the emergence and development of professions; codes, oaths, statements of purpose, and statutes adopted to guide the conduct of professionals; legal and other disciplinary records indicating the level of enforcement of such guides; expectations of professionals entertained by clients and the pub-

lic at large; cases of actual events illustrating typical and not so typical ethical issues arising on the job and various responses to them.

2.    We also focus value systems–philosophical, religious and perhaps just common sense ones.  We look at how they are constructed, what authority they claim and what actual adherence they elicit.  We sometimes trace their history.  We examine moral principles, lists of rules, and character traits or virtues said to be particularly relevant to business and professional practice and examine the reasons given to support them, and suggest how they might apply to ethical issues arising in business and professional practice.

3.    We also discuss methods of analysis, reflection and criticism, with which we examine materials from both the former categories with an eye to assessment and evaluation, which enable us to appraise such data according to criteria internal to the data and criteria from appropriate external sources.

4.    Finally, we teach, or at least encourage personal introspection in our students–hoping that as they prepare for lives in business and the professions they will try to identify their own goals, motives, and commitments and then perhaps examine them for their adequacy in light of various other considerations raised in the course.  [Student anecdote about 'making it big' but unable to answer the 'why' question.]

Now some might suggest, and some years back I might have suggested that we can break down the "what" of professional ethics much more simply than this by dividing what we teach into descriptive materials and normative materials.  Or to use other frequently used categories, we teach facts and we teach values, or we deal with the 'is' and with the 'ought' of business and professional ethics.

This may still be a helpful initial distinction.  But most of us are now aware that, like so many of the categories we have used to cut reality up into manageable chunks, this distinction too can mislead us as much as it enlightens us.  Most of us now realize that the descriptive and the normative or evaluative do not inhabit separate realms divided by an impenetrable wall which no fool could miss.  Increasingly there seems to be between the two realms (if we should even retain that language) a virtual open frontier in which fact and value, is and ought, move back and forth with a freedom that some still find scandalous, or even threatening.

For example, virtually any history of the professions and of professional ethics will have significant normative dimensions.  There will be normative considerations at work, either consciously or unconsciously, in the selection of the history we teach.  Are we interested in the typical attire of professionals of a certain sort in a certain period.  Probably not.  But if so, it is most likely because such information tells us certain potentially normative things about those professionals–it may reveal their social location, their income, their general status in the community, the models they emulate, and the other groups in the society with whom they wish or wish not to be identified.

Normative matters will also often be included in the content of histories of business or the professions–what general standards of conduct guided, or were assumed to guide the conduct of parish clergy during the late 19th century? What did the AMA principals say about performing abortions in the 1930's? How was the lawyer's being an officer of the court thought to set limits to what the criminal defense lawyer could do on behalf of the accused under the first ABA code? No history of the professions will be adequate even as descriptive history if it ignores such questions.

Any neat distinction between descriptive and normative enterprises is also shown to be too simple by the fact that we can discuss value systems, principles and virtues in largely descriptive ways. However unsystematic, the Hippocratic oath does reflect certain values and normative commitments. And we can lead students through an examination of the oath in terms of its content, its internal consistency, its frequency of use in the education, socialization and disciplining of physicians historically and currently, and through a comparison of its teachings with the general conduct of practitioners–and all this we can do in a largely descriptive fashion. That is, without explicitly endorsing the code or rejecting parts of it, without condemning the use or neglect of the oath, and without blaming or praising the conduct of professionals in proportion to its consistency with the oath. We can do the same with the A.B.A. code of professional conduct, or with the multitude of oaths, codes and statements of purposes of established and emerging professions and of business corporations. It would be difficult to understand why such matters are taught at all in the absence of any normative concerns. Nevertheless, careful descriptive treatment of such normative elements is also a legitimate, demanding and important task.

In other words, most of us now realize that when we move beyond facts about the physical world, and facts about how certain symbols are used within certain systems of meaning, and enter the area of what we might call social facts–which is certainly where we will most often find ourselves in speaking of business and the professions–we find not a neat division between two distinct realms of facts and values. We rather find ourselves dealing with a single world where what we once so confidently called facts and values, at least in any setting of real interest to us, woven into a complex, and varied fabric that frequently defies our best efforts to isolate the purely factual.

Thus perhaps we should retain our descriptive/normative distinction, but see it as applying not to different subject matters, but to different ways of treating virtually any subject matter. In a descriptive treatment, we suspend normative judgment and a focus on representing the subject matter in an accurate way that is subject to verification or falsification by generally known and accepted procedures. In a normative or evaluative treatment we acknowledge that our interests go beyond the purely descriptive and move into areas of assessment of the materials in ways and according to criteria that have the potential to shape character and influence conduct along lines set out by certain normative or value considerations.

Where then do we end on the 'what' of business and professional ethics. Descriptively we end with the knowledge that a considerable variety of subject matters are taught and that virtually all of them can be approached both descriptively and normatively. But what *ought* to be taught and how? That is the normative, and thus the more difficult question. It is to that one I now turn with regard to our three settings with the hope of doing little more than making initial observations on each.

My guess would be that a careful examination of the business and professional ethics taught in these three settings would uncover considerable overlap in terms of the subject matter itself which is presented. The interesting and, for our purposes, important question is the differences these three settings make or should make in the question of the normative treatment of the subject matter, that is, the right assumed in each setting to attempt to alter the future conduct of students, or the duty felt in them to limit such attempts. When professional ethics in any of the settings is clearly normative, we often move to a second set of questions concerning the source, authority and content of the specific norms invoked there. These questions, however, will not be taken up here.

In discussing our three settings, I consider each setting not only as the place in which the teaching occurs, but also as providing the teacher and defining what is taught. Thus, for our purposes, the university, the religious community and the business or professional group are the teachers as well as the setting.

Now in response to question concerning the mix of descriptive and normative elements, it would be very convenient if we could take our three settings and string them out, nicely spaced, on a spectrum between the descriptive and the normative. However, we know this is impossible because of the above challenge to the sort of neat distinction that separates and defines the two poles of such a spectrum.

Nevertheless, it is sometimes instructive to attempt the impossible, to learn first hand why it can't be done. (Pedagogically, stubbing one's own toe is much more effective than hearing the story of another's toe–stubbing.)

Any such attempt to locate our three settings on a normative–descriptive spectrum would almost certainly place the religious setting closest to the normative end. After all, aren't religious communities to a considerable degree defined by shared worldviews, rituals, practices and/or lifestyles that clearly imply or reflect a widely shared community consensus about values and norms, about which things in life are worthy of our attention and efforts and which ones are not; about what sorts of acts, attitudes and character are appropriate for members of that community or for humans in general as that group understands them, and which ones are not appropriate.

I assume, in other words, that Jim Gustafson's description of the Christian church as a community of moral discourse can be applied to most religious communities. The ethical impulse in different religious communities will take different shapes and play different roles in the overall life of the community. But for those which concern us here, those which do in some direct way address matters of business and professional ethics, it would be difficult to understand why they did so unless to illumine those issues with the light of their own faith and ethics, to offer their own moral tradition as a guide for the business and professional conduct of their own members and of any other persons willing to listen to them.

However, any religious community which speaks exclusively from its own internal normative tradition and never ventures toward the descriptive end of our impossible spectrum will almost certainly condemn itself to irrelevance, and will have to be content to speak only to the most devout and unquestioning of its own members. Few non–members are likely to attend to any such teaching that does not reflect an understanding of the current (factual) realities of business and professional life, and which does not engage in the difficult struggle to bring ancient wisdom to bear in appropriate and sometimes modified form on contemporary realities.

In fact, one can go a step further and suggest that the religious community frequently needs to attend to current realities, to do its 'descriptive' homework, not only in order to apply its tradition to current realities, but also in order to understand its own tradition better. Certainly the Christian doctrines of God's continuing creation, of God's ongoing governance of and involvement in human affairs–and not just in matters ecclesiastical and religious–suggests that religious communities–in this case the Christian churches–need not only to address the 'secular' world, but that they need to be open to *being addressed* by that world, to being brought to a new understanding of their own traditions through such listening to the world at large and to the persons who spend their lives dealing with it. If I read him aright, Dennis McCann has made this point persuasively in regard to some traditional teachings of the Catholic Church about money and economics.

Nevertheless, a religious community that attempted to confine itself to descriptive matters would be a strange phenomenon indeed. Not only would such a community be engaging in an enterprise for which it is unlikely, as religious community, to be particularly well qualified. It would also be short–changing its own heritage and its internal and external audiences by failing to do what it is best able to do–to bring to bear on the issues of business and professional ethics its own distinctive heritage. Thus the most appropriate location for religious communities on our spectrum would seem to be someplace toward the normative end.

The university or the academic setting is a more complex matter. We can mark off one end of the range in which we might locate the university by asserting, quite properly I believe, that the University is not a church. As an arena for free discussion, for the pursuit of truth, for the clash of ideas, for the testing of all plausible hypotheses, any university deserving of the name should have to struggle mightily with itself before it excludes any significant question from its curriculum, or any defensible position on such questions from its investigation of those areas.

But we need with equal alacrity to close off the other end of the university's range on our spectrum by asserting with similar conviction that the university is not a data bank. It is not and never has been simply a passive and neutral repository for all available facts.

I speak primarily of western universities in the following, not to exclude all others, but to restrict myself to the area of my lesser ignorance. Certainly in the west the university has often been the repository of a culture's accumulated information–but also of its knowledge, and of its wisdom. And clearly in these latter terms we move beyond merely factual matters into normative ones about how to interpret and even to assess such matters, and we find ourselves dealing with commitments about how our knowledge of such matters and the power it gives us ought to be used. And of all this rich and varied heritage, the University has not been simply a repository. It has been a channel through which such knowledge and wisdom flowed to the next generation. In fact, it was much more than a channel, it was simultaneously a proponent, and a critic of, a contributor to the heritage of the culture which founded and sustained it. A value neutral repository of data it never was.

And universities rightly continue to champion the cultural heritage with which they have been entrusted. Through the directing of its resources–especially money, and faculty, it encourages the enlargement and refinement of our knowledge and wisdom in some directions, in some areas, and not in others; it requires its students to study certain areas of human experience, and permits them to bypass others. It directs them to the use of some resources and passes over others without comment. In light of current debates about the goals and the failings of higher education, and about the so–called canon that supposedly defines education in certain fields, I would hardly assert that the universities have always done these things well. But whether well or poorly, it has done them and continues to do them. That is the present point.

The university, whatever else it is, is a contributing citizen of society and active participant in the perpetuating, refining and extending of its heritage. For our purposes it is especially significant to see this fact in relation to the university's sponsoring of professional schools. In such sponsoring, it generally endorses the way of doing medicine, or of practicing law, or engaging in business currently dominant in the society. Its openness to alternative ideas and viewpoints makes possible the nurturing of a critical edge which may help redefine such business and professional practices in the future. But in general it is hard to say that it is not predominantly on the side of the status quo in these matters. That is sometimes a good thing. It is sometimes a bad thing. But it is always a normative thing. The University is not a data bank.

Some Universities such as DePaul complicate and enrich their lives still further by publicly proclaiming certain values and commitments that help define them and their mission and which may set them off from other universities which proclaim identities based on other values, or which simply remain silent on such issues.

What now does or should happen when business and professional ethics is taken up in the setting of such a university which is normatively tied to a particular culture, but which also professes distinctive values which may go beyond or even go against some of that culture's values. Unfortunately time prevents my spelling this out in detail. But let me attempt a beginning.

1. Since it seems clear to me that we do teach business and professional ethics because we do at some level hope to make a positive difference in our students' future conduct and thereby to serve the greater social good, it is disingenuous, even unethical of us, to disclaim all such interests. Being the university, however, sets some limits on how we pursue this goal, several of which are already indicated in the

above comments. Some things such as sensitizing our students to the presence of moral and ethical issues in business and professional practice I believe can be pursued with a passion without violating the nature of the university or the freedom of conscience of our students. We must, however, be willing to listen to them when they suggest we have mislabeled some act or practice as a moral problem. For example, is there, morally speaking, such a thing as profits or professional incomes that are excessive or unfair simply because of their size. But if we are committed to letting students have their say on such an issue, which I believe we are, then I think we can insist that they let us have our say. That is, among other things, simply to educate them about the rules of civilized conversation. And certainly on matters such as the best response to specific moral problems, being the University means that we listen, and encourage our students to listen to any proposed solutions that can be supported by rational discourse.

2.   A University's own distinctive values, that is, those that depart in some significant way from the values shaping the dominant culture are probably best and most defensibly presented and urged upon students not in the classroom curriculum but in other aspects of the University's life. For example, DePaul's Vincentian personalism and its commitment to urban service are properly displayed before and even urged upon students. But except for courses specifically designed and clearly labeled as focusing on such matters, these commitments should be exhibited more in the University's life outside the classroom–in its conduct of its own affairs, in special co– and extra–curricular events–special lectures, service opportunities, and in the kinds of persons it holds up as models in the various awards and honorary degrees it gives. The obvious reason for this preference is that it avoids pairing, or even appearing to pair the University's own value commitments with the constraints and sanctions of the classroom–most obviously grades–and so protects the students' autonomy and freedom of conscience and the freedom of discussion in the classroom. These are themselves, of course, no mean expression of Vincentian personalism.

3.   In this age of multi–culturalism or cultural diversity the university needs in all its activities to be reflective, self–critical and perhaps even a bit chastened as it continues, both inadvertently and quite self–consciously, to represent the culture–however one defines it–that created and has long dominated the university as we know it. And I think we must be open to the possibility that business and professional studies, including the ethics thereof, may be some of the most resistant to, or at least the most difficult to see from the perspective of cultures just now asserting themselves. I venture this suggestion perhaps without adequate forethought. But it is based in part on the degree to which

business and the professions represent the vested interests of this nation's long dominant culture, and the degree to which the models, assumptions and values of these two areas have permeated and shaped virtually all other aspects of our society's life. Having said this, however, I also hasten to say that the University abdicates part of its historic task if it does not see to it that among the various voices speaking for the great diversity of cultures which promise to enrich us all there is not also heard the voice, even if it must be the university's own, of this perhaps chastened, but still valuable and informative attempt at creating a humane world. Does this put the university somewhere near the middle of our spectrum. Perhaps. But clearly final location is less important and less informative than are the issues that should figure into its determination.

And finally, the business corporation/professional association/group, the practitioners' setting, which is initially a puzzling case in this context. Certainly the professions have historically made and still currently make normative claims as part of their self–definition, primarily claims about a commitment to the crucial interests of their clients and or the larger society which may in some cases require a curtailing of the professional's own self interest. Businesses and business associations have made such claims less often, but they are not unheard of (see Johnson & Johnson code, the Beliefs of Borg Warner, etc.) Now when thoughtfully and sincerely done, businesses and professions are to be commended for such commitments (and are to be expected to live up to them).

The relevance of such public declarations of commitment and value–orientation is, for our purposes twofold. First, it would seem to commit the organization to encouraging, even requiring that its members know about and conduct themselves according to those declared values. Obviously something like business ethics courses or seminars would be one means of accomplishing these goals.

Secondly, such declarations in some sense seem to 'license' the organization to engage in normative discourse and to propagate its values among its members. Without such declarations, members and employees might reasonably object that in such ethical expectations/demands, requirements are being imposed on them that are not ordinarily part of the job or position they have assumed. In other words, just as students have a right to be protected from moral indoctrination and coercion (which are not the same thing as education in ethics), so workers and professionals have the right to expect some limits on what the corporation or profession can demand of them. Such limits we usually see as protecting them against demands that would violate moral norms. But might they not also function to protect the individual from what some would consider extraordinary or heroic moral performance? This sounds like a remote possibility. But what about the A.B.A.'s continuing debates over the requirement of a certain amount of *pro bono* work by its members? Or what about the continuing and I think unresolved discussions among health care professions about the duty to treat HIV positive or AIDS patients, that is, as some see it, to risk their lives in carrying out their professions?

Now neither business nor the professions seem, by definition, to be constrained in such declarations of values and commitments and in their propagation among their members by any commitment to open and free inquiry, or tolerance for all reasonable positions. At the same time, since businesses and professional organizations often have direct control over their members' means of livelihood, they must recognize their considerable potential for coercion. This is one reason public declaration of such distinctive values and commitments is significant.

Now with my next step, I need to tread carefully to avoid falling uncritically into certain stereotypes. Nevertheless, it seems to me both fair and accurate to suggest that institutionally speaking (i.e., not addressing the issue of motivations of the individuals operating in such institutions) in the case of business, and to a significant degree in that of the professions, any such altruistic normative claims that might figure in ethics courses will in a direct and obvious way be in tension with other motivations having a more central and a more legitimate role than they do in most religious communities or in the university. I have in mind of course the self interest which manifests itself in the profit motive or the desire for economic gain.

The interplay between these motives of self interest and the motives generally assumed in the teaching of business and professional ethics generate, I believe, more helpful questions about business and professional ethics in the practitioners' setting than does the descriptive/normative issue.

Now let me exclude one extreme position immediately. Does the pursuit of profit or other economic gain necessarily override all other motives, or is it, as such, so morally questionable as to disqualify any agents subject to it from all ethical discourse? Obviously the answer is no. At the same time, I believe it is naive to assume that these motives, however relabeled and redefined, are not a significant element in the institutional setting of business and professional practice and/or that they create no particular tension with other matters which one would ordinarily expect in ethics courses. Otherwise one is left without plausible explanation for the long list of abuses of the public good by business, and to a lesser degree by the professions, abuses that have been finally curbed only by legislation or the threat thereof: such a list would include child labor, monopolies, worker safety, product safety, environmental responsibility, racial and sexual and homophobic discrimination, honesty in advertising and packaging, and so on. Whatever their record of abuses and shortcomings, I can think of no parallel record of regulation in the cases of religious communities or universities.

This potential conflict among the various motives driving business and the professions has no doubt been in large part the reason such organizations have so often had to defend their ethical declarations against charges of 'window–dressing.' I suspect it is also the reason that in the granting of the privileges of autonomy or self–government, society has been most lenient with religious communities and academic institutions, less so with the professions and least with business. And finally it may explain why business and professional ethics in the practitioners' setting have so often ended up being reduced to questions of compliance with existing and enforceable laws, regulations and codes, both internal and external. Such an approach is almost always minimalist–these are the requirements, neither you nor the corporation/profession can afford to ignore them.

Let me end with two more positive observations: There clearly are businesses and professional groups which have engaged their members in ethics education and training which encouraged ethical reflection and analysis apparently unconstrained by other organization goals. I want to take nothing away from the sincerity and even the courage with which this is sometimes done. At the same time I cannot dismiss a couple of questions. Is it possible in such settings to totally neutralize such 'other' goals, even seriously to call them into question as part of the ethical reflection? And if so, what have been the outcomes for those persons or institutions and organizations which have taken a potentially costly stand on behalf of what I am calling the more altruistic goals?

Secondly, please note that many of the above observations about business and the professions has been (entirely) descriptive. We need to recognize the division of labor in our society which assigns certain tasks and even certain ways of fulfilling them to certain groups or organizations, and so limits to some extent what they can do in other areas. A business in this society that ignores profit may, in some sense, be thereby, more ethical. But if it persists in really ignoring profits it shows itself to be bad business. And if it begins cultivating among its members a kind of crypto–religious ideology or worldview, many of us get uneasy about its overstepping its proper bounds. All of this is to say that nothing said above should be taken as criticizing business or even the professions for not being the ethical ground–breakers or moral pioneers in terms of the general values that shape our life together in society. Business and professional persons may well contribute as much and as creatively to the society's ethical conversation as do any of us. But for business or the professions as such, as institutions, to do so makes me uneasy in ways that I am still struggling to articulate.

I promised, as you may recall no more than a beginning. I hope I have delivered that. I even dare to hope that this beginning raises some of the right questions and moves in some of the right directions. That, however, I did not promise.

# References

_____*The Teaching of Ethics in Higher Education: The Teaching of Ethics I*, p. 6 (Hastings–on–Hudson, New York: The Hastings Center, 1980), p.

Briloff, AJ. "Codes of Conduct: Their Sound and Their Fury," In *Ethics, Free Enterprise and Public Policy,* edited by R. T. DeGeorge and J.A. Pichler, p. 274 (New York: Oxford University Press, 1978).

# 2

# Can Business Ethics Be Taught?

**Dennis P. McCann**

## Introductory Remarks

Paul Camenisch has gotten us off to an impressive start by offering a broad picture of the contexts in which business and professional ethics are taught: the university or academic setting, the church or religious setting, and the professional association or practitioner's setting. He shows how each of these settings can shape our answers to the questions of "Where," "Why," and "How" business and professional ethics are taught.

I have a number of difficulties with Camenisch's theory, beginning with his assertion that the pursuit of profit in business is responsible for a long train of abuses, or at least a significantly longer train than he can imagine in either religious communities or universities. I doubt if Martin Luther, for example, would have agreed with him regarding the moral health of either the Roman Catholic church or the late Medieval university. But even more to the point, I doubt if the profit motive goes very far to explain the patterns of organizational behavior in business, for the very same patterns are to be seen time and again marring the performance of not–for–profit institutions. For example, I don't see how the profit motive goes very far to explain cases of employment discrimination or sexual harassment. Were the profit motive all powerful in corporate behavior, there might be a lot less of either in business.

Perhaps Camenisch and I can pursue these disagreements later on; I want to use my own time here to focus on still another setting–perhaps the most crucial one–for learning and teaching business ethics, namely, the modern business corporation itself. If we fail to appreciate the role of the corporation here, we are not likely to understand our own limited contribution as academicians either.

After reviewing the moral meaning of corporations, I will argue for the perspective on business ethics that I believe is implicit in my own teaching, which I have developed through trial and error experimentation over a dozen years here with our standard required course, RS 228: Business, Ethics and Society. I want to share with you my sense of the objectives of that course, and how it should fit into the vocational preparation that DePaul University offers the wanna–be business managers who enroll in the College of Commerce. I will seek to persuade you that teaching business ethics at the undergraduate level can be effective, only if it is oriented less to the needs of academicians out to demonstrate the applicability of their own scholarly disciplines, and more to the lived experience of managers seeking to meet their various commitments–organizational, professional, and personal–in a corporate setting.

## The Rap against Business Ethics Courses

The latest issue of the *Harvard Business Review* (May–June 1993) contains a timely article on "What's the Matter with Business Ethics?" Most of the authorities quoted in the essay–Norman Bowie, Richard DeGeorge, Michael Hoffmann, Ken Goodpaster, Robert Solomon, Tom Donaldson, Lisa Newton, Laura Nash, and Joanne Ciulla–are known personally by many of us who teach in this area. For business ethicians still form a tight little academic community, indeed, a beleaguered subculture in the groves of academia whose unique preoccupations may fail the test of political correctness on two counts: our willingness to embrace both business and ethics, simultaneously and constructively. The *HBR* article probes some of the vulnerabilities attendant upon our precarious relationship to the reigning academic orthodoxies. It argues that business ethics courses typically are "too general, too theoretical, and too impractical" to be of much use to business practitioners and wanna–be managers. We apparently give the impression of being so interested in defending our own intellectual and moral integrity that we rigorously adhere to "absolutist perspectives" implying that "a managerial act cannot be ethical unless it in no way serves the manager's self–interest." (Norman Bowie, among others, is singled out for criticism here—interestingly enough, the women authorities mentioned seem to share an aversion to this kind of misguided rigorism.)

The resulting impression, the article suggests, is that reigning academic paradigm of business ethics as a branch of applied moral philosophy is even less effective than the paradigm of corporate social responsibility that it sought to supplant. The *HBR* article does hold out some room to hope for a "new business ethics" based on "moderation, pragmatism, and minimalism." The authors cited approvingly seem to favor a return to Aristotelian understandings of virtue (as opposed to a mixed discourse composed of Kantian and Utilitarian forms of rationalism), and premise their recommendations upon an appreciative awareness of the moral values latent in the organizational strengths of many corporate cultures.

I do not feel the need to defend my course against the *HBR* article's criticisms. For I've always felt that the study of religious ethics usually avoided the obvious pitfalls of applied moral philosophy, so long as religious ethicists resisted the temptations of offering merely a pale imitation of the theories preferred by their philosophical colleagues. With a mix of empirical and normative concerns more like those of political science or anthropology than analytic philosophy, religious studies is constituted as an interdisciplinary inquiry into the religious dimensions of a variety of human cultures. To understand religious ideas is to understand the practices and social institutions in which they are generated, tested, and preserved. This heuristic bias toward culturally embedded social practices means that the religious ethicist is not likely to understand morality in abstract theoretical terms, at least not at first.

In my experience, the disciplinary bias of religious studies has opened the way for critical conversation with the theories and practices of business management, well in advance of most philosophers doing business ethics. (There are exceptions among the philosophers, e.g., Tom Donaldson, Ken Goodpaster, Laura Nash, etc., but I became intrigued by them mostly because I saw that they, too, were fighting the standard paradigm of applied moral philosophy, and attempting to achieve a closer fit with actual corporate practice.) I feel vindicated by the article's perception of a "new business ethics," for I feel this is precisely the direction that a religious approach to business ethics is likely to develop.

## Management as a Social Practice

My own attempt to clarify the significance of the modern corporation as a setting for the teaching of business ethics came as a result of a collaborator with a business executive (and now Congregationalist pastor), M. L. Brownsberger, with whom I wrote an essay, "Management as a Social Practice," published in *The Annual of the Society of Christian Ethics*, in 1990.  That essay used the managerial theories of Peter Drucker to argue that business management ought to be considered a morally constructive "social practice," in the sense defined by the neo–Aristotelian moral philosopher, Alasdair MacIntyre.  I won't bother you with the technical merits of the argument; among other things, it meant answering MacIntyre's own prejudices–typical in academia–against business and scientific management.  But the payoff was that managerial practice can be a source of moral virtue, for like other MacIntyrean social practices, it does foster certain "internal goods" that are indispensable to the common good of society.  The chief of these is the creation of new forms of association in which human and material resources can be organized more productively.  Drucker's characteristic subordination, but not denial, of the role of profit in business (It is a "way of keeping score," or measuring successful performance for economic effectiveness....) is important here, for it fits with MacIntyre's ethical subordination of "external goods" to "internal goods" in any genuine social practice.

If your are curious about this theory, and its implications, we can talk about it later.  Here, the point is that if the business corporation is an institutional setting in which a certain set of (virtuous) social practices are routinely fostered, then the organizational structure of modern business itself is the embodiment of certain moral values conducive to the common good of society.  If this inference is true, the task of teaching business ethics is not–or at least, should not be–antagonistic to routine business practice, but rather a clarification of the values already embedded in business organizations, and where necessary a challenge to higher standards or continuous improvement based on those shared values.  The business corporation itself thus can be seen as a primary resource, not the only resource, to be sure, in the intellectual and moral development of the persons who work within it. (Crudely put, business ethics can no longer be taught as if it were a game of "Cannibals and Christians.")

Now such a conclusion is hardly news to those conversant in the management literature focused on the analysis of corporate cultures, or the discipline of organizational development generally.   What

Brownsberger and I managed to pull out of Drucker is the major premise of popular tracts like Warren Bennis and Burt Nanus' book on *Leadership*, for example, or Max DePree's *Leadership is an Art*. Indeed, when one reads the corporate culture literature in light of our preoccupations one cannot help but be struck by the religious and theological appeals that are being made, regarding the significance of corporate work, implicitly in Bennis' case, explicitly in DePree's. A religious studies perspective, particularly one attuned to the significance of organization in the history of religions, can help to interpret these claims, and challenge them when they tend to become idolatrous or, if you will, borderline totalitarian.

Be that as it may, I am less interested in curbing the excesses of organizational development specialists than I am in pointing out their role in the teaching of business ethics. If the organizational structure of the business corporation is morally valenced throughout, then well focused orientation programs, professional development schemes, performance evaluations, routine accountability structures, and the corporate reward system generally, ought to become primary instruments for teaching business ethics. To the extent that corporations with a reputation for excellence normally do exhibit these indications of moral strength in their corporate culture, academic business ethics programs should be seen as laboratories or, literally, seminaries, in which wanna–be managers are prepared for the positive challenges they are likely to face in the moral environments for which they will be recruited.

Don't get me wrong: I'm not announcing the advent of utopia in American business. But it would be stupid, and distinctly ungenerous, for us to continue teaching business ethics in the classroom, as if leading business corporations had not already made enormous strides in internalizing business ethics within their own organizational routines. This trend, I must insist, is growing precisely because it goes with, and not against, the grain of sound business practice, and the principles of sound marketing. Yes, it can be the key to higher productivity and higher profits, and is often embraced precisely for those reasons. But, I would second the perspective of the *HBR* article on this: academic business ethics can rightly embrace "moderation, pragmatism, and minimalism," properly understood; for it no longer need regard itself as fighting a lonely, uphill battle. We have our allies, though they may not be found in academia today.

## The Business Ethics Program at DePaul

When RS 228 (PHL 228, M 228) was developed by an interdisciplinary committee hosted by Bro. Leo Ryan, then Dean of the College of Commerce, in 1981, we outlined a syllabus that looked more like a menu with a variety of choices, in the hopes that scholars from both philosophy and religious studies could adapt the framework to the needs of our commerce undergraduates.

If I try to chart my own development within that syllabus, I increasingly found myself disenchanted with the textbooks available (usually dominated by the applied moral philosophy paradigm), and in search of an alternative. Though I didn't know it at the time, the alternative I was seeking had to be responsive to the moral significance of business organizations and the analysis of their corporate cultures. Rather than narrate how I moved from the one to the other incrementally, let me review my current thinking regarding the objectives of the course:

(1) Design the course so that the learning process reflects your ideas of sound management. The classroom is a practitioner's laboratory. Having been impressed by Peter Drucker's evolving views of business management, I felt that if managers are educators, educators should structure the learning environment as if they were managers. Class work, where possible, must become teamwork, with the instructor serving as a facilitator and supervisor. In order to achieve the appropriate sense of ownership in our collective work in the class, I have experimented with the following strategies:

(a) Business storytelling: evoke their own moral experience in business (even if only as a customer) as a basis for thinking through the merits of various moral theories.

(b) Teamwork on case studies: corporate work gets done in teams and students need experience in collaborative learning; teamwork is also the first step in establishing a sense of mutual accountability within the class itself.

(c) Field research on local businesses: don't retreat into the library, but go out into the real world to investigate how a business defines and seeks to live up to its ethical responsibilities. (Parallel to the visit a worship service assignment in RS 100)

(d) Executive mentoring: successful business persons are more credible at communicating sound business values to our students than we academicians are. Invite your conversation partners into the classroom.

(e) Encourage self–discipline by having students participate in their own performance evaluation. If Drucker is right about self–

management, students must be encouraged to take responsibility for the quality of their own participation.

(2) In a managerially oriented class in business ethics, moral theory–both religious and philosophical–should be taught on a need to know basis, i.e., how much of a basic ethical vocabulary do they need to have to order their own moral common sense? I believe that one or two well focused classes on, e.g., the appendix on moral theory in the appendix to Goodpaster, Matthews and Nash, is sufficient for our purposes in an undergraduate course.

(3) If a decision–making paradigm is offered particularly in relationship to the analysis of business ethics case studies, it should integrate an ethical moment into a larger managerial pattern. (I have adapted Drucker's suggestions from his classic, *The Practice of Management*, for this purpose.) Above all, ethics should not be seen as an alternative paradigm for decision–making, but a clarification of certain threshold points within a common managerial paradigm.

I have my personal reservations about all decision–making paradigms, for I think that the purpose of sound organizational structure is to render such paradigms normally superfluous. Managers should have recourse them only in exceptional circumstances; otherwise, they should be carried along by the moral integrity built into their normal business routines. We can talk about this later . . . .

(4) We must be careful with the "Vision Thing" in business. The center of gravity in managerially oriented business ethics courses should be less upon "AVOID EVIL" and more upon "DO GOOD." Business ethics case studies should feature ethical successes as often as they do moral disasters. Inspirational books on successful integration of ethical and managerial concerns, e.g., Max DePree's *Leadership is an Art*, do more to unleash the residual idealism of our students (yeah, even Commerce majors!) than all stern lessons we may derive from the paradigms of ethical absolutism. We routinely fail to appeal to the creative energies of our students in this area, which are moral and intellectual, whatever else they may also be.

(5) Understand the difference between undergraduate and graduate education, and routinely respect it. The basic objective of an undergraduate course is business ethics ought to be instill a habit of mind, namely, the habit of sound business judgment. Teach them to think like a moral business person. If that means spending most of your time teaching them how to think in a business like fashion, period, then so be it. Get them to see the world differently. The primary challenge is to their intellectual capacity, first; sound business morality, I'm convinced, is not a matter of willing to do the obviously good thing, but of discovering what the good is in the first place. A graduate

course, by contrast, can attempt to sharpen their awareness of the contours of the academic discipline of business ethics. At that level, they more appropriately can be introduced to the diversity of theoretical approaches to business ethics, their strengths and weaknesses.

(6) Business ethics cannot be taught to a moral idiot, no matter how effective the pedagogical materials may be. Often in the past, analytic moral philosophy proceeded as if the only good reasons for being moral were those that even a Hitler would have to acknowledge. Obviously, I believe that test is absurd, and counterproductive. Our students come to us with their own histories of cognitive and moral development, their own personal track record for recognizing and making moral decisions. They represent various stages of preparedness for what we would like to accomplish. I believe that the most effective pedagogy is probably one that bets on their common sense, their openness, their generosity, and their residual desire to do good while doing well. Of course, we must help them to probe their own moral seriousness, to suggest that there may be fierce trade–offs morally when things fall apart. But I think it is a mistake to convey the impression that most moral decisions involve difficult, if not, impossible choices. Seek first to strengthen their own instinct for the good that can be done, and they are more likely to perform well in the corporate setting, when put to the test.

(7) Don't worry over much about critical reflection. Strengthening their capacity for sound habits of mind is far more important, I believe. Besides, most managerial decisions occur in time frames that preclude any deep reflection. An overly complicated ethical decision–making paradigm may be an obstacle to managerial (and moral) effectiveness. Reflection, and the growth of new wisdom, has its place in the aftermath of moral experience. The classroom is a laboratory for business ethics. It is not the real thing.

These pedagogical remarks (or heresies) suggest a qualified answer to the question, "Can business ethics be taught?" First, I'm inclined to agree with Socrates (I think) in answering "No" if it means communicating a moral sensibility where none existed before; "Yes" if it means provoking a recollection (whatever its ultimate source) and harnessing the power of that insight for the challenges involved in mastering new social situations. A course in business ethics is no substitute for sound moral development; nor is it likely to be effective, if its lessons are not appropriate to the realities of the moral environment the student is about to enter in beginning a career in business.

God guiding the world and that the world in time will be brought into the Kingdom of God).

These four religious virtues promote four secular virtues: (1) the intrinsic dignity of the human person; (2) principle–based ethics, (3) self–sacrificial love, and (4) a broad concept of the common good.[3]

These concepts are both supported and challenged in the Global Economy. They are supported in the movements toward a Global Ethic (led by Hans Kung and the Manifesto of the World Parliament of Religions)[4] and by the U.N. initiative, Global Compact, presented at the 1999 World Economic forum at Davos.[5] They are challenged by the prevailing spirit of a world called postmodernism, "where there are no objective moral values and no moral laws. People make up their own truths and their own values, and there is no clarity as to the way that people should live."[6]

As we face "Corporate Social Responsibility in the Global Economy" we face a problem about which Manfred Frings, the world's leading Scheler scholar, has written extensively. All great philosophers from Aristotle to the present have "focused, more or less, on the ultimate moral question of ethics, namely, what any human being, at any of its moments and situations, ought to do."[7]

Every word in the title of this presentation is worthy of a book–and many have been written on each of them. In school we were taught to parse a sentence. I shall do so by saying a few brief words about "the global economy" and conclude with thoughts on "corporate social responsibility".

I have just returned from Poland. I was struck by a comment of a speaker at a meeting sponsored by the Union of Polish Industry, Trade and Finance.

"We are moving from the world of atoms to the world of bytes; from the world of muscle to the world of brains, from the world of working hands to the world of working heads. Kilobytes, not kilograms are the basis of competition."[8]

What about the global economy: September 11, 2001 induced significant changes in the world economy. The terrorist attacks destroyed two symbols of American capitalism and damaged our symbol of military power. Pete Engardio, *Business Week* analyst wrote:

"By striking down a key pillar of America's leadership–its unbridled faith in its own security–the catastrophe has plunged the world into an uncertain new era. A decade ago, when the cold war was history and nations rushed to embrace free market; the world seemed united by shared opportunity. It now seems united by a dread of risk."[9]

This disaster came at the worst possible time in the business cycle when the U.S., Europe and Japan were sliding into a rare synchronized slump. "America's confidence in the promise of equities, the magic of technology and the brilliance of celebrity CEO's was shaken" by the economic aftermath of September 11.[10] A headline commented, "Uncertainty is spooking business and the markets" (*Business Week*, October 8, 2002). Henry Kaufman predicts that "all economic and profit forecasts are null and void".[11] Global strategist, Stephen Roach noted that the U.S. accounts for 40% of global worth since 1996 and "the world economy has become over dependent on the U.S."[12]

What then is the lookout for the global economy? Will it mean, as some suggest, that the public sector will have a bigger role in the economy? That defense and security spending will accelerate? That R&D money will shift from innovations to national security? That trade flows will be slower and more costly? That immigration will limit the entry of workers and tighten labor markets? Will expanding unemployment increase social costs? All of these have been suggested.[13] To these Pete Engardio adds: . . . commercial security, the potential "blow up" of the Japanese financial system, stagnation in the developing World and the, as yet, unclear meaning of China in the WTO and the Qatar agreement on new global talks.[14]

Is there a hopeful side? Yes. Even a mild U.S. recovery will encourage a world suffering the trauma of risk. Can we "unspook" business and the market? As the global economy unfolds in 2002 the bright side is that the worst economic fears about the impact of September 11 have not materialized. Real fears of world terrorism have accelerated.

Three recent headlines on one day (March 29, 2003) proclaimed: "U.S. Economy Picking Up Steam" (*Daily Herald*); "Economy Advances on 3 Fronts" (*Chicago Tribune*) and "Corporate Profits show Signs of Recovery" (*Wall Street Journal*).

This recovery trend offers good news for corporate social responsibility. Without profits even the best–intentioned corporation is limited in what it can do in the social–economic arena. In both management and business ethics classes, we study the definition of corporate social responsibility. That means the "classical" and, often misunderstood, Milton Friedman definition. The Friedman argument is that 'there is one and only one social responsibility of business–to use its resources and engage in activities designed to increase its profits . . .". These are the words most people associate with the Friedman theory. But the Friedman definition continues with these words: "so long as it stays within the rules of the game, which is to say, engages in open and free competition, without deception of fraud."[15] That continuation of his definition is often omitted in business discussions. Yet the vary words contained in the extension of his definition reflects Friedman's recognition of a moral agenda for business.

Even so, I do not myself favor so narrow a definition. I am more disposed to understanding CSR "as corporate social responsiveness" (the Robert Ackerman approach). Another model of responsibility is that of Professors Lee Preston and James Post, which defines as *primary* the interaction between business and market–groups and *secondary* the relations with non–market segments of society. Professor Archie Carroll would define CSR in terms of the economic, legal and ethical principles, which create a "social contract" between business and society. These evolving concepts "corporate, social, responsiveness" of CSR gave rise to various "stakeholder theories" which essentially identify individuals or groups who are affected by business organizations as they pursue their goals and whose welfare should be the concern of ethical managers.[16]

The corporate social responsibility movement has been evolving for over forty years. The concept is not new. It predates the Scientific Management era. It dates to the life of Robert Owens, the Scottish cotton mill owner, in the early 1880's.[17] The concept of CSR "was built upon deep moral ideas about the primacy of human interests over corporate one . . . . But early advocates of CSR were relatively inarticulate about the nature of its moral core. Many intellectuals of that time struggled to be inclusive and respectful of all people, all rights, all issues."[18] Initially academics advocating CSR were heavy on advice and weak on application. Without getting mired in theory, some firms simply began to act with increasing concern and care for their varied 'publics". The success of stakeholder terminology and its evolving theories have been the result of much study, including academic and corporate interaction, before arriving at the acknowledged "Clarkson Principles of Stakeholder Management".[19] Today there is increasing discussion about Corporate Citizenship and even Global Corporate Citizenship.[20]

You may ask me what advice I would give individuals in the audience about how to be responsible in their respective corporate settings. There are four steps in the ethical decision making process: (1) develop a recognition that problems have a moral dimension; (2) develop your own level of moral cognition, (3) learn to examine your own motives, i.e. your intention in any situation, and (4) consider social consensus and the impact of your moral behavior, i.e. the probable effect and the consequences of your actions in the immediate and long term future.

Regular reflections on moral issues and grappling with moral judgments–both contribute to the development of moral cognition. Reflection and judgment, together with being honest with yourself about your intentions, all contribute to the refinement of moral behavior. Recognition, reflection, self–understanding and personal honesty usually yield responsible moral decisions.[21] In even more simple terms: always consider the act, yourself as actor/agent, your intentions, the persons affected and the results.[22]

We are all challenged, "to pursue truth, to give compassionate service and to participate in the creation of a more just and humane world". In conclusion, I thank Mrs. Callista Wicklander, Jim Wicklander and the Wicklander family for their demonstration of personal and corporate social responsibility in establishing the Wicklander Chair in Business Ethics at DePaul University.

May each of us who will hold this Chair contribute to the promotion of Business Ethics and Corporate Social Responsibility in our national and global economy.

Thank you.

# Notes

1. Phillip De Vous, "Enron's Moral Lessons," *Action Institute Weekly News and Commentary*,
January 16, 2002, p. 1.

2. Vaclav Havel quoted in Timothy Radcliffe, O.P., *I Call You Friends*, New York: continuum, 2001, p. 161 (quoted during Radcliffe's lecture delivered to the European Dominican Provincials Meeting, Prague, 1993).

3. Cf. Robert J. Spitzer, S.J., "Religious Education Indispensable for Free Society", *Religion and Liberty*, Vol. 11, No. 5, Sept–Oct–2001, p. 1–2.

4. Cf. *A Global Ethic: The Declaration of the Parliament of the World's Religions with Commentaries by Hans Kung and Karl–Josef Kuschel.* New York: Continuum, 1998. "The aim of this document provides a statement of the minimal ethical consensus by the World's Religions" comments Jean Porter, "The Search for a Global Ethic," *Theological Studies*, Vol. 62, No. 1, March 2001, p. 114. The second part of the Porter article examines the work of Hans Kung implementing a Global Ethic, *ibid*, pp. 113–118.

5. Cf. Michael Jexiorski, "A Matter of Ethics", *Warsaw Voice*, No. 1 (88–89), January 6, 2002, p. 22.

6. Cf. Remarks of Cardinal Corman Murphy O'Connor of Westminster preaching Morning Prayer, St. Mary Magdalene Church, Sandringham, England, January 13, 2002, reported in *The Tablet*, Vol. 255, No. 8400. For a commentary on the varieties of postmodernism and the ethics of organizational life see "Varieties of Postmodernism: Triple–Loop Dialog III in Richard P. Nielsen, *The Politics of Ethics: Methods for Acting, Learning and sometimes Fighting With Others In Addressing Ethics Problems in Organizational Life.* New York: Oxford University Press, 1996, pp. 141–156.

7. Manfred Frings, *The Mind of Max Scheler*. Milwaukee: Marquette University Press, 2001, p. 19.

8. N. Negroponte, author of *Being Digital*, quoted by Renata Kossowics "People Make a Difference", *Warsaw Voice*, No. 43 (679). October 28, 2001, p. 20.

9. Pete Engardino, "A New World", *Business Week*, October 8, 2001, p. 32.

10. *ibid.*, p. 33. "The Nasdaq meltdown that erased $5.4 trillion in wealth between March 2000 and April 2001. Now the markets must mull the implications of $1.4 trillion in market value that vanished in the five days of panic selling after Wall Street re–opened on September 17, the biggest one–week sell–off since 1933." *ibid.*

11. Quoted in *ibid*, p. 32.

12. Quoted in Pete Engardio, "What's Next for the Global Economy", *Business Week*, February 11, 2002, p. 52.

13. Cf. "Rethinking the Economy", *Business Week*, October 1, 2001, p. 30.

14. Pete Engardino, "What's Next for the Global Economy", *op.cit.*, p. 52–53. Also, Cf. re: Japan, Mortimer B. Zuckerman, "Land of the Sinking Sun" *U.S. News and World Report*, March 11, 2002, p. 80. Also Cf. re: developing world, John Plender, "Quenching the Thirst for Capital", *Financial Times*, March 20, 2002. "For the health of the global economy, fund managers must take a more enlightened attitude to investing in developing countries–and a longer term view", p. 20. Also Cf.: "Is Latin America Losing Its Way?", *Economist*, March 2, 2002, p. 11.

15. Milton Friedman quoted in Michael Novak, *Business As A Calling· Work and The Examined Life*. New York: The Free Press, p. 140–141. The complete Friedman article appears in most ethics texts, Cf. Thomas Donaldson, Patricia Werhane, and Margaret Cording, *Ethical Issues in Business* (Seventh Edition), Upper Saddle River, N.J.: Prentice Hall, 2002, pp. 33–38.

16. Cf. James A.F. Stoner and R. Edward Freeman, *Management*, (Fifth Edition), Englewood cliffs, N.J.: Prentice Hall, 1992, p. 100 –102. For External Environments and Stakeholder Theory, p. 62–71; for Internal Stakeholders, p. 71–73 and for Multiple Stakeholders, p. 73–74.For the seminal work on Stakeholder theory cf. R. Edward Freeman, *Strategic Management· A Stakeholder Approach*. Marshfield, Mass: Pitman Publishing, 1984. For a summary cf. Freeman, "Stakeholder Theory of the Modern Corporation" in Donaldson, Werhane, Cording, *op. cit.*, pp. 38–48. For a discussion of possible "global social contract" (an extension of the Archie Carroll "social contract") cf. Michael J. Mazarr, *Global Trends 2005*, New York: Palgrave, 1999, p. 109–112.

17. *Ibid.*, p. 30. Also Cf. John Donaldson, "Multinational enterprises, Employment Relations and Ethics", *Employer Relations*, Volume 23, No. 6, 2001, p. 627–642, esp. "Corporate Social Responsibility" p. 637–639.

18. Jeanne M. Logsdon and Donna J. Woods, "Business Citizenship: From Domestic to Global Level of Analysis", *Business Ethics Quarterly*, Vol. 12, No. 2 p. 157. The authors argue for an extension of CSR to corporate citizenship and eventually to a global corporate citizenship.

19. Cf. James E. Post, "Global Corporate Citizenship· Principles to Live and Work By", *Business Ethics Quarterly*, Vol. 12, No. 2, p. 143–153.

20. Cf. Thomas Donaldson, "The Stakeholder Revolution and the Clarkson Principles", *Business Ethics Quarterly*, Vol. 12, No. 2, April 2002, p. 107–111. Also cf. Appendix "Principles of Stakeholder Management" (Clarkson Principles) presented and explained, p. 257–264.

21. J. R. Rest, *Moral Development–Advances in Research and Theory*, New York: Praeger, 1986.

22. Cf. Elizabeth D. Scott, "Organizing Moral Values", *Business Ethics Quarterly*, Vol. 12, No. 1, January 2002, p. 33–55.

# 4

## The Impartial Judge: Detachment or Passion?

### Jeffrey M. Shaman*

*[Judges] do not stand aloof on these child and distant heights; and we shall not help the cause of truth by acting and speaking as if they do. The great tides and currents which engulf the rest of men, do not turn aside in their course, and pass the judges by.*[1]

## I. Introduction

In our legal system, judicial impartiality is a fundamental component of justice. We expect our judges to be, above all else, impartial arbiters so that legal disputes are decided according to the law free from the influence of bias or prejudice. The principle of judicial impartiality is dictated by statutory and common law,[2] is required by the

*  Wicklander Professor of Law, DePaul College of Law; Senior Fellow, American Judicature Society. The author is grateful to Jodi M. Solovy who provided excellent research and editing assistance for this article.

Code of Judicial Conduct,[3] and is essential to due process of law. Thus, it is no exaggeration to say, as did the Supreme Court of New Hampshire, that "It is the *right* of every citizen to be tried by judges as impartial as the lot of humanity will admit."[4]

Like many other fundamental principles, however, this one is not always easy to translate into specific application. Pure impartiality is an ideal that can never be completely attained. Judges, after all, are human beings who come to the bench with feelings, knowledge, and beliefs that cannot be magically extirpated. They may have prior knowledge about evidentiary matters in a case, or strong beliefs about legal issues they must decide. They may have feelings about the attorneys, parties, or witnesses who appear before them. Furthermore, judges engage in extrajudicial activities that may affect their ability to be impartial.[5] They have relatives and friends who may appear before them in court. They participate in civic, charitable, and business activities that may create conflicts of interests. In sum, judges do not live in ivory towers and are not immune to the foibles of the human condition. Nonetheless, we demand that they adhere to the highest degree of impartiality that is mortality possible.[6]

## II. The Code of Judicial Conduct

In the United States, judges are governed by the Code of Judicial Conduct, which traces its roots to the Canons of Judicial Ethics originally set forth by the American Bar Association in 1924.[7] The 1924 Canons, which were drafted by a committee headed by Supreme Court Chief Justice William Howard Taft, were intended to be an ideal guide of behavior rather than an enforceable set of rules.[8] Despite their precatory intent, the Canons were officially adopted for use by a number of states, although they were rarely enforced.[9] The Canons have been criticized for their emphasis on "moral posturing" that proved to be more "hortatory than helpful in providing firm guidance fro the solution of difficult questions."[10] Moreover, the 1924 Canons reflected the traditional view of the judicial function. That is, they envisioned the ideal judge as one who dispensed justice in a mechanical, detached way. Canon 20 proclaimed:

> A judge should be mindful that his duty is the application of general law to particular instances, that ours is a government of law and not of men, and that he violates his duty as a minister of justice under such as system if he seeks to do what he may personally consider substantial justice in a particular case and disregards the general law

as he knows it to be binding on him . . . He should administer his office with a due regard to the integrity of the System of the law itself,
remembering that he is not a depository of arbitrary power, but a
judge under the sanction of law.[11]

Thus, justice was seen as an impersonal system, a system of "law
not of men."[12] A judge was expected to apply general legal principles
and to eschew any personal view of justice. Indeed, the judge's personal belief was considered arbitrary and a thing apart from the law.

The next Canon, Canon 21, was entitled "Idiosyncrasies and In-
consistencies," and included the following statement:

Justice should not be moulded by the individual idiosyncrasies of
those who administer it. A judge should adopt the usual and expected method of doing, justice, and not seek to be extreme or peculiar in his judgments, or spectacular or sensational in the conduct of
the court.[13]

No doubt, there is some sound advice in Canon 21. Certainly it is
best for a judge to avoid being "peculiar" or even "idiosyncratic," although perhaps being "spectacular" or "sensational" once in a great
while might not be so contemptible. According to Canon 21, however,
a judge should be neither individualistic nor extreme; passion and zeal
are best avoided in the ideal judge.[14]

In 1972, the ABA substantially rewrote the Canons and gave them
a new name, the Model Code of Judicial Conduct.[15] Then, in 1990, the
ABA revised the Model Code, amending some specific details and add-
ing others, while maintaining its basic standards.[16] Unlike their prede-
cessor, both the 1972 and 1990 Codes were designed to be mandatory
and enforceable.[17]

Some version of the Code of Judicial Conduct has been officially
adopted in forty–eight states, the District of Columbia, and the federal
court system.[18] Only Montana and Wisconsin remain as hold–outs in
adopting the Code, although those two states have adopted their own
rules of conduct for judges.[19] Moreover, every state, as well as the District of Columbia, has established some agency to enforce its Code or
rules, and has authorized a variety of sanctions that may be imposed
upon judges who violate ethical standards.[20] In the federal system,
judicial councils in each circuit enforce the Code and apply sanctions
for its violation.[21]

The Code of Judicial Conduct governs off–the–bench as well as
on–the–bench conduct of judges. It places restrictions upon extrajudicial activities[22] in addition to restrictions upon activities that are part of
the official judicial function.[23] Indeed, the Code expressly states that "a

judge shall avoid impropriety and the appearance of impropriety in all
of the judge's activities," and "shall act at all times in a manner that
promotes public confidence in the integrality and impartiality of the
judiciary."[24]

Certainly there are reasons to place some restrictions upon a
judge's extrajudicial activities.  Off–the–bench activity may distract a
judge or interfere with the proper performance of the duties of office.[25]
Extrajudicial activity may give rise to bias or a conflict of interest that
should be avoided, or it may demean the integrity of the judiciary.[26]
And judges should not be able to exploit their judicial office or private
gain.[27]

But that is not to say all restrictions upon a judge's off–the–bench
activities are justifiable.  As previously noted, judges do live in the real
world, and cannot be secluded from society.[28]  As individuals, judges
should be allowed outside activity and interaction with other people.
Moreover, judges can benefit society in ways that would not be possible if their extrajudicial activities are unduly restricted.  Perhaps most
important, involvement in the outside world can enrich judicial sensibility and thereby enhance judicial ability.[29]

There are those who believe that the Code of Judicial Conduct
goes too far in attempting to disengage judges from the outside
world.[30]  Professor Charles Wolfram, for one, has criticized the
Code for tipping the balance too far toward isolating judges from the
rest of society.[31]  The Code, he says, "fall[s] just short of requiring
that judges undertake a kind of monastic withdrawal from the
world."[32]

The latest version of the Code of Judicial Conduct, the 1990 version, acknowledges that "[complete separation of a judge from extra–
judicial activities is neither possible nor wise; a judge should not
become isolated from the community in which the judge lives."[33]
Furthermore, Canon 4 of the Code expressly allows judges to engage in certain extrajudicial activities, including speaking, writing,
lecturing, and teaching, so long as they do not cast doubt on judicial
impartiality, demean the judicial office, or interfere with the proper
performance of judicial duties.[34]  Commentary to Canon 4 notes
that because of their special learning, judges are in a unique position
to contribute to the improvement of the law and legal system, and
the Commentary therefore actively encourages judges to participate
in extrajudicial activities concerning the law and legal system.[35]  In
that respect, the Code of Judicial Conduct is consistent with the
principles of the First Amendment of the Constitution, according to
which there is great value in participating in public discourse.[36]  It
is by participating in public discourse, or in the marketplace of

ideas, that we improve our laws, our legal system, our government, our society, our lives.[37]

## III. The Ideal of the Disinterested Judge

The 1924 Canons envisioned an ideal judge who was neutral, impersonal, and disinterested.[38] That traditional vision of the ideal judge has persisted in more recent times. As one court put it, "[i]t is axiomatic that a judge serves as a neutral and *detached* magistrate."[39] Or, as Justice Frankfurter once noted, a judge "must think dispassionately and submerge private feelings on every aspect of a case."[40] This view of the judicial function stresses disengagement, and calls for judges who are disinterested, detached, and dispassionate.

Perhaps the most prominent jurist who embodied the ideal of the disinterested judge was the great Supreme Court Justice, Oliver Wendell Holmes, Jr. G. Edward White, a biographer of Holmes and an assiduous student of his thought, has described Holmes' approach to judging, at least on the Supreme Court, as follows:

> Detachment seems the most accurate term to characterize Holmes' stance on the Supreme Court. He was not merely skeptical; his emotions were for the most part not engaged. To put it more precisely, his emotions were stimulated by the professional features of his work but not by its substance. Few judges could pack more emotion into an opinion, but the emotion was not often generated from compassion for the litigants or concern for the seriousness of the issue at stake. *It* was the emotion of a literary talent, a person who liked the sound of memorable phrases . . . .
> One can see Holmes' stance of detachment as the culmination of his intellectual history Acquaintances of Holmes had from his early years noted his apparent indifference to others. His father thought he "look[ed] at life as at a solemn show where he is only a spectator."[41]

One of the more disquieting aspects of Holmes' detachment was his indifference to the world around him. He never read a newspaper[42] and professed that facts were a "bore."[43] Indeed, he flatly stated, "I hate facts."[44] On one occasion he bristled with indignation when Justice Brandeis suggested that he spend a summer improving his mind by studying some "domain of fact" and visiting factories to observe working conditions there.[45]

Holmes' disinterest is illustrated in an exchange he once had with another great judge, Learned Hand.[46] The two jurists had shared a ride in an old coupe, with Holmes on his way to a Supreme Court conference. As they started to walk their separate ways, Hand said, "Well, sir, good–bye. Do justice."[47] Turning sharply, Holmes called out to Hand, "Come here. Come here."[48] Then Holmes delivered a short lecture to Hand. "[Doing justice,]" Holmes said, "is not my job. My job is to play the game according to the rules."[49] On another occasion Holmes went so far as to say, "I hate justice."[50]

A similar antipathy shows up in Holmes' correspondence with the English political scientist Harold Laski. In one letter to Laski, Holmes proclaimed that: "If my fellow citizens want to go to Hell I will help them."[51] That sort of sentiment has prompted one observer to portray Holmes as "fundamentally antithetical in his detached acceptance and detached rejection of men as he saw them."[52] "To a remarkable degree, Holmes simply did not care."[53]

Holmes' detachment is apparent in his dissenting opinion in *Lochner* v. *New York,*[54] an opinion that has garnered more credit than it may deserve. In *Lochner,,* a case that led to the "New Deal Court Crisis" and has come to symbolize the excesses of judicial intervention, a slim majority of the Supreme Court ruled that a labor law setting maximum hours for bakers unduly interfered with liberty of contract and therefore was a violation of the Due Process Clause of the Fourteenth Amendment.[55] The five–person majority equated due process of law with an extremely conservative economic policy and in the bargain bestowed an undeserved constitutional status upon the concept of liberty of contract. This provided Holmes, who of course had a genius for aphorisms, with the opportunity for one of his better ripostes. "The 14th [sic] Amendment," he retorted in dissent, "does not enact Mr. Herbert Spencer's Social Statics."[56]

Another dissenting opinion written by the first Justice Harlan (and joined by Justices White and Day) was less clever but more careful.[57] Justice Harlan pointed out that liberty of contract was not absolute and could be limited by state regulations reasonably designed to protect health.[58] To demonstrate that the law in question was a reasonable health measure, Justice Harlan's dissenting opinion included a good deal of empirical evidence describing the health hazards faced by bakers and showing that in fact their health was substandard.[59]

This, of course, was of no avail to the majority.[60] To Justice Holmes, on the other hand, it was of no interest.[61] His dissenting opinion in *Lochner,* which was joined by no other justice, is a typical example of two aspects of Holmes' detachment.[62] First, "boring" facts about health hazards or working conditions find no place in his opinion. Second, "doing justice" was not his job. As Holmes put it in his *Lochner* opinion, his "agreement or disagreement has nothing to do with the right of a majority to embody their opinions in law."[63] The state may regulate life in many ways "as injudicious or if you like as tyrannical as this . . . ."[64] In other words, if his "fellow citizens want to go to Hell," Holmes may not offer them affirmative help, but he certainly was not about to lift even a little finger to stop them.[65]

It is important to note that in many respects Holmes was a great philosopher of law. His book, *The Common Law*–not to mention other works of his–was truly pathbreaking and led to the founding of modern jurisprudence. Insofar as his detachment is concerned, however, Holmes has been subject to a fair amount of condemnation.[66] He has been castigated as "a bleak, harsh figure ... a tough old party, quite aware that he was deficient in empathy."[67] He has been called "savage, harsh, and cruel, a bitter and lifelong pessimist."[68] He has been depicted as "emotionally impoverished ... a man who suppressed his own feelings and isolated himself from most of those things believed to give life meaning . . . ."[69] To be sure, there are those who see Holmes' emotional estrangement as a positive source for his judicial ability. For instance, one commentator maintains that Holmes was "a profoundly injured spirit, and his greatness as a human being can be justly viewed only in light of that fact."[70] Most observers of Holmes, however, see his emotional detachment as a decided detriment to his judicial capacity.[71]

In all probability, it is Yosal Rogat who strikes the right tone and poses exactly the right question about Holmes' dispassion when he says:

> It is true that we associate detachment with the judicial function, and require a minimum of neutrality. But Holmes more strikingly than any other judge invites a question that is rarely asked: Whether a minimum of involvement is not also required. Holmes was certainly sufficiently detached. Was he, however, sufficiently engaged?[72]

As a judge–indeed, as a human being–Holmes was truly disinterested. He was genuinely disengaged from the mortal problems that came before him for resolution in case after case. Genuine detachment such as Holmes possessed is a rare quality in judges. Most judges are more engaged than Holmes was about the issues they face. They may, however, attempt, either consciously or unconsciously, to appear detached. They may refrain from expressing their feelings and beliefs. Whether on tie bench or off, they may forgo speaking out about matters in which they believe. They may abstain from making speeches, writing articles, or engaging in associational activities that manifest their beliefs and ideas. Or, when they do venture to express their views, they may do so cautiously, being careful not to go too far, not to take a position, not to say what they really think.

By curtailing their expression in this way, judges may cultivate an appearance of neutrality when in fact they are not neutral at all. For many judges, Holmesian detachment may be a matter of appearance but not reality. It may be an outward stance that cloaks a judge's inner feelings and beliefs.

So, there are two questions that need to be asked about the ideal of the disinterested judge. First, is it desirable? And second, is it possible?

The ideal of the disinterested judge is tied to the nineteenth century view that law is a science that can be mechanically applied by judges.[73] According to this view, law and the judicial function were thought to be essentially non–ideological[74]. Law was seen as neutral, objective, and devoid of values.[75] Hence, it was for the legislative and executive branches of our government, but not the judiciary, to make value judgments or policy choices.[76] Judicial decisions, then, did not require the exercise of will or discretion,[77] and certainly had nothing to do with making values choices. Judges were expected to be unconcerned about policy, or detached from it; it simply was none of their business.

This view of the judicial function persevered through the beginning of the twentieth century. So, for example, in 1905, while striking down a maximum hours law in *Lochner v. New York* on the ground that the law unduly interfered with liberty of contract and was not a valid health measure, the Supreme Court had either the myopia or the temerity to claim that it "was not substituting the judgment of the court for that of the legislature."[78] As late as 1936, Supreme Court Justice Owen Roberts declared that when an act of Congress is challenged as unconstitutional, "the judicial branch of the Government has only one duty–to lay the article of the Constitution which is invoked beside the statute which is challenged and to decide whether the latter squares with the former . . . . This court neither approves nor condemns any legislative policy."[79]

By the time Justice Roberts uttered those infamous words, however, serious doubt about the traditional view of the judicial function was well under way.[80] Indeed, the doubt began in 1881, when

Holmes, "a generation ahead of his time"[81] and two decades before his appointment to the high Court, published his groundbreaking opus. *The Common Law.* In chapter one, Holmes proclaimed:

> [T]he life of the law has not been logic it has been experience. The felt necessities of the time, the prevalent moral and political theories, intuitions of public policy, avowed or unconscious, even the prejudices which judges share with their fellow–men, have had a good deal more to do than the syllogism in determining the rules by which men should be governed . . . .
>
> [I]n substance the growth of the law is legislative . . . . It is legislative in its grounds . . . . Every important principle which is developed by litigation is in fact and at bottom the result of more or less definitely understood views of public policy . . . .[82]

After Holmes' book, the traditional view of law came under increasing criticism. In 1908 Roscoe Pound published his seminal article, *Mechanical Jurisprudence,*[83] paving the way for a new school of thought, "Legal Realism," that was devoted to exploding the traditional myth that law was separate from policy and values [84] By today, the traditional view of mechanical jurisprudence has been thoroughly discredited as a myth that bears little relationship to the reality of the judicial function.[85] Nonetheless, the traditional view has never been entirely abandoned, and it still prevails in some corners more than others. Indeed, there seems to be a never–ending quest to make the law objective and devoid of human value judgments. For example, in the realm of constitutional law, which by character is one of the most political areas of the law, the Supreme Court and some constitutional scholars seem bent upon constructing a network of abstract rules that give the appearance of objectivity and neutrality while masking the human value choices that the Court makes.[86]

Four decades after Holmes' book lifted the veil from the judicial function, another important book about the judicial process was written by another jurist destined to become a Supreme Court Justice. Like Holmes, Benjamin Cardozo was well aware that judging necessarily entailed choosing among values. In *The Nature Of The Judicial Process,* Cardozo wrote:

> My analysis of the judicial process comes then to this, and little more: logic, and history, and custom, and utility, and the accepted standard of right conduct, are the forces which singly or in combination shape the progress of the law. Which of these forces shall dominate in any case must depend largely upon the comparative importance or value of the social

interest that will be thereby promoted or impaired.... I think that the judges themselves have failed adequately to recognize their duty of weighing considerations of social advantage. The duty is inevitable . . . [87]

Cardozo understood that in an important sense the judicial function was much like the legislative function.[88] He explained:

If you ask how [a judge] is to know when one interest outweighs another, I can only answer that he must get his knowledge just as the legislator gets it, from experience and study and reflection; in brief, from life itself. Here, indeed, is the point of contact between the legislator's work and [the judge's]. The choice of methods, the appraisement of values, must in the end be guided by like considerations for the one as for the other. Each indeed is legislating within the limits of his competence.[89]

Unlike Holmes, however, Cardozo did not shrink from the consequences of the nature of the judicial process. Here is Cardozo as seen through the eyes of yet another Supreme Court Justice, William Brennan, whose comments may be as much about himself as about Cardozo:

Having admitted and demonstrated that judges inevitably confront value choices, Cardozo did not shrink from the implications of that admission. He rejected the prevailing myth that a judge's personal values were irrelevant to the decision process, because a judge's role was . . . governed by external, objective norms. Cardozo acknowledged that judges, like common mortals, cannot divorce themselves completely from their personal, subjective vision . . . . He attacked the myth that judges were oracles of pure reason, and insisted that we consider the role that human experience, emotion, and passion play in the judicial process.[90]

Thus, if Holmes represents the ideal of judicial detachment, Cardozo represents the ideal of judicial passion. To be sure, it is a very careful passion. Cardozo was chary about his passion, but unlike Holmes, he embraced it. Whereas Holmes thought that doing justice was not his job and if his fellow citizens wanted to go to Hell he would help them, Cardozo believed that the function of judges was to enhance the well-being of their fellow humans.[91] "The final cause of the law," he stated, "is the welfare of society,"[92] and the business of judges is to promote social welfare.[93]

## IV.  The Obligation to Follow the Law

Justice Cardozo's exemplary career illustrates that detachment is not a necessary element of judicial impartiality and that passion is not incompatible with the judicial function. To be sure, there are limits to how far a judge should allow his or her passion to go. Judges are, after all, obligated to follow the law. While judges often have a good deal of discretion in interpreting and applying the law, that discretion is not boundless. Judicial discretion is abused when a judge does not comport with the dictate of Canon 3 of the Code of Judicial Conduct which states that "[a] judge shall be faithful to the law and maintain professional competence in it."[94]  Ordinarily, when a judge exercises his or her discretion incorrectly–that is, makes a legally incorrect ruling–it is a matter for appeal and does not raise a question of unethical behavior under the Code of Judicial Conduct.[95]  However, some courts have ruled that under certain circumstances legal error–an incorrect exercise of judicial discretion–may be a violation of the mandate of Canon 3 that a judge shall be faithful to the law.[96]

This is an extremely sensitive issue, because to find that the Code of Judicial Conduct may be violated by an incorrect judicial ruling seems to threaten judicial independence. In this nation, there has been a long-standing belief in judicial independence so that judges can be free to make decisions according to their consciences without undue pressure or influence. Judicial independence is a cornerstone of our legal system recognized in the Code of Judicial Conduct, Canon 1 of which expressly states that the independence of the judiciary should be preserved and that the provisions of the Code should be construed and applied to further that objective.[97]

Accordingly, it is only under limited circumstances that an incorrect legal ruling will be considered to violate the requirement of Canon 3 that a judge be faithful to the law. An incorrect legal ruling is an abuse of discretion in violation of Canon 3 if it is motivated by bad faith. For instance, unbelievable as it may seem, there are a number of cases that might be called "coin–flip cases,"–that is, instances when judges make a decision by flipping a coin in open court, or by throwing a dart at a dart board, or by taking a vote of the spectators in the courtroom.[98]  That sort of behavior goes distinctly beyond the bounds of judicial independence because it constitutes a complete abdication of the duty to exercise judgment. The essence of the judicial function is to make *judgments,* in other words, to make reasoned decisions according to the law. Deciding a case by the flip of a coin is decision–making completely without reason and that ignores the law. In fact, it violates Canon 1 of the Code of Judicial Conduct, which requires judges to uphold the integrity of the law;[99] it violates

Canon 2, which requires judges to avoid impropriety and the appearance of impropriety;[100] and it violates Canon 3, which requires judges to decide cases impartially and diligently, as well as to be faithful to the law and maintain professional competence in it.[101]

Another instance of ignoring the law occurred in a 1991 case from Massachusetts, *In re King*[102], which involved a judge who set unusually high bail for four African–American defendants in retaliation for the overwhelming rejection of his brother by African–American voters in a gubernatorial primary election. After imposing the bail, the judge said to a court clerk, "[t]hat's what blacks get for voting against my brother."[103] Unlike the coin–flip cases, here the judge had a reason for the decision he made, but it was a reason completely at odds with the law. Obviously, that the African–American community voted against the judge's brother has nothing to do with the legally appropriate amount of bail. To impose high bail for that reason is a gross abuse of judicial discretion that is unfaithful to the law and abdicates the judicial duty to exercise judgment according to the law.[104]

# V. Openmindedness

These cases remind us that judges are not autocrats.[105] They are obligated to be faithful to the law and to apply it impartially. Moreover, judges are expected to be openminded in regard to the cases over which they preside. It is often said that to maintain the requisite degree of impartiality, judges should not predetermine their decisions. In other words, they should keep an open mind about the outcome of a case until all of the evidence and arguments have been presented.

Still, as a case proceeds, it is only natural for a judge to form various opinions about it. As one court explained, any evidence heard by a judge is bound to engender a certain reaction or attitude regarding how the case may be decided, but so long as the judge is not influenced by extraneous factors and so long as the judge keeps an open mind about the final outcome of the case, the judge will be considered sufficiently impartial.[106]

If made before a jury, a judge's comments on the evidence as a case proceeds may be improper because they unduly influence the jurors, but such comments do not necessarily indicate bias on the part of the judge and are not improper where no jury is present.[107] Comments or remarks made in court that are indicative of a judge's reaction to evidence are not disqualifying so long as the judge has not made a final decision in the case.

On occasion, judges voluntarily disqualify themselves if they feel they cannot be open-minded in a case. For example, some years ago Justice Frankfurter voluntarily recused himself from a case in which two bus passengers claimed that their right of privacy was violated when a public utility commission gave its approval to a bus company to pipe music and other radio programs into its buses.[108] In stepping aside from the case, Justice Frankfurter explained: "My feelings are so strongly engaged as a victim of the practice in controversy that I had better not participate in judicial judgment upon it."[109] It is interesting that Frankfurter felt compelled to disqualify himself, but could not resist the temptation to remark in the official Supreme Court reports, no less, that he was a "victim" of the practice in controversy.[110] Still, Frankfurter deserves credit for being able to admit of his own volition that he could not be open-minded about the case.

Often it is extremely difficult to determine exactly when a judge has crossed the line and lost the requisite degree of openmindedness. Consider, for example, *Haines* v. *Liggett Group, Inc.*,[111] a 1992 decision that concerned a tort action claiming that the decedent's death had been caused by smoking cigarettes produced by the defendant company. The case had been in litigation for over four years when the United States Court of Appeals for the Third Circuit removed the trial judge, Judge Sarokin, from further presiding over the case, because he made the following statement in an interim opinion:

> In the light of the current controversy surrounding breast implants, one wonders when all industries, will recognize their obligation to voluntarily disclose risks from the use of their products. All too often in the choice between the physical health of consumers and the financial well-being of business, concealment is chosen over disclosure, sales over safety, and money over morality. Who are these persons who knowingly and secretly decide to put the buying public at risk solely for the purpose of making profits and who believe that illness and death of consumers is an appropriate cost of their own prosperity! As the following facts disclose, despite some rising pretenders, the tobacco industry may be the king of concealment and disinformation.[112]

Although professing that its decision was "most agonizing", the Court of Appeals nonetheless ordered that Judge Sarokin be removed from the case.[113] In the view of the appellate court, Judge Sarokin was disqualified because the statement he made concerned one of the "ultimate issues to be determined by a jury" in the case—whether the defendants had concealed information about the risks of smoking.[114] Therefore, the Court of Appeals concluded that the trial judge could no longer maintain the appearance of impartiality that is required by due process of law.[115]

The Court of Appeals certainly was correct that Judge Sarokin's statement concerned an ultimate issue in the case, namely, whether the defendants had fraudulently concealed information about the dangers of smoking. But, in addition to being an ultimate issue for the jury to decide, it also was an interim issue raised through a discovery motion that Judge Sarokin was required to rule upon at that point in the litigation[116]. The plaintiff in the case had asked the judge to order the defendant to produce certain documents that the plaintiff believed showed that the tobacco industry had intentionally concealed information about the dangers of smoking.[117] The defendants claimed the documents were exempt from discovery under either the attorney–client or work–product privilege, while the plaintiffs countered that those privileges were nullified by the crime–fraud exception.[118] Thus, in ruling on the discovery motion, it was necessary for Judge Sarokin to decide the question of fraudulent concealment.

One commentator has argued that Judge Sarokin's statement went too far because, in ruling on the discovery motion, all that was necessary to decide was whether there was *prima facie* evidence of fraudulent conduct.[119] But if the evidence clearly established more than a *prima facie* case of fraudulent conduct, what could be wrong about saying so?

Apparently, the judge's sin was not that he commented on an issue of ultimate fact, but rather that his comment was perceived as an overstatement. But what if his comment was supported by the evidence and was factually accurate? If so, is it fair to characterize it as "overstatement?" Moreover, it rarely is considered disqualifying when judges make extreme statements in the course of their work, even when they comment on ultimate issues of fact. So long as a judge remains openminded about the final outcome of a case, statements made by the judge in response to evidence presented in the case do not amount to disqualifying bias. Ordinarily, to be disqualifying, judicial remarks must derive from an extrajudicial source. Comments made by a judge in the context of litigation are considered a normal aspect of adjudication and are not disqualifying unless they are so egregious as to destroy all semblance of openmindedness.

The Supreme Court has said that "[j]udicial rulings alone almost never constitute valid basis for a bias or partiality motion . . . and can only in the rarest of circumstances evidence the degree of favoritism or antagonism required [for disqualification]."[120] In fact, there are a number of cases in which it has been held not to be improper bias for a judge to express extreme disapproval of a defendant's behavior. In one case, it was found not to be disqualifying for a judge to describe the defendants as part of "a large scale conspiracy composed of the most vicious individuals that this court has ever seen."[121] In another case, it was ruled not to be disqualifying for the judge to describe the defendant as "[t]he most viciously antisocial person who has ever come before me."[122] There are even several cases that go so far as to hold that it is not disqualifying for a judge to announce before all the evidence has been presented in a case that he or she believes the defendant to be guilty as charged.[123] Compared to those comments, Judge Sarokin's statement in *Haines* hardly seems to be so extreme that he should be disqualified from presiding over the case.

It is instructive to compare the *Haines* case to another federal case, *United States v. Barry*,[124] that was decided the same year, but in a different federal circuit. In *Barry,* the United States Court of Appeals for the District of Columbia found that a trial judge who states his or her views about the merits of a pending proceeding does not necessarily create an appearance of partiality that requires recusal.[125] In this case, the trial judge, Judge Jackson, was presiding over the criminal prosecution of former Washington, D.C Mayor Marion Barry, who was convicted of one misdemeanor count for possession of cocaine and acquitted of another possession charge, while the jury could not reach a verdict on twelve other counts.[126] While an appeal was pending which would eventually see the case remanded to Judge Jackson for resentencing, Judge Jackson made some public comments about the case in a speech at Harvard Law School. In the speech, the judge said that he was convinced that Barry was guilty of perjury and other crimes.[127] Judge Jackson further remarked that he had never seen a stronger government case, that some jurors had their own agendas and would not convict under any circumstances, and that some jurors were determined to acquit the petitioner regardless of the facts.[128]

Mayor Barry argued that these comments created an appearance of partiality that required disqualification of the judge.[129] The Court of Appeals, however, while noting that a judge should abstain from out–of–court public comment about a pending proceeding, concluded that the judge's remarks did not require his disqualification.[130] The appellate court pointed out that the long–standing rule is that to be disqualifying, the appearance of bias or prejudice must stem from an extrajudicial source.[131] In this case, virtually all of the judge's extrajudicial remarks were based on previous comments that he had made at the sentencing of the defendant.[132]  The Court of Appeals also noted that a judge's remarks that reflect strong views about a defendant do not call for recusal if the remarks are based on the judge's own observations during the performance of his judicial dudes.[133]  Recusal is not required unless the remarks give rise to a reasonable appearance that the judge cannot be impartial.[134]  In this instance, the court concluded that such an appearance had not been established, and that recusal was not necessary.[135]

If recusal was not necessary in the *Barry* case, it is difficult to see why it was in *Haines.*  Judge Sarokin's remarks seem to be no more closeminded or biased than Judge Jackson's, yet the former was removed from a case while the latter was not.  Such are the vagaries of a standard that is inherently subjective and is a matter of degree that cannot be determined by bright lines.

## VI. Personal Bias or Prejudice

It is possible, however, to be more definitive regarding another facet of impartiality which concerns bias or prejudice.  Although justice need not be devoid of passion, it should be applied without personal bias or prejudice toward individuals.  Judges should apply the law uniformly and consistently to all persons.  In other words, judicial impartiality should be akin to equal protection of the law.  Judges should apply the law equally or impartially to all persons.[136]

This principle is violated when a judge has a *personal* bias or prejudice concerning one of the parties to a controversy.  A feeling of ill will or, conversely, favoritism toward one of the parties is improper, and indicates that a judge does not possess the requisite degree of impartiality to decide a case fairly.

A clear example of improper personal bias can be seen in a 1987 Pennsylvania case involving a judge who was presiding over litigation involving the National Fuel Gas Supply Corporation.[137]  During the course of the litigation, the judge said: "I hate the damn gas company and if I could find a way to rule against them I would."[138]  A statement such as this one manifests improper personal bias because it shows that the judge who made the statement is predisposed against one of the parties on the basis of personal animosity.  Instead of listening to the evidence and making a ruling on the basis of law, the judge is looking for a way to rule against the gas company because he detests it.  He has gone into the case with his mind set against the gas company because he hates it.[139]

Improper personal bias has been found in several cases where judges are prejudiced against certain classes of criminal defendants. In one case, a judge announced that he would follow a policy of sentencing all violators of the Selective Service Act to at least thirty months in jail, despite any extenuating circumstances.[140] A reviewing court ruled that the judge's policy amounted to personal bias against a class of defendants that resulted in abuse of the judge's responsibility to tailor sentences to the individual defendant.[141] In another case, a judge was found to be prejudiced against a class of litigants when he expressed his disagreement with sentencing guidelines and said that the maximum penalty should be imposed in all drug cases.[142] The reviewing court found that the judge's statements indicated a predetermined policy in regard to sentencing drug offenders and a personal bias against a particular class of litigants, which required recusal from the drug case over which he was presiding.[143]

Some of the cases involve judges who are candid enough or disingenuous enough to make extremely biased remarks in the presence of others. In reviewing reported cases, it is disconcerting to see how frequently judges make biased remarks in court or elsewhere in public. Judges often express personal animosity toward attorneys,[144] or, although less frequently, toward litigants.[145] The case law is also replete with instances where judges have expressed racial, ethnic, or gender bias.[146] Perhaps this is not surprising. Judges, after all, are human beings, and, although we might hope for more from judges, it must be admitted that they are not immune to the baser motivations of human behavior. Still, judicial comments that manifest this sort of extreme and improper bias should be the basis for disqualification of a judge, not to mention further action against him or her.

Unfortunately, there are severe limitations in attempting to deal with bias and prejudice by focusing upon remarks or comments that judges make. While improper remarks or comments of judges should not be tolerated, the greater danger is the state of mind where bias and prejudice reside. These evils may be present there and may affect a judge's rulings, even though the judge makes no remark or comment to reveal them. One can get the impression from reading the case law that even though a judge has a biased state of mind, he or she can conceal it by saying as little as possible. In fact, one reviewing court has been quite forthright in stating that "in terms of [a judge's] usefulness in later cases, it would have been better had he not given voice to his sentiments."[147] Unfortunately, however, that would do nothing to alleviate the judge's state of mind. Indeed, if a judge is prejudiced, his or her silence masks a situation that calls for a strong remedy. The goal should not be to prevent or punish remarks and comments, but rather to eliminate bias and prejudice, which are the real root of the danger.

Certain kinds of bias are incompatible with the judicial function and are unacceptable in judges. Clearly, racial bias should play no part in the judicial temperament. In the vast majority of situations that come before judges, race is an irrelevant consideration that has nothing to do with the matter at hand since racial bias often is based upon misguided stereotypical thinking about groups of people. Racial bias is demeaning and offensive to the individuals to whom it is directed. It denies equal protection of the law, and simply has no place in the judicial process.

Similarly, gender bias and bias based on ethnic or religious background is inappropriate for a judge and should be excluded from the judicial process.[148] In fact, bias against any *class* of persons may be incompatible with the judicial function, because class bias incorrectly ascribes the attributes of a group of persons to individual members of the group. Where a judge has a predilection against a class of persons, it may operate to improperly predetermine the facts of individual cases and deny a litigant the right to have his or her case decided on the evidence presented at trial. Thus, the 1990 Code of Judicial Conduct expressly prohibits judges in the performance of their duties from manifesting bias or prejudice based on race, sex, religion, national origin, disability, age, sexual orientation or socioeconomic status.[149]

Further, in regard to off-the-bench activities, the 1990 Code prohibits judges from belonging to organizations that practice invidious discrimination on the basis of race, sex, religion, or national origin,[150] because membership in such organizations gives rise to the appearance of bias or prejudice.[151] Commentary to the Code explains that whether an organization practices invidious discrimination is often a complex question which cannot be resolved from a mere examination of the organization's membership rolls.[152] Rather, it may depend on how the organization selects its members, as well as other factors, such as that the organization is dedicated to the preservation of religious, ethnic or cultural values of legitimate concern to its members, or that it is a purely private organization whose membership is within the constitutional right of privacy.[153] In the absence of these factors, invidious discrimination will be found to exist if an organization excludes persons from membership for no other reason than their race, religion, sex, or national origin.[154]

In addition to prohibiting a judge from belonging to an organization that practices invidious discrimination, the 1990 Code also prohibits a judge to regularly use or to arrange a meeting at a club that the judge knows practices invidious discrimination[155]. This prohibition recognizes that any public approval by a judge of invidious discrimination diminishes public confidence in the integrity and impartiality of the judiciary.[156]

## VII. Avowals of Impartiality

When motions are made to judges to disqualify themselves on the ground of bias or prejudice, they often respond by denying the motion coupled with an avowal of openmindedness. "I have determined in my own mind" a judge might proclaim, "that I am openminded and impartial about this case, and free from bias or prejudice." One sometimes wonders if judges truly believe these statements. Given the human tendency not to admit one's own shortcomings, I suspect that most judges do believe these statements, although doubt may lurk somewhere in their heart of hearts. Moreover, even if a judge does remain openminded despite indications to the contrary, there is still an appearance of partiality, which is problematic. I wonder how many judges have considered that their avowals of openmindedness may have a very hollow ring in the public ear. And after all, the Code of Judicial Conduct does state that a judge shall disqualify himself or herself if the judge's impartiality "might reasonably be questioned."[157] Supposedly, the standard that governs the appearance of impartiality is an objective one: whether an objective observer fully informed of the relevant facts would reasonably doubt a judge's impartiality.[158]

Nonetheless, even some reviewing courts have been excessively receptive to accepting declarations of apologetic openmindedness after judges have been challenged for bias or prejudice.[159] In fact, the case law suggests that a judge can successfully fend off a charge of improper bias or prejudice merely by stating on the record that his or her mind is still open and that a final decision on the matter will not be made until the close of all the evidence. All too often, bias or prejudice can be cleansed, so to speak, merely by professing a pure heart and an open mind. While in reality these sorts of avowals of impartiality may be dubious, some reviewing courts have tended to accept them with an uncritical eye. Perhaps this leniency is rooted in the exigency of avoiding numerous recusals of judges; but whatever the reason, the fact remains that a mere recitation by a judge

that he or she remains openminded despite signs suggesting otherwise may be too readily accepted by the reviewing courts.

For example, in *People v. Hall,* the Supreme Court of Illinois
ruled that recusal of a trial judge was not required where the defendant in a criminal case had physically assaulted the judge (as well as
the public defender).[160] In refusing to disqualify the judge, the
state supreme court noted that the record failed to show any unfairness to the defendant and pointed to the judge's declaration
that "I have determined in my own mind that I shall not allow
[the defendant's behavior] to prejudice me in any way and that I will
be completely fair and impartial in this case . . . ."[161] Readily accepting the judge's avowal of impartiality, the reviewing court
asserted that "The trial court is in the best position to determine
whether it has become prejudiced against the defendant."[162] This,
of course, assumes that trial judges can look into themselves and
admit their own biases and prejudices, a practice at which human
beings are not always proficient. It also ignores that trial judges may
be in the worst position to determine whether they *appear* to be biased or prejudiced and should be disqualified on that basis.

A hypothetical situation similar to the one in *Hall* was presented
to judges in a recent survey concerning disqualification.[163] Their
responses to the hypothetical strongly favored disqualification.[164]
This suggests that the respondents either doubted that a judge could
in fact remain impartial after being assaulted by a defendant or that
if actual prejudice did not occur, the appearance of it certainly did.

Still, many appellate courts unquestioningly accept avowals of
openmindedness from trial judges. One notable and recent exception is *In re Schenck,*[165] a 1994 Oregon decision. This case concerned
a number of incidents with escalating ramifications between a judge
and an attorney. After several of the incidents had occurred, the
attorney filed a complaint with the Oregon judicial commission,
asserting that the judge had violated the Code of Judicial Conduct by
incorrectly refusing to recuse himself in a case. The next day, the
judge and attorney had a telephone conversation, during which the
judge said, "Who in the hell made you God's gift to the legal profession?"[166] And about a week later, the judge sent a letter to the local
bar association with a copy of the attorney's complaint, which the
judge described as "pathetic" and "petulant."[167]

When the attorney subsequently had another case assigned to
the same judge, he made a motion to disqualify the judge on the
ground that the judge was biased against him by virtue of their previous confrontations.[168] The judge denied this motion, and in a relatively lengthy statement, explained that whatever may have tran-

spired between him and the lawyer, the judge believed that he could be fair and impartial in presiding over the case at bar.[169]

The Supreme Court of Oregon, however, disagreed, and found that the judge's refusal to recuse himself was a violation of Canon 3C of the Code of Judicial Conduct.[170] The court noted that a judge is not ordinarily disqualified from presiding over a case where one of the attorneys has filed a disciplinary complaint against the judge, because to do so would allow attorneys to "judge shop" by creating disqualifying bias.[171] The court also noted that harsh words between a judge and lawyer do not usually call for recusal.[172] However, if a judge responds to a complaint filed by an attorney against the judge by affirmatively publicizing it and by angrily rebuking the attorney who filed it, the cumulative effect may be enough to establish disqualifying bias on the part of the judge.[173] Thus, in the aggregate the judge's actions created an appearance of bias, if not actual bias, that required his recusal from the case.

Moreover, in addition to finding that there were reasonable grounds to question the impartiality of the judge, the Oregon Supreme Court further ruled that the judge's refusal to recuse was misconduct in wilful violation of Canon 3C and therefore subject to sanction. The judge's expressed avowal that he could be impartial was not convincing to the court; notwithstanding the judge's protestations to the contrary, the court thought that his impartiality could reasonably be questioned and that he should have known as much.[174] Thus, his refusal to recuse himself was a wilful violation of Canon 3.

Under this approach, a judge's statement that he or she can maintain impartiality will not be accepted by a reviewing court at face value, and if a judge's avowal of impartiality is contradicted by the surrounding circumstances, the judge's refusal to step aside can amount to a wilful violation of Canon 3C.

At this point in the *Schenck* case, the judge argued that to discipline him for violating Canon 3C would take him by surprise and hence deprive him of due process of law.[175] But the Oregon Supreme Court thought otherwise. The court stated that there are objective standards by which the judge should have realized that his impartiality was subject to reasonable question.[176] These objective standards, the court thought, provide sufficient notice to a judge as to when recusal is required.[177]

# VIII. Conclusion

The *Schenck* case is an example of a judge whose passion was misdirected. This happens, probably more often than we would like, but perhaps not more often than we should expect. Judging, after all, is a difficult and consuming task. Making decisions about other people's lives is a serious responsibility that engages both intellect and emotion. This author believes that the judicial task of making difficult decisions is advanced when judges care about the law as well as about facts–in short, when they have a passion for life. Judicial passion, however, must be tempered. It should not be infested with hostility, hatred, bias, or prejudice.

Justice Holmes represents the apotheosis of the traditional concept of judicial detachment. That sort of detachment in any human being is extremely rare, if not impossible. Moreover, it is hardly an essential element of judicial impartiality. As Justice Cardozo knew well, passion enriches the judicial temperament and enhances the law.

# Notes

1. Benjamin J. Cardozo, The Nature of The Judicial Process 168 (1921).

2. *See* Jeffrey M. Shaman Et Al, Judicial Conduct and Ethics *passim* (1990).

3. Model Code of Judicial Conduct Canon 3 (1990) [hereinafter Model Code].

4. *In re* Mussman, 302 A.2d 822, 824 (N.H. 1973) (citing N.H. Const. Pt. 1, art, 35) (emphasis added).

5. For example, some extrajudicial activities identified in the Model Code include speaking engagements, written commentary, participation in charitable or civic groups and related activities, financial and business dealings, and other activities outside a judge's official duties. See Model Code Canon 4.

6. *See, e.g.,* Model Code Canon 3E cmt. (stressing the importance of judicial impartiality by requiring disqualification in proceeding "whenever the judge's impartiality might reasonably be questioned").

7. Robert J. Martineau, *Enforcement of the Code of Judicial Conduct,* 1972 Utah L. Rev. 410.

8. *See* Canons of Judicial Ethics (1924) for a statement from the Preamble regarding original intent: "The [American Bar] Association accordingly adopts the following Canons, the spriti of which it suggests as a proper guide and reminder for judges, and as indicating what the people have a right to expect from them."

9. *See* Martineau, supra note 7 and accompanying text (commenting that based on the Canons' suggestive versus regulatory nature, the states adopted what the ABA originally intended, that is, guidelines for judicial conduct).

10. Robert B. McKay, *Judges, the Code of Judicial Conduct, and Nonjudicial Activities*, 1972 Utah L. Rev. 391.
11. Canons of Judicial Ethics Canon 20 (1924.)
12. *Id.*
13. *Id.* Canon 21.
14. *Id.*
15. See *generally* E. Wayne Thode, Reporter's Notes to Code of Judicial Conduct (1973) (compiling notes and documents underlying the 1972 Code of Judicial Conduct).
16. Lisa L. Milord, The Development of the ABA Judicial Code 7 (1992).
17. *See id.* at 8 (explaining the 1990 Code Committee's decision to maintain the enforceable nature of the 1972 Code by keeping the Canons clear and distinct from their corresponding sections); Thode, supra note 15, at 43 (making special note of the 1972 Code Committee's insistence on including a system of enforceable standards).
18. *See* Shaman Et Al, supra note 2, at 3–4 (stating that this near nationwide adoption of the Code helps standardize judicial conduct from state–to–state).
19. *Id.* at 4.
20. *Id.* at 5–7.
21. *Id.* at 7–8.
22. *See* Model Code Canon 4 (covering all areas of extrajudicial conduct, including quasijudicial behavior, nonjudicial activities, and financial disclosure).
23 *See id.* Canon (dividing these official duties into six general categories including duties in general, adjudicative responsibilities, administrative obligations, disciplinary rules, and disqualification duties).
24. *Id.* Canon 2 (emphasis added).
25. *See*, e.g., Shaman Et Al, supra note 2, at 277 (listing potential judicial distractions as business involvement, investments, and participation or membership in charitable or civic organizations).
26. *See id.* at 268–70 (noting that Canon 5 of the Model Code has been interpreted to require judges to abstain from membership in such organizations as the Ku Klux Klan, as well as from serving as board members to groups, such as a legal aid society or Mothers Against Drunk Drivers that are engaged in frequent litigation).
27. *See*, *e.g.*, *In re* Yaccarino, 502 A.2d (1985) (disciplining judge for using confidential information from a case before him to pressure a litigant in the case to sell him real property at an extremely favorable price).
28. *See* McKay, *supra* note 10 (commenting that judges must be familiar with the world outside of the courtroom in order to properly settle the disputes over which they preside).
29 *See* Hon. Shirley S. Abrahamsom, *Refreshing Institutional Memories: Wisconsin and the American Law Institute*, 1995 Wis. L. Rev. 1, 25–30 (illustrating the delicate balance between judicial observation of debates outside the courtroom and the appearance of improper ex parte communication with a story about Judge Benjamin Cardozon and his attendance, not participation, at pre–Palsgraf debates).

68 Jeffrey M. Shaman

30. *See* Charles Wolfram, Modern Legal Ethics 980 (Practitioner ed. 1986) (referring to a comment by Jerome Frank that a judge could only achieve this "ideal" disengagement through death).

31. *See id.* (criticizing the "idealized model" for forcing judges to discontinue valuable outside commitments).

32. *Id.*

33. Model Code Canon 4A cmt.

34. *Id.* Canon 4A.

35. *Id.* Canon 4B cmt.

36. *See. e.g.*, Whitney v. California, 274 U.S. 3S7 (1927) {Brandeis. J. concurring) (asserting that "a fundamental principle" of the American government is freedom of expression and that "public discussion is a political duty" of its citizens).

37. *See* Abrams v. United States, 250 U.S. 616 (1919) (Holmes, J., dissenting) ("[T]he ultimate good desired is better reached by free trade of ideas—that the best test of truth is the power of the thought of get itself accepted in the competition of the market...").

38. *See* Canons of Judicial Ethics Canons 20, 21, 25–33 (1924) (governing neutrality in decisions, consistency in judgments, and detachment from many community activities).

39. West Va. Judicial Inquiry Comm'n. v. Dostert. 271 S.E.2d 427,434 (W. Va. 1980) (emphasis added).

40. Public Utilities Comm'n v. Pollak, 343 U.S. 451,466 (1952).

41. G. Edward White, Intervention And Detachment–Essays In Legal History And Jurisprudence 88 (1994).

42. Yosal Rogat, *The Judge As Spectator*, 31 U. Chi. L. Rev. 213, 244 (1964).

43. II Holmes–Pollock Letters 14 (Howe ed. 1941).

44. *Id.* at 13.

45. *Id.*

46. Learned Hand, *A Personal Confession*, in The Spirit of Liberty 302, 306–07 (3d ed. 1960).

47. *Id.* at 307.

48. *Id.*

49. *Id.*

50. *Id.* at 306.

51. *See* I Holmes–Laski Letters 249 (Howe ed. 1953) (explaining to Laski how he (Holmes) hoped he was not influenced by his personal opinion in the *Steel Trust* case since he knew the nation "liked" the law).

52. *See* Rogat, *supra* note 42, at 226 (concluding that Holmes accepted the transgressions of humankind white refusing to be concerned with the destruction between humans).

53 *Id.* at 255.

54. 198 US. 45, 74–76 (1905) (Holmes, J, dissenting).

55. *Id.*

56. *Id.* at 75 (Holmes, J., dissenting).

57. *Id.* at 65–74 (Harlan. J, dissenting).

58. *See id.* at 66–67 (Harlan, J., dissenting) (citing numerous authorities which supported state regulations "designed and calculated to promote the general welfare or to guard the public health").

59. *See id.* at 70 (Harlan, J., dissenting) ("Professor Hirt in his treatise... has said: "The labor of the bakers is among the hardest and most laborious imaginable, because it has to be performed under conditions injurious to the health of those engaged in it.").

60. *See id.* at 59 ("We think that there can be no fair doubt that the trade of a baker... is not an unhealthy one.... There must be more than a mere fact of the possible existence of some small amount of unhealthiness to warrant legislative interference with liberty.").

61. *See id.* at 75 (Holmes, J., dissenting) (stating that he (Holmes) did not find it his duty to analyze the proposed economic theory or other debated rationales, such as the health hazards of bakers). In fact, Justice Holmes explicitly declined to address the health rationale at all.

62. *Id.* at 74–76 (Holmes, J., dissenting).

63. *Id.* at 75 (Holmes, J., dissenting).

64. *Id.* (Holmes, J., dissenting).

65. I Holmes–Laski Letters, *supra* note 51, at 249.

66 Rogat. *supra* note 42, at 225–26; *see also* Benjamin Kaplan, *Encounters with O. W. Holmes, Jr.*, in Holmes And The Common Law: A Century Later (1983); Grant Gilmore, The Ages Of American Law (1977); Gary J. Aichele, Oliver Wendell Holmes. Jr. Soldier, Scholar, Judge (1989).

67. Kaplan, *supra* note 66. at 12–14. After an awakening to Holmes' truer, non–paternalistic, attributes, Kaplan seeks what he calls a "more balanced appreciation of Holmes." *Id.* at 15–16.

68. Gilmore, *supra* note 66, at 48–49. Gilmore exposes Holmes' truer, less commendable, attributes in contradistinction to his legendary status at the lime of World War 1. Id.

69. Aichele, *supra* note 66, at 164. Aichele concludes that Holmes' deference to the political majority and "deaf–ear" to the plight of the minority was the most troubling aspect of Holmes' approach to the law. Id.

70. Saul Touster, *In Search of Holmes from Within*, 18 Vand. L. Rev. 437, 470–71 (1965).

71. See, e.g.. Rogat. supra note 42, at 243 (highlighting Holmes' detachment from society as the major limitation to his role in the judiciary).

72. *Id.*

73. *See* Roscoe Pound, *Mechanical Jurisprudence*, 8 Colum. L. Rev. 605.605–11 (1908) ("Law is scientific in order to eliminate so tar as may be the personal equation in judicial administration, to preclude corruption and to limit the dangerous possibilities of magisterial ignorance.").

74. *See* Morton J.Horwitz, The Transformation Of American Law 1870–1960: Crisis of Legal Orthodoxy ch. 1 (1992) (stating that although the judicial function was to remain neutral, the judiciary was challenged at times with Legal issues that fell outside "core" areas of (he law and were, thus, unequipped to analyze those issues).

75. *Id.* at 15.

76. *Id.* at 18.

77. *Id.*

78. Lochner v. New York, 198 U.S. 45, 56–57 (1905).

79. United States v. Butler, 297 U.S. I. 62–63 (1936).

80. *See generally* Horwitz, *supra* note 74.

81. Henry Steele Commager, The American Mind 376 (1950).

82. Oliver Wendell Holmes, Jr., The Common Law 1, 35 (1881).

83. *See* Pound, *supra* note 73.

84. *See* White, *supra* note 41, at 166 (describing Legal Realism as a late 1920s and 1930s jurisprudential movement driven by the principle that "individuals 'made a difference' in politics that government").

85. *Id.* at 289.

86 *See* Morton Horwitz, *The Constitution of Change: Legal Fundamentally Without Fundamentalism*, 107 Harv. L. Rev. 30 (1993) ((racing the 1992 Supreme Court Term's decisions, and some Justices' apparent reliance on "mechanical jurisprudence" to employ a technical equation that ultimately eliminates their personal values): Jeffrey M. Shaman, *Constitutional Fact: The Perception of Reality by the Supreme Court*, 35 U. Fla. L, Rev. 236,252–53 (1983) (stating that "through the manipulation of constitutional fact, the Supreme Court obscures its own creative function in interpreting the Constitution"); Jeffrey M. Shaman, *Cracks in the Structure: The Coming Breakdown of the Levels of Scrutiny*, 45 Ohio St. LJ. 161.174 (1984) (finding that a major problem of the Supreme Court's multi–tier review is its focus on abstractions in which the Justices become "primarily concerned with the problem of judicial review, to the exclusion of the specific disputes that gave rise to them").

87. Cardozo, *supra* note 1, at 112,11849.

88. *Id.* at 119.

89. *Id.* at 113. It is correct that immediately after (he quoted passage, Cardozo went on to say:

"No doubt the limits for the judge are narrower. He legislates only between gaps. He fills the open spaces in the law." *Id.*

However, shortly after that passage, Cardozo continued to say. "None the less [sic], within the confines of these open spaces and those of precedent and tradition, choice moves with a freedom which stamps its action as creative. The law which is the resulting product is not found, but made. The process, being legislative, demands the legislator's wisdom." *Id.* at 115.

90. William J. Brennan, Jr., *Reason. Passion, and The Progress of the Law: The Forty–Second Annual Benjamin N. Cardozo Lecture*, 10 Cardozo L. Rev. 3. 4–5 (1988); see generally Hon. Shirley S. Abrahamson, *Judging in the Quiet of the Storm*, 24 St. Mary's L.J. 965 (1993) (acknowledging that the judiciary is vulnerable to personal judgments, predilections and experiences even though numerous constraints exist to limit such subjective influences).

91. *See* Cardozo, *supra* note 87, at 66–67 (noting that the extent a judge's duty is to extend or restrict existing rules as society deems appropriate rather than to fabricate rules on a whim).

92. *Id.* at 66.

93. *See id.* at 67 (arguing that judges should allow the welfare of society lo dictate the direction and scope of existing rules).

94. Model Code Canon 3B{2}.

95. *See In re* Benoit, 487 A.2d 1158 (Me. 1985) (acknowledging that judges occasionally will commit legal errors, and judicial discipline is inappropriate in those cases where something more than mere legal error is absent); *In re* Thomson, 494 A.2d 1022 (NJ. 1985) (holding that if a judge's ruling regarding a defendant's constitutional rights is incorrect, it may be reversed on appeal and does not automatically constitute judicial misconduct).

96. *See In re* Scott. 366 N.E.2d 218 (Mass. 1979) (acknowledging that a pattern of disregard or indifference to (act or law, especially in juvenile and criminal cases, has led to discipline under the Code of Judicial Conduct); *In re* Troy, 306 N.E.2d 203 (Mass. 1973) (holding that a judge's misapplication of bail statutes was a gross abuse of discretion and warranted sanctions).

97. Model Code Canon 1 cmt.

98. *See In re* Daniels, 340 So. 2d 301 (La. 1976) (holding that coin–flipping or holding a spectator ballot prior to a judge's ruling on a defendant's guilt or innocence gives the public the improper impression that the outcome of cases is arbitrary and injures the public confidence in the integrity and impartiality of the judiciary); Currin v. Commission on Judicial Fitness & Disability. 815 P.2d 212 (Or. 1991) (holding that plaintiff is entitled to examine complaints and depose complainants regarding a judge's practice of coin–flipping in traffic infraction cases); *see* also *In re* Rose, unreported determination (N.Y. 1979) (telling defendant in open court that the judge was dismissing defendant's criminal charges because it was the judge's first case).

99. Model Code Canon 1.

100. *Id.* Canon 2.

101. *Id.* Canon 3.

102. 568 N.E.2d 588 (Mass. 1991).

103. *Id.* at 594.

104. *Id.* at 599. The Supreme Judicial Court of Massachusetts found that the judge in this case had committed a number of violations of the Code of Judicial Conduct and therefore censured him and permanently enjoined him from sitting in his court. *Id.*

105. *See. e.g.* Judicial Inquiry & Review Bd. v. Fink. 532 A.2d 358, 373 (Pa. 1987): Judges are not autocrats; they are not police forces; they are not religious advisors; and they do not legislate their own rules and statutes. Rather, they are impartial arbiters under the precedents, rules of court and statutes of this Commonwealth to insure that those who appear before them receive justice. The power of a judge is enormous, and concomitantly, no position in our society demands higher standards. *Id.*

106. Banks v. Department of Human Resources, 233 S.E.2d 449, 450 (Ga. 1977); *see also In re* J. P. Linahan, Inc., 138 F.2d 650. 653–54 (2d Cir. 1943): The court room is a place of surging emotions.... [T]he parties are keyed up to the contest, often in open defiance; and the topics at issue are often calculated to stir up the sympathy, prejudice, or ridicule of the tribunal.... If the judge did not form judgments of the actors in those court–house dramas called trials, he could never render decisions. *Id.*

107. *Banks*, 233 S.E.2d at 450.

108. Public Utils. Comm'n v. Pollak, 343 U.S. 451 (1952).

109. *Id.* at 467 (separate opinion of Frankfurter, J.)

110. *Id.*

111. 975 F26 81 (3d Cir. 1992).

112. *Id.*

113. The Court of Appeals also noted that Judge Sarokin was "a distinguished member of the federal judiciary for almost 15 years and... is well known and respected for magnificent abilities and outstanding jurisprudential and judicial temperament." *Id.* ac 98. In disqualification cases, this sort of praise coming from an appellate court often » the kiss of death for trial judges. In another case, for example, an appellate court began its opinion by describing the trial judge as "one of the ablest and most experienced judges of [a] distinguished trial bench," before quickly moving on to order his disqualification from the case. *In re* International Bus. Machines Corp. 45 F.3d 641.642 (1995). In the case of Judge Sarokin. however, sometime after *Haines* he was promoted to the Court of Appeals in an apparent confirmation of his ability as a judge. Stephen Gillers, Regulation Of Lawyers: Problems Of Law And Ethics 591 (4th ed. 1995).

114. *Haines*, 975 F.2d at 98.

115. *Id.*

116. *Id.* at 85.

117. Id.

118. *Id.* at 85–86.

119. *Panel Discussion–Disqualification of Judges (The Sarokin Matter): Is It A Threat To Judicial Independence?*, 58 Brook. L. Rev. 1063,1081 (1993) (noting that Judge Sarokin's comments lashing out at the tobacco industry and displaying his outrage were inappropriate at the beginning of a trial where the jury had not yet been selected).

120. Liteky v. linked States, 114 S. Ct. 1147, 1157 (1994).

121. United States v. Archbold Newball, 554 F.2d 665, 681 (5th Cir. 1977).

122. United States v. Antonelli, 582 R Supp. 880,881 (N.D. HI. 1984).

123. *See, e.g.* Stale v. Smith, 242 N.W.2d 320 (Iowa 1976) (holding that the trial judge did abuse his discretion in sentencing the defendant to life imprisonment even though he told defense counsel that the defendant may stand a better chance with a jury); Commonwealth v. Leventhal, 307 N.E.2d 839 (Mass. 1974) (holding that a judge's prejudicial remarks during trial displaying to the jury his belief in the defendant's guilt did not affect the disposition of the case); United States v. Sutherland. 463 F.2d 641 (5th Cir. 1972) (acknowledging that a judge does reach some conclusions as to guile before the dose of the trial, and thus, a judge's statement that a defendant is guilty during pre–trial hearings does not deprive the defendant of a fair and impartial trail); People v. Diaz, 427 P2d 505 (Cat. 1967) (holding that a judge's comment while in his chambers that everyone is convinced of the defendant's guilt before the trial ended did pot show that the judge was prejudiced in denying defendant's motion for a new trial).

124. 961 F.2d 260 (D.C. Cir. 1992).

125. *Id.* at 263.

126. *Id.* at 261.

127. *Id.* at 264.

128. *Id.*
129. *Id.* at 262.
130. *Id.* at 265.
131. *Id.* at 263.
132. *Id.* at 264.
133. *Id.* at 263.
134. *Id.*
135. *Id.* at 265.
136. *See* U.S. Const, amend. XIV (providing that "[n]o state shall . . . deny to any person within its jurisdiction the equal protection of the laws").
137. Judicial Inquiry & Review Bd. v. Fink, S32 A.2d 358 (Pa. 1987).
138. *Id.* at 366.
139. The judge later asserted that his remark about the gas company was inconsequential and was being blown out of proportion. He claimed that he made the remark "with tongue in cheek," and that eventually he ruled in favor of the gas company. *Id.* at 367. Nonetheless, the Pennsylvania Supreme Court found that "tongue–in–cheek remarks which announce that the judge will favor one party over another are grossly improper, and if such remarks are made, the judge who makes them must stand down from any controversy in which he has indicated a bias." *Id.*
140. United States v. Thompson, 483 F.2d 527, 528 (3d Cir. 1973).
141. Id. at 529.
142. Pennsylvania v. Lemanski, 529 A.2d 1085,1088 (Pa. 1987).
143. *Id.* at 1089.
144. *See. e.g.* Judicial Inquiry & Review Bd. v. Fink, S32 Aid 358,362–66 (Pa. 1987) (finding that judge's personal dislike for attorney contributed to the judge's abuse of the criminal contempt powers).
145. *See, e.g., In re* Sutler, 543 Fid 1030 (overturning trial judge's assessment of $1,500 against appellant for three–day delay in trial because the fine seemed colored by personal animosity on the part of the judge).
146. *See, e.g.,* Catchpole v. Brannon, 36 Cal. App. 4th 237 (1995) (holding that judicial stale–menu suggesting gender bias warranted reversal of court's ruling because the average person might have justifiably doubted whether trial was impartial); Iverson v. Iverson. 11 Cal. App. 4th 1495 (1992) (holding that language used by trial judge indicated gender bias affecting resolution of credibility issues thus requiring reversal of court's ruling); *In re* Stevens, 31 Cal. 3d 403 (1982) (holding that repeated use by judge of racial and echoic epithets to counsel and court personnel in in–chambers conferences, although performing judicial duties fairly and equitably and free from actual bias, warrants public censure).
147. Commonwealth v. Dane Entertainment Servs., Inc. 467 N.E.2d 222, 225 (Mass. 1984). The court stated that the judge's expression of sentiments about defendant's films was not advisable but this alone did no! disqualify the judge. *Id.*
148. *See* Hon. Shirley S. Abrahamson. *Toward A Courtroom of One's Own: An Appellate Court Judge Looks At Gender Bias*, 61 U. of Cin. L Rev. 1209 (1993) (demonstrating how women face condescension, indifference and

hostility in all judicial system roles–from attorneys and judges to jurors and litigants)

149. Model Code Canon 3B(5) states that

[a] judge shall perform judicial duties without bias or prejudice. A judge shall not, in the performance of judicial duties, by words or conduct manifest bias or prejudice, including but not limited to bias or prejudice based upon race, sex, education, national origin, disability, age, sexual orientation or socioeconomic status, and shall not permit staff, court officials and others subject to the judge's discretion and control to do so. *Id.*

150. Model Code Canon 2C provides: "[a] judge shall not hold membership in any organization that practices invidious discrimination on the basis of race, sex. religion or national origin." *Id.*

151. Model Code Canon 2C cmt.

152. *Id.*

153. *Id.*

154. *Id.*

155. *Id.*

156. *Id.*

157. *Id.* Canon 3E.

158. *See* Pepsico, Inc. v McMillan, 764 F.2d 458.460 (7th Cir. 1985} (holding that a judge's allowance of an inquiry by a third party for possible future employment with a law firm involved hi the proceeding before him created an appearance of impartiality and warranted the judge's recusal).

159 *See, e.g.,* United States v. Sturman.951 F.2d 1466, 1482 (6th Cir. 1991) (accepting judge's statement that he set aside his feelings toward defendant as factor supporting finding that judge was impartial); People v. Hall, 499 N.E.2d 1335,1347 (Ill.1986) (accepting trial judge's statement that he would not allow himself to be prejudiced by defendant physically assaulting him); Banks v. Department of Human Resources, 233 S. E.2d 449, 450 (Ga. 1977) (accepting trial judge's statement that despite strong remarks disapproving of defendant's behavior, "his mind was not closed on the subject..."): State v. Smith, 242 N.W.2d 320, 323 (Iowa 1976) (accepting trial judge's explanation for bis statement that "the defendant may stand a better chance with a jury than with me"); Commonwealth v. Leventhal. 307 N.E. 2d 839, 842–43 (Mass. 1974} (accepting trial judge's explanation for his statement "that doesn't give a person a license to steal"); *see also In re* Gridley, 417 So. 2d 950, 955 (Fla. 1982) (finding that trial judge's strenuous public criticism of death penalty did not interfere with the performance of judicial duties or decrease public confidence in the impartiality of the judiciary where judge included statement that he would do his duty as a judge to follow the law as written).

160. 499 N.E.2d at 1335, 1347.

161. *Id.*

162. *Id.*

163. Jeffrey M. Shaman & Jona Goldschmidt, Judicial Disqualification: An Empirical Study Of Judicial Practices And Attitudes 33 (1995).

164. *See id.* (reporting that judge–respondents expressed a strong disposition to disqualify themselves from a case when the criminal defendant had previously physically assaulted the judge).

165. 870 P.2d 185 (Cir. 1994).
166. *Id.* at 192.
167. *Id.*
168. *Id.*
169. *Id.* at 195.
170. *Id* at 195.
171. *Id* at 194–95.
172. *Id.* at 195.
173. *Id.*
174. *Id.*
175. *Id.*
176. *Id.* at 196.
177. *Id.*

# 5

## How to Read a Contract: From Self–Interest to Fairness and Decency

### Kenneth D. Alpern

### A. Introduction

The aim of the Wicklander Chair is to promote excellence in the teaching of ethics in the professions. Accordingly, I have decided for today's presentation not to offer the standard sort of scholarly lecture in which I would report directly on the conceptual inquiries on which I have been working–inquiries addressing the concepts of trust, forgiveness, decency, fairness, and justice. Such abstract, conceptual studies are essential to effective and creative teaching, and I, at least, find such studies fascinating. But to make those studies exciting and to show their relevance in the detail that I think is necessary to avoid superficiality would take much longer than we have this afternoon. So, instead of delivering the standard sort of scholarly lecture, I have decided to try something different and experimental; indeed, I am not exactly sure what it is going to turn out to be–you will help determine what we do.

What I want to try to do is to teach a class, to teach a class in professional ethics, specifically a class in business ethics. I will frame the class, and, perhaps, from time to time draw back to comment on the lessons, strategies, and pedagogy involved, and to point out directions of development. But for the most part I want simply to *teach*, with the aims of exhibiting an approach to teaching ethics in the professions and of contributing toward the improvement of that teaching.

Before proceeding, I would like to formally and publicly thank the Wicklander family and the Wicklander Chair selection committee for providing me the opportunity to pursue my conceptual studies, to consider the teaching of professional ethics, to bring the two together, and to be able to work with you today in elaborating one small dimension of these activities. I hope and expect to learn from you today.

If a normal class lecture and discussion goes on from about sixty to ninety minutes, I will try to guide us in within that time limit. What I envisions is: I will frame the class, commenting on goals and problems for a course in business ethics; teach the class, with us all interacting as we would in a classroom situation; and I will try to leave some time for questions and comments that you might wish to raise outside the framework of the "class session."

## B. Framing the Class

### B1. *Aims of the Course and Obstacles to Meeting those Aims*

*As a course in Liberal Studies*

The course Philosophy/Religious Studies/Management 228: "Business, Ethics, and Society," is a part of the Liberal Studies Program required of all students at DePaul. Among the general educational aims of any course in the Liberal Studies Program is gaining skills in reading, writing, and speaking, skills of cogency, analysis, interpretation, critical reflection, imagination, and judgment.

Among the obstacles to developing such skills is a curriculum that calls for and rewards formulaic, routinized regurgitation of information that has been placed before students in short readings, in textbook formulations, and that is tested in multiple–choice examinations that call on at most the ability to remember answers already given and which does not call for the exercise of understanding or imagination in applying and extending that understanding.

Among the aims of the Liberal Studies Program and the Business Ethics course is critical reflection—developing the ability to formulate ideas with clarity and precision, to understand and appreciate different perspectives on an issue, and not just to "hear where you are coming from," but to actually engage with alternatives ideas and perspectives, to learn from that engagement, to potentially change, and in the end, to be able to *judge* better and worse based on sound and well–articulated reasons.

This judgment of better and worse, however, is often abandoned out of a misplaced deference to relativism and to an utterly confused thought that one cannot be respecting if one does not allow the validity of all points of view, somehow losing track of the perspective of Nazis, ethnic cleansers, and those who would deny the very respect that is supposed to be valued. Respect just does not demand abdication of critical judgment. But it is a long haul to show how that is so and to fight back the ideology of verbal tolerance that yet masks intolerance and dismissal of true diversity in thought and action.

## As a specifically philosophy course

As a specifically philosophy course and an ethics course, an aim of the Business Ethics course is understanding morality, especially moral theory: to learn what ethical theory is and why it matters. To learn to conceptualize in terms of useful concepts and categories such as rights, interests, justice, and freedom; to begin to explore the relations among such concepts and others such as desire, need, oppression, liberty, exploitation, alienation, respect, and esteem. To acquire a battery of perspectives on morality, including understanding and ability to deploy conceptions of objectivism, relativism, subjectivism, and other approaches to value and to be able to draw insights from theories such as utilitarianism, deontology, and character–ethics.

Among the obstacles to such university education is narrow vocational focus: just give me a diploma, get me a job. At it's worst: I'm interested in the real world, not in learning anything.

It is a real job to bring people with such a narrow view even of what an economic vocation entails to appreciate that they have minds and that university is one of the few places left in which that mind will be valued, nurtured, and used under the scrutiny of critical reflection. As I tell my students the first day of class: "I am going to make a controversial assumption. I am going to assume that you are not business students, but that you are human beings." That usually gets a rise. The point, as I explain to them, is that I will not treat them as if their sole purpose in being alive is to make money—for themselves or for anyone else—but that I will rather treat them as capable of understanding and choice embraces the whole of their humanity, and that it is only in that context that I will address human activities of production and making wealth.

*As a course of philosophical ethics concerning business practice*

The aim in this connection is to illuminate the ethical dimensions of business practice and the organization of human society to produce, exchange, and consume. Here we examine specific areas of business practice, including finance, accounting, marketing, and advertising. But we also attend to the broader social context of business, historically and conceptually. Here we take up concrete issues such as the morality of layoffs and plant closing, to more general issues such as contemporary problems of poverty, to abstract issues such as the meaning of capitalism.

In all of this, we philosophers remain convinced of the relevance of theory to practice, and that, too, is part of the aim of the course: to show that we need theory and that theory illuminates our lives. This is not an easy task. We only have one term. And the often simple applications that we can examine can end up sounding simplistic to anyone with business experience and recognition of the multitude of values that come to bear in almost any real–life situation and the nuance that is necessary to judge their application.

I will, in this connection, elaborate just a bit to take up one of my pet peeves: the insidious use of case studies. I do believe that case studies can be educationally valuable. But, in the vast majority of uses, case studies are damaging to real understanding. For case studies are generally the spectacular cases, and so tend to foster fascination more than inquiry. They set people in opposition, and so tend to foster disputatiousness. They tend to focus on the "correct" solution, and so tend to turn students and faculty away from the conditions that created the problems in the first place. And as removed from the details of the actual cases and in seeking the "fix," case studies tend to be insensitive to nuance and subtlety of judgment. Indeed, case studies are often approached as opportunities to "apply" theories, typically utilitarianism and some version of deontology (or rights–based approach). As if ethical insight and sensitivity were more like a problem of engineering than like judgment in music. We do need theory and principles, but we also need nuance, perceptiveness, sensitivity, maturity, and judgment to use those theories and principles well. Such qualities of liberal humanness are not developed in a single class.

*Expanded Vision*

A further aim of the course is at the express request of the College of Commerce. This, in my opinion, laudable aim is that we *take them out of Chicago*. The College of Commerce means by this: make sure that the course addresses business in an international context. But I take the charge in a more general sense: *enliven the students to possibilities*, possibilities that they may never have considered or even imagined. And here I mean not just to specific creative alternatives, but to a whole frame of mind, to a frame of mind that probes beyond clichés, slogans, and platitudes, that probes beyond what is normally taken for granted, that inquires about what is ideal as well as what is mundane and, so it might be said, "practical." In this class, I want to push students beyond "that's the way it's always been done," and "I can't do anything about it, so I'll just accept it."

These loftier, perhaps more idealistic, perhaps unrealistic aims encounter considerable obstacles. For one thing,  students are challenged in the very commitments that brought them to major in commerce to begin with. They are brought to real critique of the business activities upon which they hang their dreams. And thus, business students sense that their entrenched, if uncritiqued, interests are threatened by the course even more than they would be in a normal philosophy course. Thus, the course is open to the charge first lodged against Socrates, of corrupting the youth, of turning them away from the realities (so believed) of their elders.

*Make Them Moral*

Finally, an aim underlying the instigation of a required course in business ethics for undergraduate majors in commerce: make them moral. That is, make them more aware of and sensitive to moral issues, make them care, make them motivated, and make them more likely to act morally—in their business activities and in their lives in general.

That's a pretty tall order. We don't expect biology classes to turn smokers into abstainers, but many people seek such change from a course in applied ethics. Even the few who think that instruction alone can transform a life–Socrates, for example–think it takes longer than 20 class sessions. And the task goes up against much of the ethos and mythology of current business practice: look out for number one; grab for all the gusto one can get. Further, most of these students are still not entirely out of adolescence. Aristotle points out the hopeful immaturity of the young, and that and ethos was certainly exhibited in a recent class of mine when 22 of 39 students asserted with some confidence that they would become wildly rich. These are students, many of whom resonate positively with my formulation of an appeal for them to their elders: "Take me. Use me. Abuse me. Just give me an MBA and a BMW!" These are not the experienced learners that Aristotle thinks are necessary for benefiting from instruction in ethics. (I tend to do much

better with—there's almost one in every class—the divorced women
with two or three kids, trying to gain advancement through education.
She's seen the losing side of extolling unfettered power.) Finally,
among obstacles, remember that Socrates succeeded in turning souls
through instruction of one or two at a time, not forty. The alternative,
he thought, was sophistry and hypocrisy.

## B2. Types of Course

Very briefly and in broadest outline, two different approaches are
commonly taken to this course. The first is an *historical–sociological
approach.* Here, the focus is on how ethical consciousness is formed by
historical and ideological influences. In its lowest form, this sort of
course can sink to the level of simple consciousness raising by watching films in which some one or group is shown suffering. That may be
a useful sort of experience, but it is hardly higher education.

A second sort of focus is on moral reasoning and character development that issues out of understanding, not being molded by cultural
pressures. Sticking just with moral reasoning is easier and cleaner. But
concern with the person and character is threatening: "You are trying to
change me!" But, believing with Aristotle that understanding in the
area of ethics and character development are inseparable, I take up the
full task: these ideas matter to your lives, to what you do and even more
fundamentally to what you are. And, I recognize along with Plato, that
such an approach will be difficult, frustrating, threatening and therefore
resisted and ridiculed. It is an intellectual enterprise, but not only an
intellectual enterprise: it is understanding in the service of making our
lives different and better.

Now, on to one small illustration: a class in business ethics.

## C. Class

Any good class needs an assignment. So, I am passing out yours.
There's an assignment sheet and a reading. The assignment includes
written answers. You are going to have to write fast.... Actually, I'll
take us through just a part of the assignment, to illustrate some lessons
in education in professional ethics.

Please take a quick look at the assignment and the reading, [respec-
tively, Appendix A: Assignment for Apartment Lease and Appendix B:
Apartment Lease].

## 1. Design of the Assignment

### a. Pedagogical

The design of the assignment, pedagogically, is to start from a type of document that is or should be familiar to business students. At least it is the sort of reading that they can't justifiably balk from, as it is the sort of document common to many business situations. Also, this document allows us to work from the concrete, which students recognize, toward seeing the relevance of the abstractions that are introduced to aid critical examination.

### b. Skills

Through this assignment students will learn to read:

> analytically
> from multiple perspectives
> critically, toward reasoned judgment
> which require remedy, and
> generalization for broader application

I point out to students that these different conceptual activities can be seen to mimic, at least roughly, different roles in a social system that they largely recognize:

| | |
|---|---|
| analysis | detective |
| multiple perspectives | lawyer (own, client's, oppo- |
| critique and judgment | nent's, jury) |
| remedy | judge and jury |
| generalization | legislator |
| | philosopher |

### c. Content

The subject matter is a lease, and so, more generally, bargains, and contracts, a important dimension of business practice. And the ethical examination of the lease addresses fairness, justice, and decency. Exactly what we take up depends to a large extent on what the class–or in this case, you, my "class for the day"–take up and find interesting.

## 2. Discussion

*[At this point, the lecture followed the audience's line of inquiry. What follows in the present text are illustrations and lessons from my own examination.]*

Is the lease fair and just? Consider some of the following provisions of the lease and comment on those provisions.

INDEMNIFICATION OF ATTORNEY'S FEES (§25C)

Perhaps this is a minor provision, not at the heart of the substance of the lease, but it is straightforward and instructive. The provision reads:

Tenant shall pay Lessor all Lessor's costs, expenses and attorney's fees in and about the enforcement of the covenants and agreements of this Lease.

What do you think?

In itself, the lessor has an interest–to recover the cost she [for ease of reference, let the lessor or landlord be female, the lessee or tenant be male] might have to expend in enforcing the lease. And, in that light, the protection that the provision provides would seem to be legitimate: the landlord shouldn't have to incur unreimbursed costs to get the tenant to do follow the lease.

But, now, (a) that legitimacy is compromised if the landlord is in the wrong. If the landlord takes the tenant to court, but loses, then it is prima facie unfair that the tenant should have to pay the landlord's costs. But even more telling, perhaps, (b) though the tenant has the exact same interest in recovering costs of enforcing the lease upon the landlord, look through the whole lease and you will find that it provides no parallel protection to the tenant to recover his costs. Intuitively, this is an unfair difference in protection. And this intuitive unfairness suggests a prima facie principle of fairness: parallel interests call for parallel protection. If both parties have a legitimate claim of protection against the other for imposing costs, then, other things being equal, the lease should stipulate the same protections for both of them. In short, we get the general principle: Parallel protection for parallel interests.

Further examination could address whether, indeed, there are disparities, say in the likelihood or number or burdensomeness of enforcement under which things would not be equal.

But in assessing such inequalities beware of presuppositions: is it more or less likely that one or the other party is to be in breach of the contract? Why do you say that? What contexts do you have in mind? Which party do you most easily identify with? –If I am lucky, a typical class of forty students will contain students who are (themselves or their parents) tenants and students who are or have been associated with landlords. One of the key lessons is to more from one's own perspective and a small number of experiences and anecdotes to general rules and principles designed for the common good.

SECURITY DEPOSIT (§5)

The provision of a security deposit is pretty standard stuff, and on their first reading, few students find any problem here. The landlord has a legitimate interest that the tenant comply with the lease and, as above, the landlord has an interest in not losing due to the tenant's non–compliance. The security deposit gives the landlord immediate protection: motivation to the tenant not to violate the lease and compensation to the landlord readily available if he does. That sounds legitimate enough.

Or is it? Can we apply our principle of parallel interests call for parallel protection? After all, the tenant, too, has an interest that the he not incur losses because of the landlord's non–compliance. But the lease does not give the tenant any power like the security deposit. Claim: it would be parallel protection for the tenant's parallel interest for the lease to stipulate that the tenant may *withhold rent* similar to the landlord's power under the lease to hold and apply the damage deposit. Yet, the lease emphatically excludes such a power to the tenant. Note section 24:

24. TENANT'S WAIVER: Tenant's covenant to pay rent is and shall be independent of each and every other covenant of this Lease.

Tenant agrees that Tenant's damages for Lessor's breach shall in no case be deducted from rent nor set off for purposes of determining whether any rent is due in a forcible detainer action brought on the basis of unpaid rent.

The lease contains no parallel "Lessor's Waiver." And then, section 6D contains this inestimable language:

It is, however, understood and agreed that buildings are physical structures subject to aging, wear, tear, abuse, inherent defects, and numerous
forces causing disrepair or breakdown beyond Lessor's reasonable control, and that components and skilled workmen are not always immediately available. It is further understood and agreed that for the most part
Lessor's costs of operation are fixed and unavoidable and to permit rent
abatement or damages to Tenant would create an intolerable burden on
Lessor, other tenants and surrounding neighborhood.

Legitimate interests of the landlord are here–the rest of the section
bears reading–inflated and made impregnable. The landlord controls
the security deposit as leverage, the tenant has no such control under
the lease.
    But wait, what about the fact that the tenant holds the landlord's
apartment. That is of considerable value and could be damaged by the
tenant. –Yes, and the landlord has the security deposit, the law, and
recommendations to use against the tenant should he seek to coerce the
landlord through threat of damage to her apartment. The lease gives the
landlord easy and legal means of protecting herself. The lease does not
give, indeed expressly denies, such easy and legal means to the tenant.
Of course, other things may not be equal. I have identified one consideration toward the conclusion that things are in fact sufficiently equal to
justify parallel protection, but much more analysis of that issue is
needed. [A possible homework assignment–or hint for the more engaged student to follow out.][1]

APPLICATION (§3)
The requirement of an application on the part of the tenant is, again, a
standard provision, commonly accepted by all. And it does protect legitimate interests of the landlord in gaining assurance of the tenant's
reliability and ability to pay. But, again, the doesn't the tenant have
parallel interests in assurance of the landlord's reliability: her record of
upkeep and compliance with leases? Is it outrageous to expect that a
fair lease would provide for disclosure, under penalty of voiding the
lease, by the landlord, say, of court actions against the landlord or other
infractions? How about recommendation letters from former tenants? Is
such information readily available to prospective tenants just by asking
current tenants? Perhaps, to some extent. But asking strangers for criticism of the very person who holds power over them is not always so
easy. Nor is it all that easy to find out who even owns the building in
many large scale operations.

Again, these considerations are the *start* of inquiry, not the final conclusion on the provisions addressed or on dozens of other potentially problematic and potentially defensible provisions.

### 3. Lines of Development

a. We have already formulated one potentially useful principle of fairness and justice: parallel protection for parallel interests. It may be that parallel interests do not receive parallel protection, as an imbalance toward one party in one part of the lease is balanced by an imbalance elsewhere in favor of the other party, or that rather than piece by piece, the lease as a whole gives reasonably equitable protection. I leave estimation as an exercise for the audience, (though you can easily enough guess my own conclusion).

b. What shall we say, what principles shall we be guided by when interests or position are not comparable? How for example, compare the provisions governing subletting (§12) or bankruptcy (§25B) by the tenant in relation to the arguably parallel provisions governing sale (§5) or condemnation (§16), involving the landlord? We can say that each party should receive appropriate protection or protection that is fair and just? But what how should those values be judged?

One avenues that could be pursued is that of impartiality, sometimes put in terms of the Golden Rule, but treated with more sophistication by approaches such as that of John Rawls' choice of principles behind a veil of ignorance. Though designed for judging principles of justice for the basic structure of society, Rawls' procedure is appealing for particular decisions as well. The idea is simply that the principles are just that would be chosen by people who did not know which position they held in a contractual situation. Roughly, if one did not know whether one is to be landlord or tenant, which provisions would one choose? The decision of this fair procedure supposedly identifies principles that are fair.

Another avenue–which, perhaps, could be conceived under suitable restrictions as a guide in practice to what such a "veiled" decision would be–is to look at statute. That is, to look at what is said by the law, if one can see law not as merely the expression of power, but as the expression of an attempt by the society to protect fairly. In the present case, we do have "The Chicago Landlord and Tenant's Ordinance." And there we find many of the provisions that we have questioned redrafted in ways we have suggested. For example, rent withholding is allowed and any interest on security deposits accrues to the tenant, not the landlord. Other suggestions, such as parallel "applications" by tenant and landlord, do not appear. Whether that is a result of excessive protection such a provision would give to the tenant or lack or imagination or will or power on the part of the drafters of the Ordinance, is another issue that must be left to discussion.

c. It might be objected to the whole thrust of my discussion, that we do not need criteria of fairness and justice. Rather, appropriate protection, fairness, and justice are *whatever is agreed to*. If you voluntarily sign the lease, then  you are justly held to its terms. If you do not like the terms, you are free to not sign. If you sign, then it is fair to hold you to the terms of the lease. Such an approach, it might be claimed, respects the person: each individual is autonomous and responsible. Parties pursue their interests according to their own conception of what that interest is and of how to promote it.

Many lines may be followed in responding to this position. I will suggest a few:

i. Signing that is coerced would not be seen as valid or demonstrating that it is just to enforce the terms of the lease. Now, what constitutes coercion? Only the proverbial gun at the head? Must it be the party who benefits who exercises the coercive pressure? Or, could coercion be constituted by such things as lack of alternative housing, lack of opportunity to negotiate leases with different terms, lack of time to seek alternatives, or lack of access to information?

ii. A different line of thought derives from the transience of many renters. Given that the rental for many tenants will be for only a short period of time, it may be that tenants are willing to sign to and endure unjust provisions: "Since I'll be gone in a year or two, it's not worth fighting against the system. I'll just buck up, get through it, and get out." This attitude, by the way, is common among college students, who may accept tuition hikes in their junior and senior years that are (seen by them as) unfair. They do not fight the perceived unfairness because they think of themselves of being soon gone, and the fight is just not worth it.

It might be responded on the side of landlords that these conditions are not of their making, that they are in competitive positions, and that it is not their responsibility to be paternalistic. So, they press for the advantages that they can get, and that is just.

Back on the other side, it might yet be said, that even if landlords may not create such conditions, they exploit them and are predators on the vulnerable. Indeed, it might be claimed that the ethos of such inequality between landlord and tenant becomes inculcated in us, so that we do not even recognize that the relationship is exploitative.

As a landlord, in a competitive condition, what is fair competition, what is fair bargaining, and what is treating other people with decency? Can a competitor afford to be decent? The law and common decency recognize that even if a person signs a contract with an escalator clause (say, rent of one cent the first day, doubling each day of the month), the contract will not and should not be enforced–to allow rent of $9,395.240.96 per month would be unconscionable, even if freely and voluntarily agreed to.

d. Another line of thought concerns indeterminacy. However precisely terms are specified, there will always be indeterminacy in provisions: how often is too often to allow showing of the apartment for re–rental? How much wear and tear is reasonable? The general problem is one of the discretion: it is not eliminable and it is useful for flexibility, as is the discretion in allowing merge lanes for traffic, in place of traffic lights. But as the analogy of the merge lane exhibits, if certain parties regularly exercise their discretion maximally for their own benefit–say, the drivers in the highway never let in driver from the ramp, then the value of the flexible arrangement is lost and more rigid, authoritarian techniques–e.g. a traffic light–have to be invoked to secure efficiency and justice. Thus, again, in the area of indeterminacy, lack of decency, that is, lack of voluntary accommodation of one's own interests to the interests of others, will result in injustice that is to remedied only by more coercive, rigid, and less efficient techniques.

### D.  Closing

I must draw back for the conceit of teaching a class. I arbitrarily cut off discussion at this point–and I don't even have the possibility of continuing discussion next class.

A final comment though on the nature of teaching ethics. As intimated above, principles cannot cover everything. As Aristotle points out in his *Nicomachean Ethics* Book 5, chapter 10, written codes, laws, and general principles cannot capture the nuances of the particular. Rules for merges are not precise, any more than are rules for how to hug. Rules can help, but ultimately we must also exercise judgment, practical wisdom, and decency. Such qualities of character, Aristotle thought, come from a combination of study and experience. And that is why he thought that instruction in ethics of the sort he offers in the *Nicomachean Ethics* is not suitable for the young–they do not have the experience, nuance, and judgment necessary to understand and flexibly apply principles to particular cases. And, further, that is one of the reasons courses on professional ethics of the sort we teach at DePaul are so hard and in the end must fail for many of the students.

A then a final comment about our present undertaking. One purpose of an occasion like this that hasn't been enough noted is that it is a celebration, and a celebration in several senses. It is a celebration in the sense of honoring the people who made it and the professorship possible–the celebration is to honor the Wicklanders. And this occasion is a celebration in the sense of a festivity, an opportunity for us to enjoy together an intrinsically valuable activity.

But more fundamentally–etymologically and conceptually–to celebrate is to keep, to hold. I originally sought out my students, past and present, to populate a mock class for you this afternoon. In self–interest, I contact my best students, the ones who hardly learned anything from me because they already know it and just needed an excuse to do it well. And many of your have been able to come. Thank you. Your being here allows me to remember you more securely. And so, keeping you in my thoughts and appreciation is to celebrate you. Thank you.

## APPENDIX A

## ASSIGNMENT FOR APARTMENT LEASE
**Part A**

1. **Provision.** Make a list of all those provisions of the lease that might be found objectionable from the point of view of the landlord, the tenant, or others. List the items in the order they appear on the lease and give the number or other reference for the provision in question. Put a star beside the items on your list that you think are most important.

2. **Objection(s).** For each item on your list, state from whose point of view it might seem objectionable and state why it might seem so.

3. **Defense.** For each item on your list, state what, if anything, could be said in defense of the provision.

4. **Judgment.** Having surveyed objections and defense for each provision on your list, render a reasoned judgment stating whether the provision is, all things considered, acceptable or unacceptable, and explaining why that judgment should be accepted.

5. **Remedy.** For each item on your list that is in some respect unacceptable, suggest changes that should be made in the lease itself or in the circumstances surrounding the making of leases that would make that part of the lease acceptable.

6. **Comments.** Add any further comments that you think useful.
**Part B**

7. **Fair Lease.** Considering your answers to Part A, as well as the overall nature of the business relationship between landlord and tenant, would you say that the original lease represents a *fair* bargain? Why/Why not?

8. **Supplementation.** Is the relation of landlord and tenant as defined by a written document, i.e. the lease, in itself sufficient to secure fairness? Of what value might be integrity, judgment, and decency of the parties to the lease; special laws governing leases; tenants' organizations; landlords' trade groups; or other institutions, policies, or personal traits?

9. **Fair Bargains.** Now try to move to a more general level. Think not just of a lease, but also of other sorts of bargains for goods and services. With what you have learned by answering the preceding questions in mind, make a list of the general conditions which you think must be satisfied in order for a bargain of any sort to be a fair bargain. In short, what are the *general conditions* for a *fair bargain* of any kind.

# APPENDIX B

# APARTMENT LEASE
# NOT FURNISHED

DATE OF LEASE      TERM OF LEASE      MONTHLY RENT    SECURITY DEPOSIT*

BEGINNING              ENDING

*IF NONE, WRITE "NONE". Paragraph 5 of Lease Agreements and Covenants then INAPPLICABLE

|  | TENANT | LESSOR |
|---|---|---|
| **TENANT** | A | .........................................................A |
| **APARTMENT** | A | .........................................................A |
| **BUILDING** | A | .........................................................A |
| **CITY** | A | .........................................................A |

In consideration of the mutual agreements and covenants set forth below and on the reverse side hereof (the same being fully included as part of this Lease) Lessor hereby leases to Tenant and Tenant hereby leases from Lessor for use in accordance with paragraph 8 hereby the Apartment designated above, together with the fixtures and accessories belonging thereto, for the above Term. All parties listed above as Lessor and Tenant are herein referred to individually and collectively as Lessor and Tenant respectively.

ADDITIONAL AGREEMENTS, AND COVENANTS (including DECORATING AND REPAIRS), if any.
THIS LEASE IS EXECUTED BY THE OWNER WITH THE DISTINCT UNDERSTANDING ON THE PART OF THE TENANT THAT NO DOG, CAT, OR ANY OTHER ANIMAL WILL BE KEPT ON THE PREMISES AND THAT A VIOLATION OF THIS UNDERSTANDING WILL GIVE THE OWNER THE RIGHT TO FORTHWITH CANCEL THIS LEASE.

SIGNATURES                        LESSORS

_____(SEAL)

_____(SEAL)    _____(SEAL)

## LEASE AGREEMENTS AND COVENANTS

**1. RENT:** Tenant shall pay to the Lessor at the above address (or such other address as Lessor may designate in writing) the monthly rent set forth above on or before the first day of each month in advance. THE TIME OF EACH AND EVERY PAYMENT OF RENT IS OF THE ESSENCE OF THIS LEASE. ALL RENTAL PAYMENTS SHALL BE DUE PROMPTLY ON THE DATE SPECIFIED HEREIN. LESSOR SHALL CHARGE A MONTHLY LATE FEE OF TEN ($10.00) DOLLARS OR TWELVE PERCENT (12%) PER ANNUM, WHICHEVER IS GREATER, OF ALL RENTALS NOT RECEIVED BY THE TENTH DAY OF ANY MONTH AND OF ANY BALANCE REMAINING FOR PREVIOUS MONTHS' RENTALS AND CHARGES. ALL SUCH CHARGES AND LATE FEES SHALL BE DEEMED TO BE ADDITIONAL RENT, AND SHALL BE IMMEDIATELY DUE AND PAYABLE

**2. POSSESSION:** At the commencement of the term of this Lease, Lessor shall deliver possession of the Apartment to Tenant. If Lessor fails to do so within 10 days from the date thereof, this Lease shall terminate unless reaffirmed in writing within an additional 5 days by Tenant. Upon such termination Lessor shall refund all prepaid rent and security, which shall be Tenant's sole remedy. It is understood that decorating, if any, to be performed by Lessor shall not be a condition precedent to possession or rent

**3. APPLICATION:** The application for this Lease and all representations and promises contained therein are hereby made a part of this Lease. Tenant warrants that the information given by Tenant in the application is true. If such information is false, Lessor may at Lessor's option terminate this Lease by giving Tenant not less than 30 days' prior written notice, which shall be Lessor's sole remedy.

**4. PROMISES OF THE PARTIES:** The terms and conditions contained herein shall be conclusively deemed the agreement between the Tenant and the Lessor and no modification, waiver or amendment of this Lease or any of its terms, conditions or covenants shall be binding upon the parties unless made in writing and signed by the party sought to be bound.

**5. SECURITY DEPOSIT:** Tenant has deposited with Lessor the Security Deposit in the amount set forth above for the performance of each and every covenant and agreement to be performed by Tenant under this Lease Lessor shall have the right, but not the obligation, to apply the Security Deposit in whole or in part as payment of such amounts as are reasonably necessary to remedy Tenant's defaults in the payment of rent or in the performance of the covenants or agreement contained herein Lessor's right to possession of the Apartment for non-payment of rent or any other reason shall not be affected by the fact that Lessor holds security Tenant's liability is not limited to the amount of the Security Deposit.

Lessor shall give Tenant written notice of the application of the Security Deposit or any part thereof within thirty (30) days of said application. If the application is on account of maintenance, repairs or replacements necessitated by Tenant, said notice shall include the estimated or actual cost of the same, attaching estimates or paid receipts. Upon receipt of said notice, Tenant shall at once pay to Lessor an amount sufficient to restore the Security Deposit in full. Upon termination of this Lease, full payment of all amounts due and performance of all

Tenant's covenants and agreements (including surrender of the Apartment in accordance with Paragraph 15), the Security Deposit or any portion thereof remaining unapplied shall be returned to Tenant within thirty (30) days of said termination without interest except as provided by law. If Lessor fails to return all or a portion of Tenant's Security Deposit, Lessor shall pay to Tenant an amount equal to two (2) month's rent as liquidated damages.

In the event of a sale, lease, or other transfer of the Building, Lessor may transfer or assign said Security Deposit to Lessor's grantee, lessee, or assignee, provided said grantee, lessee or assignee by written undertaking addressed to Lessor assumes all Lessor's obligations hereunder Tenant agrees to look to such grantee, lessee or assignee solely for the return of said Security Deposit. The provisions hereof shall apply to each and every sale, lease, or other transfer of the Building

SECURITY DEPOSIT SHALL NOT BE DEEMED OR CONSTRUED AS ADVANCE PAYMENT OF RENT FOR ANY MONTH OF THE LEASE TERM.

## 6. LESSOR TO MAINTAIN:

**A.**       Tenant hereby declares that Tenant has inspected the Apartment, the Building, and all related areas and grounds and that Tenant is satisfied with the physical condition thereof. TENANT AGREES THAT NO REPRESENTATIONS, WARRANTIES (EXPRESSED OR IMPLIED) OR COVENANTS WITH RESPECT TO THE CONDITION, MAINTENANCE, OR IMPROVEMENTS OF THE APARTMENT, BUILDING, OR OTHER AREAS HAVE BEEN MADE TO TENANT EXCEPT THOSE CONTAINED IN THIS LEASE, THE APPLICATION, OR OTHERWISE IN WRITING SIGNED BY LESSOR.

**B.**       Lessor agrees that Lessor will perform work set forth in this Lease within a reasonable time not to exceed 60 days from the commencement of the Term unless otherwise agreed

**C.**       Lessor covenants that at all times during the Term hereof, the Lessor shall maintain the Apartment and the Building to the following minimum standards

     (1)   Effective weather protection, including unbroken windows and doors;

     (2)   Plumbing facilities in good working order,

     (3)   A water supply which either under the control of the Tenant is capable of producing hot and cold running water, or under the control of the Lessor produces hot and cold running water, furnished to appropriate fixtures, and conducted to a sewerage system,

     (4)   Heating (and, if furnished, air conditioning and ventilation) facilities in good working order which, if under the control of the Tenant, are capable of producing, or if under the control of the Lessor, produce heat (and, if furnished, air conditioning and ventilation) in fixtures provided (and no other) within reasonable accepted tolerances and during reasonable hours.

     (5)   gas and/or electrical appliances which are supplied by Lessor in good working order, and appropriate gas piping and electrical wiring system to the extent existing in the Building maintained in good working order and sound condition;

     (6)   Building, grounds and areas under the control of the Lessor in clear, sanitary and safe condition free from all accumulations of debris, filth, rubbish, garbage, rodents and vermin,

     (7)   Adequate and appropriate receptacle(s) for garbage and rubbish, and, if under the control of the Lessor, in clean condition and good repair;

     (8)   Floors, stairways, and railings and common areas in good repair;

     (9)   Apartment floors, walls and ceilings in good repair and safe condition, and

     (10)   Elevators (if existing) in good repair and safe condition

**D.**       It is, however, understood and agreed that buildings are physical structures subject to aging, wear, tear, abuse, inherent defects, and numerous forces causing disrepair or breakdown beyond Lessor's reasonable control, and that components and skilled workmen are not always immediately available. It is further understood and agreed that for the most part Lessor's costs of operation are fixed and unavoidable and to permit rent abatement or damages to Tenant would create an intolerable burden on Lessor, other tenants and surrounding neighborhood It is, therefore, understood and agreed that Lessor's delay in performing agreements set forth in 6B, interruptions in services provided by Lessor, breakdowns of equipment or disrepair caused by (1) conditions caused by Tenant, members of Tenant's household, guests or other persons on the premises with Tenant's consent or other tenants; (2) Tenant's unreasonable refusal of or other interference with entry of Lessor or Lessor's workmen or contractors into the Apartment or Building for purposes of correcting defective conditions, (3) lack of reasonable opportunity to Lessor to correct defective conditions: (4) conditions beyond Lessor's reasonable control, including strikes or lockouts, (5) Lessor's not having actual knowledge of such defective conditions; or (6) Lessor's having exercised due care but such defective condition(s) continuing to persist, shall be an absolute defense in any action against Lessor for breach of covenant based upon the duties of Lessor to maintain the Apartment or Building. Lessor's failure or inability to make repairs or provide services in any of the just described circumstances shall in no event form the basis of any claim or setoff for damages against Lessor nor a basis for an abatement of rent nor a cause for termination of the Lease

**E.**       Nothing herein contained shall in the event of fire, explosion or other casualty impose upon Lessor any obligation to make repairs which are more extensive or different from those required by the provisions of paragraph 14 of this Lease (Fire & Casualty).

**7. UTILITIES:** Unless otherwise agreed in writing, if the Apartment is individually metered, payment to the utility company or authorized metering agency of the applicable charges for gas, electricity or water consumed by the Tenant in the Apartment, including, if applicable, current used for electric heating, ventilation, air conditioning, hot water, etc., shall be Tenant's sole responsibility.

**8. TENANT'S USE OF APARTMENT:** The Apartment shall be occupied solely for residential purposes by Tenant, those other persons specifically listed in the Application for this Lease, and any children which may be born to or legally adopted by Tenant during the Term. Unless otherwise agreed in writing, guests of Tenant may occupy the Apartment in reasonable numbers for no more than three weeks each during each year of the Term hereof. Neither Tenant nor any of these persons shall perform nor permit any practice that may damage the reputation of or otherwise be injurious to the Building or neighborhood, or be disturbing to other tenants, be illegal, or increase the rate of insurance on the Building.

**9. TENANT'S UPKEEP:** Tenant covenants to perform the following obligations during the term hereof· (A) maintain the Apartment and appurtenances in a clean, sanitary and safe condition; (B) dispose all rubbish, garbage and other waste in a clear and sanitary manner from the Apartment to the refuse facilities; (C) properly use and operate all appliances, electrical, gas and plumbing fixtures; (D) not place in the Apartment or Building any furniture, plants, animals, or any other things which harbor insects, rodents, or other pests, (E) keep out of the Apartment and Building materials which cause a fire hazard or a safety hazard and comply with reasonable requirements of Lessor's fire insurance carrier; (F) not destroy, deface, damage, impair, nor remove any part of the Building or Apartment or facilities, equipment or appurtenances thereto, and (G) prevent any person in the Apartment or Building with Tenant's permission from violating any of the foregoing Tenant obligations. Tenant shall not suffer or commit any waste in or about the Apartment or Building and shall at Tenant's expense keep the

Apartment in good order and repair (except to the extent Lessor has in this Lease agreed to do so). On termination of this Lease, Tenant shall return the Apartment to Lessor in like condition, reasonable wear excepted.

**10. ALTERATIONS, ADDITIONS, FIXTURES, APPLIANCES, PERSONAL PROPERTY:** Tenant shall make no alterations or additions nor install, attach, connect, or maintain in the Apartment or any part of the Building, interior or exterior, major appliances or devices of any kind without in each and every case the written consent of the Lessor and then, if granted, only upon the terms and conditions specified in such written consent All alterations, additions and fixtures (including security devices) whether temporary or permanent in character, made by Lessor or Tenant, in or upon the Apartment shall, unless otherwise agreed or unless Lessor requests their removal, become Lessor's property and shall remain in the Apartment at the termination of the Lease without compensation to Tenant. The foregoing notwithstanding, neither Lessor nor Lessor's insurance carrier shall be liable to Tenant for the replacement of such alteration, addition, or fixtures in the event of casualty loss unless Tenant notifies Lessor of the replacement value and pays, as additional rent, the resultant premium increase, if any. If Lessor shall permit or demand removal, Tenant shall put that part of the Apartment into like condition as existed prior to the installation of such alteration, addition, or fixture

**11. ACCESS:** Lessor reserves the right in accordance herewith to enter the Apartment in order to inspect same, make necessary or agreed repairs, decorations, alterations, or improvements, supply necessary or agreed services, or exhibit the Apartment to prospective or actual purchasers, mortgagees, tenants, workmen, or contractors, or as is otherwise necessary in the operation and/or protection of the Building, its components or persons therein. At Lessor's discretion, Lessor shall be provided with and may retrain and use copies of any keys necessary for access to the Apartment. In the event of apparent or actual emergency, Lessor may enter the Apartment at any time without notice At any time within 90 days prior to the end of the term hereof, after a single general notice, Lessor may as often as necessary show the Apartment for rent between the hours of 9 AM and 8 PM on not less than 15–minute specific notice if Tenant or other person is in the Apartment, without limitation as to days At other times, entry shall be in accordance with agreement with Tenant or if same is impractical or refused, after 24 hours' notice and only during the period of 7 AM to 7 PM Monday through Saturday In the event of the willful or negligent breach of this provision, the non–breaching party shall at once be entitled to actual damages or liquidated damages in the amount of two month's rent and an injunction, if necessary, to prevent continuation of such breach

**12. ASSIGNMENT, SUBLETTING, AND RELETTING:** Tenant may substitute a new tenant for the balance of the Term provided (a) Lessor consents to the prospective new tenant, and (b) Tenant upon demand pays (i) in advance, the deficiency if the aggregate rent from the reletting for the balance of the Term hereof is less than the aggregate rent then remaining to be paid under this Lease, and (ii) all expenses of reletting (if any) including decorating, repairs, replacements, commissions, and/or an administrative fee for performing the details attendant to such a transaction. Lessor at its option may determine whether said transaction shall be in the form of a subletting, assignment or reletting

Lessor may at any time and for any reason reject any prospective new tenant offered by Tenant or by others, provided, however, that if Lessor shall do so WITHOUT CAUSE, Tenant shall be liable to Lessor only for the deficiency and/or actual or estimated expenses described in (b) (i) and (ii) of this Paragraph 12 which would have been due from Tenant had the prospective new tenant been accepted Cause shall be deemed to be the failure, based on information and data made available to the Lessor, of such prospective new tenant to meet the criteria customarily employed by the Lessor to evaluate the acceptability of prospects as tenants for similar apartments in the Building. During the last three months of the Term, Lessor shall be obligated to accept an otherwise qualified prospective new tenant only if said prospective new tenant enters into a lease for a term for which leases are customarily offered for similar apartments in the Building Unless otherwise agreed by Lessor in writing, Lessor shall have no duty to procure prospective new tenants for Tenant or otherwise mitigate damages Lessor's attempt to procure such prospective new tenants shall in no event constitute a new agreement by Lessor to assume such duty. Lessor may let other vacancies in the Building first before reletting or subletting or attempting to relet or sublet the Apartment.

Tenant shall neither sublet the Apartment nor any part thereof nor assign this Lease nor permit by any act or default of himself or any person any transfer of Tenant's interest by operation of law, nor offer the apartment or

any part therefor for lease or sublease except in accordance herewith

**13. ABANDONMENT:** Ten days' physical absence by Tenant with rent being unpaid, or removal of the substantial portion of Tenant's personal property with rent being paid, and, in either case, reason to believe Tenant has vacated the Apartment with no intent again to reside therein shall be conclusively deemed to be an abandonment of the Apartment by Tenant In such event, and in addition to Lessor's remedies set forth in Paragraphs 15 and 25. Lessor may, but need not, enter into the Apartment and act as Tenant's agent to perform necessary decorating and repairs and to relet the Apartment in accordance with the terms and conditions set forth in Paragraph 12 Tenant shall be conclusively deemed to have abandoned any personal property remaining in the Apartment and Tenant's title thereto shall thereby pass under this Lease as a bill of sale to Lessor without additional payment or credit by Lessor to Tenant.

**14. FIRE AND CASUALTY:** If the Apartment is damaged or destroyed by fire or casualty and
**A.** the Apartment is only partially damaged and is inhabitable and the Lessor makes full repairs within 60 days, this Lease shall continue without abatement nor apportionment of rent.
**B.** if the Apartment is rendered (1) uninhabitable, (2) continued occupancy would be illegal, or (3) Lessor cannot or does not repair within 60 days, Tenant may immediately vacate the Apartment and notify Lessor in writing within five days thereafter of his intent to terminate, in which case this Lease shall terminate as of the date of vacating and all prepaid rent and unapplied Security Deposit shall be returned to Tenant.

**15. TERMINATION AND RETURN OF POSSESSION:**
**A.** Upon the termination of this Lease, whether by lapse of time or otherwise, or upon termination of Tenant's right of possession without termination of this Lease, Tenant shall yield up immediate possession to Lessor and deliver all keys to Lessor at the place where rent is payable, or as otherwise directed by Lessor. The mere retention of possession thereafter shall constitute a forcible detainer. Lessor shall have the right and license with process of law (and if Tenant abandons the Apartment, Tenant grants Lessor and Lessor shall have such right and license with or without process of law) to enter into the Apartment and to be returned the Apartment as of Lessor's former estate and to take possession of the Apartment and to expel and remove Tenant and any others who may be occupying or within the Apartment and any and all property from the Apartment, without relinquishing Lessor's right to rent or any other right given to Lessor hereunder or by operation of law. If Tenant abandons the Apartment and Lessor exercises the right and license to enter without process of law, Lessor may use such force as may be necessary without being deemed in any manner guilty of trespass, eviction, or forcible entry or detainer.

**B.** Tenant shall agree that in the event Tenant fails to vacate the Apartment upon termination of this Lease or Tenant's right of possession, that:
(1) Tenant shall pay as liquidated damages for the entire time that possession is withheld a sum equal to three times the amount of rent herein reserved, pro rated per day of such withholding, or Lessor's actual damages if same are ascertainable; or
(2) Lessor, at it sole option, may upon giving Tenant written notice, extend the term of this Lease for a like period of time not to exceed one year at such rent as Lessor has stated prior to said termination date, or
(3) If Lessor fails to notify Tenant within 45 days of said termination date of Lessor's election under either (1) or (2), Tenant's continued occupancy shall be for a month–to–month term.
(4) No action or non–action by Lessor except as herein provided shall operate as a waiver of Lessor's right to termination this Lease or Tenant's right of possession nor operate to extend the term of hereof.
    **16. EMINENT DOMAIN (CONDEMNATION):** If the whole or any substantial part of the Building is taken or condemned by any competent authority for any public use or purpose, or it any adjacent property or street shall be so condemned or improved in such a manner as to require the use of any part of the Building, the term of this Lease shall at the option of the Lessor or the condemning authority be terminated upon, and not before, the date when possession of the part so taken shall be required for such use or purpose and Lessor shall be entitled to receive the entire award without apportionment with Tenant Rent shall be apportioned as of the date of Tenant's vacating as the result of said termination
    **17. LESSOR'S MORTGAGE:** This Lease is not to be recorded and is subordinated to any present or future mortgages on the real estate (or any part of it) upon which the Building is situated and to all advances upon the security of such mortgages
    **18. LEASE BINDING ON HEIRS & ETC.:** All the covenants and agreements of this Lease shall be binding upon and inure to the benefit of the heirs, executors, administrators, successors, and assigns of Lessor and Tenant, subject to the restrictions set forth in Paragraph 12 hereof, except that where there are only one or two persons named or remaining as Tenants herein, then, in the event of the death of one or both Tenant(s), the surviving Tenant and/or heirs or legal representatives of the deceased Tenant may terminate this Lease at the end of any calendar month within 120 days of said occurrence by giving Lessor not less than 45 days prior written notice
    **19. NOTICES:** Notices, including those provided by statute, shall be in writing and served by delivery (A) In person or (B) By both (1) United States regular and (2) certified or registered mail, postage prepaid, at the addresses shown for Lessor and Tenant at the beginning of this Lease or at such other addresses as either party may designate to the other party by written notices If services is by mail, the mailing shall be deemed delivery and the date of mailing the date of delivery. Notices served in person on Tenant may be served if left with some person residing in or in possession of the Apartment above the age of 12 years, and in the event of an apparent abandonment then notice may be served by posting same on the door to the Apartment in addition to (B) above Notices served in person on Lessor may be served on any office employee of Lessor, or if Lessor receives rent at his home, in the same manner as on Tenant.
    **20. RULES AND REGULATIONS:** The rules and regulations at the end of this Lease shall be a part of this Lease Tenant covenants and agrees to keep and observe these rules and regulations Tenant also covenants and agrees to keep and observe such further reasonable rules and regulations as may later be promulgated by Lessor or Lessor's agent for the necessary, proper and orderly care of the Building (provided such later rules do not materially change the terms contained in the body of this Lease)
    **21. RESIDENT TO INSURE POSSESSIONS:** Lessor is not an insurer of Tenant's person or possessions Tenant agrees that all of Tenant's person and property in the apartment or elsewhere in the Building shall be at the risk of Tenant only, and that Tenant will carry such insurance as Tenant deems necessary therefor Tenant further agrees that except for instances of negligence or willful misconduct of Lessor, its agents or employees, Lessor, its agents and employees shall not be liable for any damage to the person or property of Tenant or any other person occupying or visiting the Apartment or Building, sustained due to the Apartment or Building or any part thereof or any appurtenances thereof becoming out of repair (as example and not by way of limitation, damage caused by water, snow, ice, frost, steam, sewerage, sewer gas or odors, heating, cooling, and ventilation equipment, bursting or leaking of pipes, faucets, and plumbing fixtures, mechanical breakdown or failure, electrical failure, security services or devices or mailboxes being misused or becoming temporarily out of order, and fire) or due to the happening of any accident in or about the Building or due to any act or neglect of any other tenant or occupant of said Building or any other person.
    **22. REMEDIES CUMULATIVE. NON–WAIVER:**
**A.** (1) All rights and remedies given to Tenant or to Lessor shall be distinct, separate, and cumulative, and the use of one or more thereof shall not exclude or waive any other right or remedy allowed by law, unless specifically limited or waived in this Lease; (2) no waiver of any breach or default of either party hereunder shall be implied from any omission by the other party to take any action on account of any similar or different breach or default; (3) the payment or acceptance of money after it falls due after knowledge of any breach of this Lease by Lessor or Tenant, or after termination in any way of the Term or of Tenant's right of possession hereunder, or after the service termination in any way of the Term or of Tenant's right of possession hereunder, or after service of any notice, or after the commencement of any suit or any right hereunder not expressly waived; (4) no express waiver shall affect any breach other than the breach specified in the express waiver and that only for the time and to the extent therein stated.
**B.** Tenant's obligation to pay rent during the Term or any extension thereof or any holdover tenancy shall not be waived, released or terminated by the service of any five–day notice, demand for possession, notice of termination of tenancy, institution of any action of forcible detainer, ejectment or for any judgment for possession, or any other act or acts resulting in termination of Tenant's right of possession.
    **23. TENANT'S REMEDIES:** If Lessor:
(1) defaults in its duty to maintain the Apartment or Building or in its agreements to perform repairs, remodeling, or decorating as set forth in Paragraph 6 and such default is not cured by Lessor within 30 days after notice from Tenant to Lessor (unless such default involves a hazardous condition or failure to furnish heat, hot water or essential services, which shall be cured forthwith) and provided Lessor's failure to cure is not excused on account of one or more of the defenses set forth in Paragraph 6 **(D)**, in which case Lessor shall notify Tenant of specific facts constituting such excuse within said 30–day period (or in the case of a hazardous condition, or failure to furnish heat, hot water or essential services, within 5 days of Tenant's notice), or
(2) defaults in the performance of any other covenant or agreement hereof and such default is not cured by Lessor within 10 days after written notice from Tenant to Lessor.
Tenant may treat such event as a breach of this Lease and, in addition to all other rights and remedies provided at law or in equity (including without limitation those provided in Chapter 24, Section 11–13–15 of the Illinois

Revised Statutes relating to building code violations) may, by giving Lessor not less than 10 days prior written notice terminate this Lease and the Term created hereby by setting forth the date of said termination in the said 10 days' notice, and vacating on or before said date, with rent paid to said termination date Prepaid rent and Security Deposit, if any, shall be promptly refunded to Tenant

**24. TENANT'S WAIVER:** Tenant's covenant to pay rent is and shall be independent of each and every other covenant of this Lease.

Tenant agrees that Tenant's damages for Lessor's breach shall in no case be deducted from rent nor set off for purposes of determining whether any rent is due in a forcible detainer action brought on the basis of unpaid rent.

**25. LESSOR'S REMEDIES: A.** If Tenant·

(1) defaults in the payment of any single installment of rent or in the payment of any other sum required to be paid under this Lease or under the terms of any other agreement between Tenant and Lessor and such default is not cured within five days of written notice; or

(2) defaults in the performance of any other covenant or agreement hereof, and such default is not cured by Tenant within 10 days after written notice to Tenant from Lessor (unless the default involves a hazardous condition which shall be cured forthwith):

Lessor may treat such event as a breach of this Lease and Lessor shall have any one or more of the following described remedies in addition to all other rights and remedies provided at law or in equity.

(a) Lessor may terminate this Lease and the term created hereby, in which event Lessor may forthwith repossess the Apartment in accordance with Paragraph 15(A) hereof and Tenant agrees to pay to Lessor damages in an amount equal to the amount of rent provided in this Lease to be paid by Tenant for the balance of term as set forth in this Lease, less the fair rental value of the Apartment for said period, and in addition, any other sum of money and damages owed by Tenant to Lessor.

(b) Lessor may terminate Tenant's right of possession and may repossess the Apartment in accordance with Paragraph 15(A) hereof without further demand or notice of any kind to Tenant and without such entry and possession terminating this Lease or releasing Tenant in whole or in part from Tenant's obligation to pay rent hereunder for the full Term  Upon and after such entry into possession without termination of this Lease, Lessor may, but need not, relet the Apartment as Tenant's agent and may, but need not, make repairs, alterations and additions in or to the Apartment and redecorate, all under the same terms and conditions as set forth in Paragraph 12 hereof. Tenant shall on demand pay to Lessor damages and all Lessor's expenses of reletting as set forth and described in Paragraph 12 hereof. If the consideration collected by Lessor from any such reletting for Tenant's account is not sufficient to pay the amount provided in the Lease to be paid monthly by Tenant together with all such expenses, Tenant shall pay to Lessor, as damages, the amount of each monthly deficiency. Tenant agrees that Lessor may from time to time file suit to recover any such sums falling due under the terms of this paragraph and that no suit or recovery of any portion due Lessor hereunder shall be a defense to any subsequent action brought for any amount not theretofore reduced to judgment in favor of Lessor except that Lessor shall not be permitted more than one recovery in the aggregate amount so due.

**B.** If Tenant is the subject of any involuntary proceeding under any section of any bankruptcy act and any court or tribunal shall adjudge Tenant insolvent or unable to pay Tenant's debts and such order is not vacated within 30 days after its entry, or if Tenant files any voluntary petition or similar proceedings under any section of any bankruptcy act in any court or tribunal to delay or reduce or modify Tenant's debts or obligations, or if Tenant is declared insolvent according to law, or if any assignment of Tenant's property shall be made for the benefit of creditors, or if any receiver or trustee is appointed for Tenant or his property, this Lease shall automatically terminate without need of an election by Lessor and Lessor's remedy shall be as set forth in Subparagraph **(A)** above.

**C.** Tenant shall pay Lessor all Lessor's costs, expenses and attorney's fees in and about the enforcement of the covenants and agreements of this Lease.

**26. OTHER AGREEMENTS:**

**A.** The headings or captions of paragraphs are for identification purposes only and do not limit or construe the contents of the paragraphs.

**B.** "Lessor" as used herein shall refer to the person, partnership, corporation or trust hereinabove set forth in that capacity  If such person be designated an agent, Lessor shall also refer to and include the principal. Obligations and duties to be performed by Lessor may be performed by Lessor, its agents, employees or independent contractors. Only Lessor or its designated agent may amend or modify this Lease or Lessor's obligations thereunder.

**C.** All rights and remedies of Lessor under this Lease, or that may be provided by law, may be exercised by Lessor in Lessor's own name individually, or in Lessor's name by Lessor's agent, and all legal proceedings for the enforcement of any such rights or remedies, including distress for rent, forcible detainer, and any other legal or equitable proceedings, may be commenced and prosecuted to final judgment and execution by Lessor in Lessor's own name individually, or by agent of any Lessor who is a principal.

**D.** Tenant agrees that Lessor may at any time and as often as desired assign or re–assign all of its rights as Lessor under this Lease.

**E.** The words "Lessor" and "Tenant" as used herein shall be construed to mean plural where necessary and the necessary grammatical changes required to make the provisions hereof apply to corporations or persons, women or men, shall in all cases be assumed as though in each case fully expressed.

**F.** The obligations of two or more persons designated Tenant in this Lease shall be joint and several. If there be more than one party named as Tenant, other than children in a family, all must execute this Lease and any modification or amendment hereto.

**G.** "Apartment" used herein shall refer to the dwelling unit leased to Tenant.

**H.** Tenant's occupancy of any storeroom, storage area or garage space in or about Building shall be as licensee only  Tenant understands that due to the construction, location and use of storeroom, storage area or garage spaces, Lessor cannot and shall not be liable for any loss or damage of or to any property placed therein. DO NOT STORE VALUABLE ITEMS IN SUCH AREAS. The termination of this Lease for any reason shall also serve to terminate Tenant's right to use such storeroom, storage area, or garage space.

**I.** "Building" as used herein shall include the entire physical structure located at and about the address hereinabove stated, including machinery, equipment and appurtenances which are a part thereof, grounds, recreational areas and facilities, garages and out–buildings, and other apartment buildings which form a complex owned and operated as a single entity.

**J.** The invalidity or unenforceability of any provision hereof shall not affect or impair any other provision.

# RULES AND REGULATIONS

**These rules are for the mutual benefit of all tenants. _____ Please cooperate.**

**Violations may cause termination of your Lease.**

1. No animals without written consent of Lessor or Lessor's agent (which may be revoked on (10) ten day's notice at any time) No animals without leash in any public area of the Building
2. Passages, public halls, stairways, landings, elevators and elevator vestibules shall not be obstructed or be used for children's play or for any other purpose than for ingress to and egress from the Building or apartments, nor shall children be permitted to congregate or play in or around the common interior areas of the Building All personal possessions must be kept in the Apartment or in other storage areas if provided
3. All furniture, supplies, goods and packages of every kind shall be delivered through the rear or service entrance, stairway or elevator
4. Carriages, velocipedes, bicycles, sleds and the like shall not be allowed in the lobbies, public halls, passageways, courts or elevators of the Building and are to be stored only in places designated for their storage by the Lessor
5. Laundry and drying apparatus shall be used in such a manner and at such times as the Lessor may clearly post in such area Clothes, washers and dryers, and dishwashers, unless installed by Lessor, cannot be kept in the Apartment.
6. The use of garbage receptacles or incinerators shall be in accordance with posted signs and only garbage and refuse wrapped in small, tight parcels, may be placed in garbage receptacles or incinerator hoppers Aerosol cans or inflammable materials shall be placed in garage receptacles or dropped into the incinerator only if so posted They are highly explosive
7. No sign, signal, illumination, advertisement, notice or any other lettering or equipment shall be exhibited, inscribed, painted, affixed or exposed on or at any window or on any part of the outside or inside of the Apartment or the Building without the prior written consent of the Lessor
8. No awnings or other projections including air conditioner, television or radio antennas or wiring shall be attached to or extend from or beyond the outside walls of the Building
9. The Tenant shall not alter any lock or install a new lock or a knocker or other attachment on any door of the Apartment without the written consent of the Lessor.
10. No waste receptacles, supplies, footwear, umbrellas or other articles shall be place in the halls, on the staircase landings, nor shall anything be hung or shaken from the windows or balconies or placed upon the outside window sills
11. No noise, music or other sounds shall be permitted at any time in such manner as to disturb or annoy other occupants of the Building
12. The water closets, basin and other plumbing fixtures shall not be used for any purpose other than for those for which they were designed, no sweepings, rubbish, rags or any other improper articles shall be thrown into them Any damage resulting from misuse of such facilities shall be paid for by the Tenant.
13. There shall be no cooking or baking done in or about the Apartment except in the kitchen COOKING ON A BARBEQUE OR OTHER SIMILAR EQUIPMENT ON A PORCH, TERRACE, OR BALCONY IS EXPRESSLY FORBIDDEN
14. If Lessor provides television master antenna hookup, only Lessor's authorized agent shall install Tenant's television set to master antenna and Tenant agrees to pay installation cost and annual maintenance fee Tenant shall permit access to disconnect hookup for non–payment. Tenant agrees to pay $50 00 liquidated damage to Lessor's authorized agent for each illegal hookup in Tenant's Apartment.
15. No furniture filled with a liquid or semi–liquid shall be brought in or used in the Apartment.

## GUARANTEE

On this _____, 19____, in consideration of Ten Dollars ($10 00) and other good and valuable consideration, the receipt and sufficiency of which is hereby acknowledged, the undersigned Guarantor hereby guarantees the payment of rent and performance by Tenant, Tenant's heirs, executors, administrators, successors or assigns of all covenants and statements of the above Lease

_____(SEAL) _____(SEAL)

## Apartment Lease
## Lease Agreements and Covenants

**1. RENT:** Tenant shall pay to the Lessor at the above address (or such other address as Lessor may designate in writing) the monthly rent set forth above on or before the first day of each month in advance. The time of each and every payment of rent is of the essence of this lease. All rental payments shall be due promptly on the date specified herein. Lessor shall charge a monthly late fee of ten ($10.00) dollars or twelve percent (12%) per annum, whichever is greater, of all rentals not received by the tenth day of any month and of any balance remaining for previous months' rentals and charges. All such charges and late fees shall be deemed to be additional rent, and shall be immediately due and payable.

**2. POSSESSION:** At the commencement of the term of this Lease, Lessor shall deliver possession of the Apartment to Tenant. If Lessor fails to do so within 10 days from the date thereof, this Lease shall terminate unless reaffirmed in writing within an additional 5 days by Tenant. Upon such termination Lessor shall refund all prepaid rent and security, which shall be Tenant's sole remedy. It is understood that decorating, if any, to be performed by Lessor shall not be a condition precedent to possession or rent.

**3. APPLICATION:** The application for this Lease and all representations and promises contained therein are hereby made a part of this Lease. Tenant warrants that the information given by Tenant in the application is true. If such information is false, Lessor may at Lessor's option terminate this Lease by giving Tenant not less than 30 days' prior written notice, which shall be Lessor's sole remedy.

**4. PROMISES OF THE PARTIES:** The terms and conditions contained herein shall be conclusively deemed the agreement between the Tenant and the Lessor and no modification, waiver or amendment of this Lease or any of its terms, conditions or covenants shall be binding upon the parties unless made in writing and signed by the party sought to be bound.

**5. SECURITY DEPOSIT:** Tenant has deposited with Lessor the Security Deposit in the amount set forth above for the performance of each and every covenant and agreement to be performed by Tenant under this Lease. Lessor shall have the right, but not the obligation, to apply the Security Deposit in whole or in part as payment of such amounts as are reasonably necessary to remedy Tenant's defaults in the payment of rent or in the performance of the covenants or agreement contained herein. Lessor's right to possession of the Apartment for non–payment of rent or any other reason shall not be affected by the fact that Lessor holds security. Tenant's liability is not limited to the amount of the Security Deposit.

Lessor shall give Tenant written notice of the application of the Security Deposit or any part thereof within thirty (30) days of said application. If the application is on account of maintenance, repairs or replacements necessitated by Tenant, said notice shall include the estimated or actual cost of the same, attaching estimates or paid receipts. Upon receipt of said notice, Tenant shall at once pay to Lessor an amount sufficient to restore the Security Deposit in full. Upon termination of this Lease, full payment of all amounts due and performance of all Tenant's covenants and agreements (including surrender of the Apartment in accordance with Paragraph 15), the Security Deposit or any portion thereof remaining unapplied shall be returned to Tenant within thirty (30) days of said termination without interest except as provided by law. If Lessor fails to return all or a portion of Tenant's Security Deposit, Lessor shall pay to Tenant an amount equal to two (2) month's rent as liquidated damages.

In the event of a sale, lease, or other transfer of the Building, Lessor may transfer or assign said Security Deposit to Lessor's grantee, lessee, or assignee, provided said g4rantee, lessee or assignee by written undertaking addressed to Lessor assumes all Lessor's obligations hereunder. Tenant agrees to look to such grantee, lessee or assignee solely for the return of said Security Deposit. The provisions hereof shall apply to each and every sale, lease, or other transfer of the Building.

Security deposit shall not be deemed or construed as advance payment of rent for any month of the lease term.

## 6. LESSOR TO MAINTAIN:

**A.**        Tenant hereby declares that tenant has inspected the apartment, the building, and all related areas and grounds and that tenant is satisfied with the physical condition thereof. Tenant agrees that no representations, warranties (expressed or implied) or covenants with respect to the condition, maintenance, or improvements of the apartment, building, or other areas have been made to tenant except those contained in this lease, the application, or otherwise in writing signed by lessor.

**B.**        Lessor agrees that Lessor will perform work set forth in this Lease within a reasonable time not to exceed 60 days from the commencement of the Term unless otherwise agreed.

**C.**        Lessor covenants that at all times during the Term hereof, the Lessor shall maintain the Apartment and the Building to the following minimum standards:

(1)   Effective weather protection, including unbroken windows and doors;

(2)  Plumbing facilities in good working order;
(3)  A water supply which either under the control of the Tenant is capable of producing hot and cold running water, or under the control of the Lessor produces hot and cold running water, furnished to appropriate fixtures, and conducted to a sewerage system;
(4)  Heating (and, if furnished, air conditioning and ventilation) facilities in good working order which, if under the control of the Tenant, are capable of producing, or if under the control of the Lessor, produce heat (and, if furnished, air conditioning and ventilation) in fixtures provided (and no other) within reasonable accepted tolerances and during reasonable hours.
(5)  gas and/or electrical appliances which are supplied by Lessor in good working order, and appropriate gas piping and electrical wiring system to the extent existing in the Building maintained in good working order and sound condition;
(6)  Building, grounds and areas under the control of the Lessor in clear, sanitary and safe condition free from all accumulations of debris, filth, rubbish, garbage, rodents and vermin;
(7)  Adequate and appropriate receptacle(s) for garbage and rubbish, and, if under the control of the lessor, in clean condition and good repair;
(8)  Floors, stairways, and railings and common areas in good repair;
(9)  Apartment floors, walls and ceilings in good repair and safe condition; and
(10)  Elevators (if existing) in good repair and safe condition.
**D.**      It is, however, understood and agreed that buildings are physical structures subject to aging, wear, tear, abuse, inherent defects, and numerous forces causing disrepair or breakdown beyond lessor's reasonable control, and that components and skilled workmen are not always immediately available. It is further understood and agreed that for the most part lessor's costs of operation are fixed and unavoidable and to permit rent abatement or damages to tenant would create an intolerable burden on lessor, other tenants and surrounding neighborhood. It is, therefore, understood and agreed that lessor's delay in performing agreements set forth in 6b, interruptions in services provided by lessor, breakdowns of equipment or disrepair caused by (1) conditions caused by tenant, members of tenant's household, guests or other persons on the premises with tenant's consent or other tenants; (2) tenant's unreasonable refusal of or other interference with entry of lessor or lessor's workmen or contractors into the apartment or building for purposes of correcting defective conditions; (3) lack of reasonable opportunity to lessor to correct defective conditions: (4) conditions beyond lessor's

reasonable control, including strikes or lockouts; (5) lessor's not having actual knowledge of such defective conditions; or (6) lessor's having exercised due care but such defective condition(s) continuing to persist, shall be an absolute defense in any action against lessor for breech of covenant based upon the duties of lessor to maintain the apartment or building. Lessor's failure or inability to make repairs or provide services in any of the just described circumstances shall in no event form the basis of any claim or setoff for damages against lessor nor a basis for an abatement of rent nor a cause for termination of the lease.

E.       Nothing herein contained shall in the event of fire, explosion or other casualty impose upon lessor any obligation to make repairs which are more extensive or different from those required by the provisions of paragraph 14 of this lease (fire & casualty).

7. UTILITIES: unless otherwise agreed in writing, if the apartment is individually metered, payment to the utility company or authorized metering agency of the applicable charges for gas, electricity or water consumed by the tenant in the apartment, including, if applicable, current used for electric heating, ventilation, air conditioning, hot water, etc., shall be tenant's sole responsibility.

8. TENANT'S USE OF APARTMENT: the apartment shall be occupied solely for residential purposes by tenant, those other persons specifically listed in the application for this lease, and any children which may be born to or legally adopted by tenant during the term. Unless otherwise agreed in writing, guests of tenant may occupy the apartment in reasonable numbers for no more than three weeks each during each year of the term hereof. Neither tenant nor any of these persons shall perform nor permit any practice that may damage the reputation of or otherwise be injurious to the building or neighborhood, or be disturbing to other tenants, be illegal, or increase the rate of insurance on the building.

9. TENANT'S UPKEEP: tenant covenants to perform the following obligations during the term hereof: (a) maintain the apartment and appurtenances in a clean, sanitary and safe condition; (b) dispose all rubbish, garbage and other waste in a clear and sanitary manner from the apartment to the refuse facilities; (c) properly use and operate all appliances, electrical, gas and plumbing fixtures; (d) not place in the apartment or building any furniture, plants, animals, or any other things which harbor insects, rodents, or other pests; (e) keep out of the apartment and building materials which cause a fire hazard or a safety hazard and comply with reasonable requirements of lessor's fire insurance carrier; (f) not destroy, deface, damage, impair, nor remove any part of the building or apartment or facilities, equipment or appurtenances thereto, and (g) prevent any person in the apartment or building with

tenant's permission from violating any of the foregoing tenant obligations. Tenant shall not suffer or commit any waste in or about the apartment or building and shall at tenant's expense keep the apartment in good order and repair (except to the extent lessor has in this lease agreed to do so). On termination of this lease, tenant shall return the apartment to lessor in like condition, reasonable wear excepted.

**10. ALTERATIONS, ADDITIONS, FIXTURES, APPLIANCES, PERSONAL PROPERTY:** Tenant shall make no alterations or additions nor install, attach, connect, or maintain in the apartment or any part of the building, interior or exterior, major appliances or devices of any kind without in each and every case the written consent of the lessor and then, if granted, only upon the terms and conditions specified in such written consent. All alterations, additions and fixtures (including security devices) whether temporary or permanent in character, made by lessor or tenant, in or upon the apartment shall, unless otherwise agreed or unless lessor requests their removal, become lessor's property and shall remain in the apartment at the termination of the lease without compensation to tenant. The foregoing notwithstanding, neither lessor nor lessor's insurance carrier shall be liable to tenant for the replacement of such alteration, addition, or fixtures in the event of casualty loss unless tenant notifies lessor of the replacement value and pays, as additional rent, the resultant premium increase, if any. If lessor shall permit or demand removal, tenant shall put that part of the apartment into like condition as existed prior to the installation of such alteration, addition, or fixture.

**11. ACCESS:** lessor reserves the right in accordance herewith to enter the apartment in order to inspect same, make necessary or agreed repairs, decorations, alterations, or improvements, supply necessary or agreed services, or exhibit the apartment to prospective or actual purchasers, mortgagees, tenants, workmen, or contractors, or as is otherwise necessary in the operation and/or protection of the building, its components or persons therein. At lessor's discretion, lessor shall be provided with and may retrain and use copies of any keys necessary for access to the apartment. In the event of apparent or actual emergency, lessor may enter the apartment at any time without notice. At any time within 90 days prior to the end of the term hereof, after a single general notice, lessor may as often as necessary show the apartment for rent between the hours of 9 am and 8 pm on not less than 15–minute specific notice if tenant or other person is in the apartment, without limitation as to days. At other times, entry shall be in accordance with agreement with tenant or if same is impractical or refused, after 24 hours' notice and only during the period of 7 am to 7 pm monday through saturday. In the event of the willful or negligent breach of this provision, the non–breaching party shall at once be entitled to actual damages or liquidated damages in the amount of two month's rent and an injunction, if necessary, to prevent continuation of such breach.

**12. ASSIGNMENT, SUBLETTING, AND RELETTING:** tenant may substitute a new tenant for the balance of the term provided (a) lessor consents to the prospective new tenant, and (b) tenant upon demand pays (i) in advance, the deficiency if the aggregate rent from the reletting for the balance of the term hereof is less than the aggregate rent then remaining to be paid under this lease, and (ii) all expenses of reletting (if any) including decorating, repairs, replacements, commissions, and/or an administrative fee for performing the details attendant to such a transaction. Lessor at its option may determine whether said transaction shall be in the form of a subletting, assignment or reletting.

Lessor may at any time and for any reason reject any prospective new tenant offered by tenant or by others, provided, however, that if lessor shall do so without cause, tenant shall be liable to lessor only for the deficiency and/or actual or estimated expenses described in (b) (i) and (ii) of this paragraph 12 which would have been due from tenant had the prospective new tenant been accepted. Cause shall be deemed to be the failure, based on information and data made available to the lessor, of such prospective new tenant to meet the criteria customarily employed by the lessor to evaluate the acceptability of prospects as tenants for similar apartments in the building. During the last three months of the term, lessor shall be obligated to accept an otherwise qualified prospective new tenant only if said prospective new tenant enters into a lease for a term for which leases are customarily offered for similar apartments in the building. Unless otherwise agreed by lessor in writing, lessor shall have no duty to procure prospective new tenants for tenant or otherwise mitigate damages. Lessor's attempt to procure such prospective new tenants shall in no event constitute a new agreement by lessor to assume such duty. lessor may let other vacancies in the building first before reletting or subletting or attempting to relet or sublet the apartment.

Tenant shall neither sublet the apartment nor any part thereof nor assign this lease nor permit by any act or default of himself or any person any transfer of tenant's interest by operation of law, nor offer the apartment or any part therefor for lease or sublease except in accordance herewith.

**13. ABANDONMENT:** ten days' physical absence by tenant with rent being unpaid, or removal of the substantial portion of tenant's personal property with rent being paid, and, in either case, reason to believe tenant has vacated the apartment with no intent again to reside therein shall be conclusively deemed to be an abandonment of the apartment by tenant. In such event, and in addition to lessor's remedies set forth in paragraphs 15 and 25, lessor may, but need not, enter into the apartment and act as tenant's agent to perform necessary decorating and repairs and to relet the apartment in accordance with the terms and conditions set forth in paragraph 12. Tenant shall be conclusively deemed to have abandoned any personal property remaining in the apartment and tenant's title thereto shall thereby pass under this lease as a bill of sale to lessor without additional payment or credit by lessor to tenant.

**14. FIRE AND CASUALTY:** if the apartment is damaged or destroyed by fire or casualty and:

**A.** the apartment is only partially damaged and is inhabitable and the lessor makes full repairs within 60 days, this lease shall continue without abatement nor apportionment of rent.

**B.** if the apartment is rendered (1) uninhabitable, (2) continued occupancy would be illegal, or (3) lessor cannot or does not repair within 60 days, tenant may immediately vacate the apartment and notify lessor in writing within five days thereafter of his intent to terminate, in which case this lease shall terminate as of the date of vacating and all prepaid rent and unapplied security deposit shall be returned to tenant.

**15. TERMINATION AND RETURN OF POSSESSION:**

**A.** Upon the termination of this lease, whether by lapse of time or otherwise, or upon termination of tenant's right of possession without termination of this lease, tenant shall yield up immediate possession to lessor and deliver all keys to lessor at the place where rent is payable, or as otherwise directed by lessor. The mere retention of possession thereafter shall constitute a forcible detainer. Lessor shall have the right and license with process of law (and if tenant abandons the apartment, tenant grants lessor and lessor shall have such right and license with or without process of law) to enter into the apartment and to be returned the apartment as of lessor's former estate and to take possession of the apartment and to expel and remove tenant and any others who may be occupying or within the apartment and any and all property from the apartment, without relinquishing lessor's right to rent or any other right given to lessor hereunder or by operation of law. If tenant abandons the apartment and lessor exercises the right and license to enter without process of law, lessor may use such force as may be necessary without being deemed in any manner guilty of trespass, eviction, or forcible entry or detainer.

**B.** Tenant shall agree that in the event tenant fails to vacate the apartment upon termination of this lease or tenant's right of possession, that:

(1)   Tenant shall pay as liquidated damages for the entire time that possession is withheld a sum equal to three times the amount of

rent herein reserved, pro rated per day of such withholding, or lessor's actual damages if same are ascertainable; or

(2)   Lessor, at it sole option, may upon giving tenant written notice, extend the term of this lease for a like period of time not to exceed one year at such rent as lessor has stated prior to said termination date, or

(3)   If lessor fails to notify tenant within 45 days of said termination date of lessor's election under either (1) or (2), tenant's continued occupancy shall be for a month–to–month term.

(4)   No action or non–action by lessor except as herein provided shall operate as a waiver of lessor's right to termination this lease or tenant's right of possession nor operate to extend the term of hereof.

**16. EMINENT DOMAIN (CONDEMNATION):** if the whole or any substantial part of the building is taken or condemned by any competent authority for any public use or purpose, or it any adjacent property or street shall be so condemned or improved in such a manner as to require the use of any part of the building, the term of this lease shall at the option of the lessor or the condemning authority be terminated upon, and not before, the date when possession of the part so taken shall be required for such use or purpose and lessor shall be entitled to receive the entire award without apportionment with tenant. Rent shall be apportioned as of the date of tenant's vacating as the result of said termination.

**17. LESSOR'S MORTGAGE:** this lease is not to be recorded and is subordinated to any present or future mortgages on the real estate (or any part of it) upon which the building is situated and to all advances upon the security of such mortgages.

**18. LEASE BINDING ON HEIRS & ETC.:** all the covenants and agreements of this lease shall be binding upon and inure to the benefit of the heirs, executors, administrators, successors, and assigns of lessor and tenant, subject to the restrictions set forth in paragraph 12 hereof, except that where there are only one or two persons named or remaining as tenants herein, then, in the event of the death of one or both tenant(s), the surviving tenant and/or heirs or legal representatives of the deceased tenant may terminate this lease at the end of any calendar month within 120 days of said occurrence by giving lessor not less than 45 days prior written notice.

**19. NOTICES:** notices, including those provided by statute, shall be in writing and served by delivery (a) in person or (b) by both (1) united states regular and (2) certified or registered mail, postage prepaid, at the addresses shown for lessor and tenant at the beginning of this lease or at such other addresses as either party may designate to the other party by written notices. If services is by mail, the mailing shall be deemed delivery and the date of mailing the date of delivery. Notices served in person on tenant may be served if left with some person residing in or in possession of the apartment above the age of 12 years, and in the event of an apparent abandonment then notice may be served by posting same on the door to the apartment in addition to (b) above. Notices served in person on lessor may be served on any office employee of lessor, or if lessor receives rent at his home, in the same manner as on tenant.

**20. RULES AND REGULATIONS:** the rules and regulations at the end of this lease shall be a part of this lease. Tenant covenants and agrees to keep and observe these rules and regulations. Tenant also covenants and agrees to keep and observe such further reasonable rules and regulations as may later be promulgated by lessor or lessor's agent for the necessary, proper and orderly care of the building (provided such later rules do not materially change the terms contained in the body of this lease).

**21. RESIDENT TO INSURE POSSESSIONS:** lessor is not an insurer of tenant's person or possessions. Tenant agrees that all of tenant's person and property in the apartment or elsewhere in the building shall be at the risk of tenant only, and that tenant will carry such insurance as tenant deems necessary therefor. Tenant further agrees that except for instances of negligence or willful misconduct of lessor, its agents or employees, lessor, its agents and employees shall not be liable for any damage to the person or property of tenant or any other person occupying or visiting the apartment or building, sustained due to the apartment or building or any part thereof or any appurtenances thereof becoming out of repair (as example and not by way of limitation, damage caused by water, snow, ice, frost, steam, sewerage, sewer gas or odors, heating, cooling, and ventilation equipment, bursting or leaking of pipes, faucets, and plumbing fixtures, mechanical breakdown or failure, electrical failure, security services or devices or mailboxes being misused or becoming temporarily out of order, and fire) or due to the happening of any accident in or about the building or due to any act or neglect of any other tenant or occupant of said building or any other person.

**22. REMEDIES CUMULATIVE. NON–WAIVER:**

**A.** (1) all rights and remedies given to tenant or to lessor shall be distinct, separate, and cumulative, and the use of one or more thereof shall not exclude or waive any other right or remedy allowed by law, unless specifically limited or waived in this lease; (2) no waiver of any breach or default of either party hereunder shall be implied from any omission by the other party to take any action on account of any similar or different breach or default; (3) the payment or acceptance of money after it falls due after knowledge of any breach of this lease by lessor or tenant, or after termination in any way of the term or of tenant's right of possession hereunder, or after the service termination in any way of the term or of tenant's right of possession hereunder, or after service of any notice, or after the commencement of any suit or any right hereunder not expressly waived; (4) no express waiver shall affect any breach other than the breach specified in the express waiver and that only for the time and to the extent therein stated.

**B.** Tenant's obligation to pay rent during the term or any extension thereof or any holdover tenancy shall not be waived, released or terminated by the service of any five–day notice, demand for possession, notice of termination of tenancy, institution of any action of forcible detainer, ejectment or for any judgment for possession, or any other act or acts resulting in termination of tenant's right of possession.

**23.  TENANT'S REMEDIES:** if lessor:

(1)  defaults in its duty to maintain the apartment or building or in its agreements to perform repairs, remodeling, or decorating as set forth in paragraph 6 and such default is not cured by lessor within 30 days after notice from tenant to lessor (unless such default involves a hazardous condition or failure to furnish heat, hot water or essential services, which shall be cured forthwith): and provided lessor's failure to cure is not excused on account of one or more of the defenses set forth in paragraph 6 (**d**), in which case lessor shall notify tenant of specific facts constituting such excuse within said 30–day period (or in the case of a hazardous condition, or failure to furnish heat, hot water or essential services, within 5 days of tenant's notice); or

(2)  defaults in the performance of any other covenant or agreement hereof and such default is not cured by lessor within 10 days after written notice from tenant to lessor.

Tenant may: treat such event as a breach of this lease and, in addition to all other rights and remedies provided at law or in equity (including without limitation those provided in chapter 24, section 11–13–15 of the illinois revised statutes relating to building code violations) may, by giving lessor not less than 10 days prior written notice terminate this lease and the term created hereby by setting forth the date of said termination in the said 10 days' notice and vacating on or before said date, with rent paid to said termination date. Prepaid rent and security deposit, if any, shall be promptly refunded to tenant.

**24. TENANT'S WAIVER:** tenant's covenant to pay rent is and shall be independent of each and every other covenant of this lease.

Tenant agrees that tenant's damages for lessor's breach shall in no case be deducted from rent nor set off for purposes of determining whether any rent is due in a forcible detainer action brought on the basis of unpaid rent.

**25. LESSOR'S REMEDIES: A.** If tenant:

(1)   defaults in the payment of any single installment of rent or in the payment of any other sum required to be paid under this lease or under the terms of any other agreement between tenant and lessor and such default is not cured within five days of written notice; or

(2)   defaults in the performance of any other covenant or agreement hereof, and such default is not cured by tenant within 10 days after written notice to tenant from lessor (unless the default involves a hazardous condition which shall be cured forthwith):
   Lessor may treat such event as a breach of this lease and lessor shall have any one or more of the following described remedies in addition to all other rights and remedies provided at law or in equity:

(a)   Lessor may terminate this lease and the term created hereby, in which event lessor may forthwith repossess the apartment in accordance with Paragraph 15(A) hereof and tenant agrees to pay to lessor damages in an amount equal to the amount of rent provided in this lease to be paid by tenant for the balance of term as set forth in this lease, less the fair rental value of the apartment for said period, and, in addition, any other sum of money and damages owed by tenant to lessor.

(b)   Lessor may terminate tenant's right of possession and may repossess the apartment in accordance with paragraph 15(a) hereof without further demand or notice of any kind to tenant and without such entry and possession terminating this lease or releasing tenant in whole or in part from tenant's obligation to pay rent hereunder for the full term. Upon and after such entry into possession without termination of this lease, lessor may, but need not, relet the apartment as tenant's agent and may, but need not, make repairs, alterations and additions in or to the apartment and redecorate, all under the same terms and conditions as set forth in paragraph 12 hereof. Tenant shall on demand pay to lessor damages and all lessor's expenses of reletting as set forth and described in paragraph 12 hereof. If the consideration collected by lessor from any such reletting for tenant's account is not sufficient to pay the amount provided in the lease to be paid monthly by tenant together with all such expenses, tenant shall pay to lessor, as damages, the amount of each monthly deficiency. Tenant agrees that lessor may from time to time file suit to recover any such sums falling due under the terms of this paragraph and that no suit or recovery of any portion due lessor hereunder shall be a

defense to any subsequent action brought for any amount not
theretofore reduced to judgment in favor of lessor except that lessor shall not be permitted more than one recovery in the aggregate
amount so due.

**B.**          If tenant is the subject of any involuntary proceeding under
any section of any bankruptcy act and any court or tribunal shall adjudge tenant insolvent or unable to pay tenant's debts and such order is
not vacated within 30 days after its entry, or if tenant files any voluntary petition or similar proceedings under any section of any bankruptcy act in any court or tribunal to delay or reduce or modify tenant's
debts or obligations, or if tenant is declared insolvent according to law,
or if any assignment of tenant's property shall be made for the benefit
of creditors, or if any receiver or trustee is appointed for tenant or his
property, this lease shall automatically terminate without need of an
election by lessor and lessor's remedy shall be as set forth in subparagraph **a** above.

**C.**          Tenant shall pay lessor all lessor's costs, expenses and attorney's fees in and about the enforcement of the covenants and agreements of this lease.

## 26. OTHER AGREEMENTS:

**A.** The headings or captions of paragraphs are for identification purposes only and do not limit or construe the contents of the paragraphs.

**B.** "Lessor" as used herein shall refer to the person, partnership, corporation or trust hereinabove set forth in that capacity. If such person be
designated an agent, lessor shall also refer to and include the principal.
Obligations and duties to be performed by lessor may be performed by
lessor, its agents, employees or independent contractors. Only lessor or
its designated agent may amend or modify this lease or lessor's obligations thereunder.

**C.** All rights and remedies of lessor under this lease, or that may be
provided by law, may be exercised by lessor in lessor's own name individually, or in lessor's name by lessor's agent, and all legal proceedings
for the enforcement of any such rights or remedies, including distress
for rent, forcible detainer, and any other legal or equitable proceedings,
may be commenced and prosecuted to final judgment and execution by
lessor in lessor's own name individually, or by agent of any lessor who
is a principal.

**D.** Tenant agrees that lessor may at any time and as often as desired
assign or re–assign all of its rights as lessor under this lease.

**E.** The words "lessor" and "tenant" as used herein shall be construed to
mean plural where necessary and the necessary grammatical changes
required to make the provisions hereof apply to corporations or per-

sons, women or men, shall in all cases be assumed as though in each case fully expressed.

**F.** The obligations of two or more persons designated tenant in this lease shall be joint and several. If there be more than one party named as tenant, other than children in a family, all must execute this lease and any modification or amendment hereto.

**G.** "Apartment" used herein shall refer to the dwelling unit leased to tenant.

**H.** Tenant's occupancy of any storeroom, storage area or garage space in or about building shall be as licensee only. Tenant understands that due to the construction, location and use of storeroom, storage area or garage spaces, lessor cannot and shall not be liable for any loss or damage of or to any property placed therein. Do not store valuable items in such areas. The termination of this lease for any reason shall also serve to terminate tenant's right to use such storeroom, storage area, or garage space.

**I.** "Building" as used herein shall include the entire physical structure located at and about the address hereinabove stated, including machinery, equipment and appurtenances which are a part thereof, grounds, recreational areas and facilities, garages and out–buildings, and other apartment buildings which form a complex owned and operated as a single entity.

**J.** The invalidity or unenforceability of any provision hereof shall not affect or impair any other provision.

## RULES AND REGULATIONS

1. No animals without written consent of lessor or lessor's agent (which may be revoked on (10) ten day's notice at any time). No animals without leash in any public area of the building.

2. Passages, public halls, stairways, landings, elevators and elevator vestibules shall not be obstructed or be used for children's play or for any other purpose than for ingress to and egress from the building or apartments, nor shall children be permitted to congregate or play in or around the common interior areas of the building. All personal possessions must be kept in the apartment or in other storage areas if provided.

3. All furniture, supplies, goods and packages of every kind shall be delivered through the rear or service entrance, stairway or elevator.

4. Carriages, velocipedes, bicycles, sleds and the like shall not be allowed in the lobbies, public halls, passageways, courts or elevators of the building and are to be stored only in places designated for their storage by the lessor.

5.  Laundry and drying apparatus shall be used in such a manner and
    at such times as the lessor may clearly post in such area. Clothes,
    washers and dryers, and dishwashers, unless installed by lessor,
    cannot be kept in the apartment.

6.  The use of garbage receptacles or incinerators shall be in accor-
    dance with posted signs and only garbage and refuse wrapped in
    small, tight parcels, may be placed in garbage receptacles or in-
    cinerator hoppers. Aerosol cans or inflammable materials shall be
    placed in garage receptacles or dropped into the incinerator only if
    so posted. They are highly explosive.

7.  No sign, signal, illumination, advertisement, notice or any other
    lettering or equipment shall be exhibited, inscribed, painted, af-
    fixed or exposed on or at any window or on any part of the out-
    side or inside of the apartment or the building without the prior
    written consent of the lessor.

8.  No awnings or other projections including air conditioner, televi-
    sion or radio antennas or wiring shall be attached to or extend
    from or beyond the outside walls of the building.

9.  The tenant shall not alter any lock or install a new lock or a
    knocker or other attachment on any door of the apartment without
    the written consent of the lessor.

10. No waste receptacles, supplies, footwear, umbrellas or other arti-
    cles shall be place in the halls, on the staircase landings, nor shall
    anything be hung or shaken from the windows or balconies or
    placed upon the outside window sills.

11. No noise, music or other sounds shall be permitted at any time in
    such manner as to disturb or annoy other occupants of the build-
    ing.

12. The water closets, basin and other plumbing fixtures shall not be
    used for any purpose other than for those for which they were de-
    signed; no sweepings, rubbish, rags or any other improper articles
    shall be thrown into them. Any damage resulting from misuse of
    such facilities shall be paid for by the tenant.

13. There shall be no cooking or baking done in or about the apart-
    ment except in the kitchen. cooking on a barbeque or other similar
    equipment on a porch, terrace, or balcony is expressly forbidden.

14. If lessor provides television master antenna hookup, only lessor's
    authorized agent shall install tenant's television set to master an-
    tenna and tenant agrees to pay installation cost and annual main-
    tenance fee. Tenant shall permit access to disconnect hookup for
    non–payment. tenant agrees to pay $50.00 liquidated damage to
    lessor's authorized agent for each illegal hookup in tenant's apart-
    ment.

**15.**   No furniture filled with a liquid or semi–liquid shall be brought in or used in the apartment.

## Notes

1. In passing, I'll just point out further, that under the lease, any interest on the security deposit may be kept by the landlord. Is this fair–it is the *tenant's* money, held by the landlord. That the tenant does not get the interest is a pure grab of benefit by the landlord. In the interest of full disclosure, perhaps I should mention that I have been, myself, both renter and landlord.

# 6

# What is Evil?

## Ms. Daryl Koehn

Simone Weil once remarked that literary treatments of evil are un-trustworthy. They make evil people more interesting than they actually are. A number of theorists writing about evil have taken Weil's warning to heart and appear intent on reducing evil to something simple and codifiable. While I do not wish to glorify evil, I do want to warn against assuming that we know exactly what it is. And if we do not know what evil is, then we should not be to quick to dismiss any portrayal of evil—be it literary or theological. These other disciplines may very well offer important insights into evil, insights overlooked by those who are analyzing evil using a rather one–dimensional criminological model. In the first half of the talk, I will both sketch and analyze one variant of the criminological model as it has appeared within the business ethics field. In the second half, I will explore three very different understandings of evil drawn from the novelists Jim Thompson and Henry James and the theologian Martin Buber. Since the topic of evil is so vast and since my focus today is on professional ethics, I will draw most of my examples from the world of business.

## Part One:  Using A Criminological Approach to Think about Evil in the Workplace

One recent argument regarding the nature of evil in the workplace runs as follows:  actions of vicious employees take one form–these actions are breaches of trust or betrayals.  Trust lies at the heart of many relations, including business relationships among stakeholders (Barber, 1983; Fukuyama, 1995; Hosmer, 1995; Koehn, 1996).  So, when an employee betrays trust, an organization's ability to thrive can be seriously impaired.  If the acts are such as to place significant organizational resources at risk, these betrayals should be thought of as acts of "high betrayal."  High betrayals include, but are not limited to, embezzlement, insider trading, self–dealing, lying about facts, failure to disclose significant facts, treason, employee espionage, corruption, whistle–blowing,  and cover–ups.  "Low betrayals," by contrast, can be absorbed with minimal disruption to corporate life.  This class includes shirking, various strategies of bureaucratic opposition, padded expense accounts, strikes, symbolic acts of exiting the corporation, organized slow–downs, sick–outs, and moves to favor one's own subunit over other groups within the organization.

Having found a shared, common form to employee and managerial vice, the theorist's next move is to locate a common character flaw present in those who betray organizations.  What is this character flaw?  "Low self–control."  Low self–control is said to account for many of the betrayals–and thus much of the evil–within organizations.

We have, then, a simple model of evil: evil lies within the individual and is identical with inadequate self–control on the part of the individual resulting in betrayal.  This lack of self–control is the result of the trust violator developing a defective self–narrative.  This self–narrative goes awry because the evil person persists in a juvenile or adolescent state of egocentrism (Moberg, 1997).  When asked why they committed some crime, evil individuals respond like juvenile delinquents.  They do not mention their victims but instead cite their desire to obtain what they want and their belief that they could get away with the act.  This script is consistent with low self–control understood as a willingness or propensity to seize upon "opportunities for immediate gratification accomplished by risky and uncomplicated means requiring little skill or planning that create pain for their victims but merely transitory benefits for the perpetrator" (Moberg, 1997).  Those who suffer the vice of low self–control frequently "mislabel" their actions and tend to externalize blame.  They invoke cultural myths in order to rationalize their actions.  These myths include "the Robin Hood myth, . . . notions that organizations can absorb loss with no problems, that the organization systematically takes advantage of its employees no matter what they do, that the organization always budgets for loss contingencies", etc. (Moberg, 1997). In the event the vicious agent is caught, he typically will transfer responsibility from himself to the victim.

The low self–control model has a number of strengths. It acknowledges that all agents act upon some narrative which represents the world and their role in it. Their plans and courses of action are not only regulated by constraints implicit in this world–narrative (e.g., "The police usually hang out at 18th and California so I won't steal a car at that intersection") but also receive their meaning within this myth ("I deserve to have a car. Society has not provided me with one so I am entitled to fend for myself, even if that means taking someone else's car").

The low self–control model has a second strength. It goes some way toward accounting for why many white collar and blue collar criminals do not confine themselves to just one type of crime. They may begin with petty theft but then graduate to arson, assault and murder (Moberg, 1997). Since the lack of self–control stems from a *general* worldview, we would expect that the evildoer could rationalize many types of acts by appealing to this worldview. The account gains plausibility precisely because it is so general. For, as others have noted, the idea that white–collar crime is somehow less criminal and wicked than blue collar crime is dubious. While popular culture may romanticize the unappreciated brilliant technologist who is driven to turn against his masters who have stolen his ideas, espionage is frequently committed for reasons of plain old greed, rather than out of revenge (Herbig, 1994). Nor does there seem to be any especially compelling reason why we should distinguish a pharmacist's theft of drugs from a carpenter's theft of lumber (Gottfredson and Hirschi, 1990).

However, this model of low self–control makes several important and non–obvious assumptions:

1. Evil lies largely, if not exclusively, in the agent who is judged to be morally bad, wicked, evil, vicious, etc;
2. Evil deeds are those that fall short of being deeds the majority of us would deem morally good or appropriate;
3. Evil results *primarily* from a failure of self–control understood as an inability or unwillingness to bring the self into compliance with socially accepted or normal expectations.

In a sense, this third claim is not an assumption but rather the conclusion the theorists draw. But, in another important sense, it is largely an assumption, for the theorists have not explored other alternative and plausible accounts of evil.

None of these assumptions is trivial, so each ought to be closely considered.

### Assumption 1: Evil Resident Primarily in the Individual

On the criminological account, an agent who betrays others is vicious or evil. The account, however, tends to equivocate as to where exactly the locus of evil is. Is it in the agent's intention/ juvenile mode of self–representation. Or is the evil identical with the harm generated by betrayal (i.e., located in the act and its consequences)? The former seems more likely for several reasons. First, it is easy to imagine cases of unintentional betrayal. The wife trusts the husband to bring home some groceries, but he forgets that he has committed to do so. Few would term the husband "evil" or "vicious," although he did betray the trust. If these memory lapses occur frequently, then we may have some ground for wondering about the husband's character or mental health. But notice that in this latter case we have shifted the locus of evil away from the act of betrayal and toward the intention or motivation of the forgetful spouse.

Moreover, while some actions may be unambiguously evil (e.g., child molestation), it is often times difficult to judge whether an act has been, on the whole, harmful or helpful. A thief may steal my car, only to have the brakes fail on him. If he dies instead of me, was his theft– which the low self–control model would have us view as a betrayal of my and other citizens' trust in property rights–morally good or evil? If we are inclined to judge it evil despite the good consequences for me, then it must be because we have located the evil in the intention or reasoning of the car thief. We might argue, for example, that the harm was the direct result of a malformed intention voluntarily acted upon by the thief, while the benefit to the victim was merely accidental and should not redound to the thief's credit.

Yet locating evil exclusively in the agent–more precisely, in a self–narrative replete with "mis–labelings"–is, I think, misleading. This formulation completely ignores the role social representations of events and phenomena play in self–narratives. While people do invent portions of their narratives, this process of invention is not a pure act of fabrication by the individual. All of us adopt and mold various ideas and accounts we have drawn from literature, sermons, advertisements, parental advice, and so forth into our ever–evolving self–narrative. Our experiences in the larger society affect which of these accounts we find especially promising. Timothy McVeigh's experiences in the army during Desert Storm, including driving tanks over trenches filled with Iraqis and burying them alive, may have helped to convince him that killing is not such a bad thing if one's cause is good, an interpretation supported by much of the American rhetoric during this war. It is too simple to say that the Army made McVeigh into a terrorist, given that many who participated in the same maneuvers as McVeigh have not become domestic bombers. On the other hand, it would be equally naive to talk as though experiences, which the larger society both *provides* and *glosses*, are irrelevant to our self–narratives. After all, our individual imaginations and interpretative processes have to work on something and that something comes in part from society.

In other words, "The [self's] narrative does not arise *de novo* but is constructed and reconstructed *as a result of commerce between self and others in everyday world and in imaginary worlds*" (Sarbin, 1994). Thus, it is an over–simplification to speak as if all of people's badness somehow resides exclusively in them. At a minimum, the larger social setting affects people's ability to recognize their own actions as bad. As Hannah Arendt has argued, the law courts' standards for attributing responsibility were woefully inadequate in the context of Nazi Germany (Arendt, 1964). Soldiers historically have been held to have a duty to resist superiors' orders if and when these orders are "manifestly unlawful." The courts have interpreted unlawful to mean naturally unjust, as well as conventionally unlawful. Either way, the central idea is that the *glaringly* immoral quality of an order or law justifies holding a soldier responsible for failing to resist the order. When the larger social setting and legal framework is itself corrupt (as it was in Nazi Germany), then no single command is going to stick out as *manifestly* immoral. And, if it does not, then we are faced with the question of what justifies holding some particular individual who obeys orders to be evil. The evil would seem to be in both the agent and the larger milieu.

### *Assumption 2: Evil Acts Are Those That Deviate from the Norm*

The low self–control model assumes that we can identify certain actions as unproblematically "evil" and then proceed immediately to identification of the evildoer: the evildoer is the one who performs acts that most people (or people in the know) would judge to be betrayals. If we look closely at the list of "betrayals," a problem emerges. Even if we grant that treason is evil, what exactly counts as treason and who gets to decide that issue? Markham, the protagonist in Barry Unsworth's novel *The Rage of the Vulture*, adopts measures that do not appear to be consistent with the official British policy towards the Sultan in Constantinople (Unsworth, 1982). Yet Markham "betrays" the policy of his British superiors out of his sense that this policy is not a decent one likely to promote human rights in Asia in the long run. From exactly whose perspective is Markham a traitor? Is that perspective a sound one? The difference between a traitor and a revolutionary may be a matter of calendar days. A similar point can be made about many of the supposed acts of employee evil. There unquestionably are many temptations to lead a would–be whistleblower astray (Koehn, 1995). However, in some cases, whistleblowers are unjustly character- ized by fellow workers as traitors. When the whistleblower's options are few and when he or she has carefully documented a series of ex- tremely harmful corporate practices, whistleblowing might be the right course. The same point will apply to strikes, work slowdowns, etc.[1] In such cases, the vilified traitor may actually be a hero.

*A crucial and perhaps central dimension of the ethical problem is figuring out what qualifies as a betrayal and why.* While someone may think his trust has been abused, this perception is not sufficient for charging the alleged violator with betrayal and imputing viciousness or evil to that person. We can think of many cases where people's expec- tations are violated and where the alleged violator turns out to appear to be the morally superior party (e.g., when the trustor's expectations are malformed, are manipulative, etc.) (Koehn, 1996). The current discus- sion of evil in the workplace relies too heavily on the criminology lit- erature. By definition, this literature deals with people whom society has convicted as "criminal." Yet many of the supposed acts of corpo- rate betrayal are not obviously criminal. Talking as though there is a common standard of deviance compounds the ethical difficulty in such cases because such talk assumes what must be shown—namely, that the deviant offender, in fact. acted badly.

In business, the ethical problem may not be one of low self–control and subsequent betrayal of majority norms. The more pressing prob- lem may be a failure by both the employee and those who would judge her behavior to acknowledge the host of difficulties inherent in assess- ing human behavior. This lack of awareness may itself be a form of betrayal. After all, rigid mindless agents are unlikely to act in their or the organization's long–term interests. However, now the account of evil will have to be much more nuanced, taking into account a wide variety of judgment–distorting behaviors, not just those of mislabeling caused by juvenile egocentrism. We will have to examine distortions in the worldview of the judge as well as of the employee.

### Assumption 3: The Problem of Evil is a Problem of Self–control

While it is true that many criminals either ignore or blame their victims; and while it is plausible to associate these tendencies with the search for immediate gratification, there may be other features of evil not so plausibly attributed to low self–control. Consider the following features of evil (or evil agency) discussed by theologians, philosophers, novelists, and other thinkers who are not inclined to romanticize evil:

1.  Evil acts are mechanical or repetitive. The agent might be described as an automaton (Ouspensky, 1949).
2.  Evil acts arise out of identification with a group. Fidelity to the group results in agents who are willing to commit all sorts of atrocities in the name of protecting the group (Unsworth, 1982).
3.  Evil involves ignoring an inner voice that warns against some act (Unsworth, 1982; Plato, trans. 1971; Thompson, 1952) and/or external voices that counsel against performing the action (Thompson, 1952 ; Lewis, 1992).
4.  Evil people construe themselves as largely passive beings who are under some compulsion to perform an act judged by others to be bad. They may act because of the appearance of some "omen" or "sign" (Thompson, 1952).
5.  Evil acts are done by agents operating in a dreamlike state (Unsworth, 1982; Thompson, 1952; Ouspensky, 1949).
6.  Evil is done out of a belief that anything is possible (Sereny, 1995; Buber, 1953; Arendt, 1979).
7.  Evil stems from the agent's certainty that his or her action is absolutely justified (Plato, trans. 1971; James, 1986).
8.  The agent who has done what is deemed evil uses the language of morality to justify the immorality (Sereny, 1995; Aristotle, trans. 1975).
9.  Evil involves an element of bad faith (Sartre, 1993).
10. The evil person attributes to another person or group exactly the deed he himself is about to perform, a deed which victimizes this person or group (Arendt, 1979; Young–Bruehl, 1996).
11  Evil agents cast themselves in the role of a benefactor. The evil person demands "purity" from others and then promises continued beneficence if only the other party will remain pure. The continued beneficence is often made contingent upon the party's willingness to openly "confess" any and all past impurities (Lifton, 1989; James, 1984).

This list is not meant to be exhaustive. It is intended only to point to a number of other interesting features sometimes attributed to evil. While some of these features may be connected with low self–control, others appear in connection with agents who are "hyper–controlled"– e.g., ideologues who are willing to brainwash others (trait 11), who are completely certain of the rightness of their cause (trait 7), and who are perfectly willing to forego short–term gratification for long–term success in getting what they think they want. The list also suggests that the cause of evil may not be mislabelings of a particular act or a tendency to self–indulgence. Agents genuinely may feel themselves to be under some external compulsion (trait 5) to do an action that some other part of them is resisting. This state of affairs would help explain agents' felt sense that they are moving in a dream (trait 5). In many cases, the ethical problem may take the form of a radically defective understanding of what is meant by a self–e.g., a tendency to construe the self as a completely passive being at the mercy of external forces (trait 4) and who receives guidance from some mysterious force or being who speaks through omens (trait 4).

While low self–control may adequately model certain acts of betrayal–e.g., impulsive embezzling–, it does a poorer job of describing and analyzing other actions that we might want to criticize. We need to be extremely cautious then when identifying evil persons and when discussing the aetiology of evil. Precisely because evil appears to be a very complex phenomenon, we should keep ourselves open to the possibility that evil has different forms and should remain willing to entertain a variety of accounts of evil.

## Part Two: Alternative Models of Evil

### Henry James: Evil as Dreadful Portentousness

Henry James never gives a definition of evil. He does something more powerful. He shows evil at work. James' novella *The Turn of the Screw* tells the tale of a young governess in her twenties who assumes the responsibility of caring for two young parentless children living on an English country estate (James, 1986). During the course of the tale, the governess comes to suspect that "evil" servants–specifically, the previous governess and the estate owner's valet–have monstrously abused the children. She encounters the ghosts of these servants and believes these ghosts have returned to torment the children. She takes upon herself the task of saving the children from these corrupters.

It may be, however, that she herself is the children's greatest tormentor. James hints that the real evil lies not in the abuse of children–although he is only too willing to concede that such abuse does occur–but rather in what might be termed the "infinite imaginings" of the human soul. When the small boy Miles is dismissed from school for a reason never fully specified, the governness imagines that he has acted badly, reproducing some horrible behavior he has learned from an adult. Soon she is following the children everywhere, never allowing them to be unobserved. Then, one day, the governess suddenly discerns a man on the tower of the house, an intruder. When she speaks to the housekeeper about this invader, the housekeeper mentions Peter Quint, a now dead valet who, the housekeeper hints, took liberties with the children. The governess seizes upon this hint and becomes convinced that this wicked servant has come back to abuse the children again. She watches the children ever more closely, continually clutching at them, looking to see whether they, too, behold the ghost of Quint. Later the governess confronts the ghost of someone she infers to be Miss Jessel, the former governess who is rumored to have been "corrupted" by Quint. She watches to see whether the little girl, who was cared for by Miss Jessel, perceives the ghost of this corrupted governess. When the girl gives no evidence of seeing the ghost, the governess entertains the possibility–soon to become a certainty–that the girl really does see the ghost but is pretending not to do so. Why would the child engage in such a deceit? Why, to lull the governess into a false sense of security in order that the child may slip away to play with the wicked Miss Jessel! The governess' imagination takes another step. The only way to save the children is to force them to confess that they have been cavorting with the ghosts. Increasingly she haunts the children's presence, detecting evidence of corruption, denial, or manipulation in their every statement or playful gesture. All events become luminous with the various possibilities the governess entertains. These possibilities take on a life of their own and become "evidence" for additional, more monstrous possibilities. At the end, the governess grabs the child Miles, clutching him to her in order to "protect" him from the ghost of Peter Quint whom she sees lurking at the window. The boy dies in her clutch, perhaps from seeing the "ghost," or perhaps because the governess has so strong a hold on him that he can no longer breathe.

James does not equate the imagination *per se* with evil. But he does intimate that the imagination, *when unchecked by other people's insights and questions and when publicly unaccountable*, is the same thing as evil. Evil grows out of and engenders dread (James, 36; 40) where dread is understood as our response to perceived portentousness. What is most portentous are those events or actions that are adumbrated by imagination (James, 41). When given a free hand, our imagination will generate its own material for speculation. This speculative process is infinitely shadowed–infinitely suggestive–because the individual imagination is not self–regulating. (Or at least its "laws" are not of the sort to introduce doubts that can be resolved by appeals to objective evidence.) Unless "the full–blown flower of high fancy" (James, 36) is checked by external forces and external demands for physical proof, high fancy will spin its tale, imbuing events with infinite horror. Children, and human beings in general, will be "as exposed as we can humanly imagine them to be."[2] How exposed is that? As exposed as the unfettered human imagination will make them. Since the human imagination has the capacity to represent things to itself in a highly abstract, relatively unspecified way, the danger cannot be quantified. It is no accident that, throughout the tale, James never names the suspected evil. "It" remains an "it" or "this", which both we and the governess readily flesh out as we see fit.

Evil lies not only in the unfettered imagination but also in whatever forces or institutions conspire to give imagination a free hand. James scrupulously avoids locating the evil only in a single individual (e.g., the governess) or only in the social environment. Evil resides in both. For example, the children's guardian acts callously when he washes his hands of any concern for his wards, requiring the newly hired governess to pledge that she will never contact him about any matter whatsoever. The governess is an inexperienced young woman in desperate need of employment. The guardian uses his position of superior power to extort her acquiescence to his stipulation, a concession that leaves her with almost no one to share her worries about the children. When young Miles is dismissed from school, she feels that she cannot take up the question of his dismissal with the child's guardian or with school representatives. So she is left to indulge her imaginings. Society's sexism contributes to the tragedy. The governess is loathe to speak with the child's guardian in part because she fears that any attempt by her to contact him will be viewed as a ploy to catch this desirable bachelor. Class differences and attitudes enter the picture as well. The governess apparently feels herself above speaking to some household members and puts on airs to distance herself from them. She does speak with the housekeeper, but the housekeeper does not feel entirely free to share her suppositions with the governess. And, in any case, the governess is quite willing to dismiss some of the housekeeper's ideas or objections because the woman is less educated than she, a genteel parson's daughter.

James' conception of evil is more applicable to organizations than one might initially suppose. Managers who are in the care–taking business or who run daycare centers for their employees certainly should take heed. There have been a number of cases where caregivers have been accused not only by parents but also by their fellow employees of ritually abusing children. In the "Little Rascals" day care case, more than 90 children have accused 20 adults of 429 instances of child sexual abuse.[3] Just as the governess' suspicions become increasingly monstrous, so, too, the number of supposed victims and offenses in child abuse cases have escalated as the children have been intensively questioned by parents, officials, and therapists. Daycare providers have been accused of killing a baby with a handgun and of hanging a child upside down from a tree and then setting the child on fire. Children have reported being taken on board a space ship and flown into outer space where they were abused and of being taken out to sea and abused while trained sharks swam around the boat.[4] Such claims might be amusing if it were not for the fact that juries so very often convict in cases involving alleged child abuse. In the Little Rascals case, 7 of the 20 accused adults were arrested and several are serving life sentences in prison. Others escaped prosecution by confessing their participation in the abuse perpetrated by their fellow employees.[5] Managers ought to be very careful about leveling charges of abuse (harassment, discrimination, molestation, etc.) and skeptical when evaluating charges made by clients or fellow employees. As James realized, the human imagination is perfectly capable of manufacturing its own "evidence" of dreadful crimes. Surely it is not a mere coincidence that, in a response to critics, James linked his ghosts with witches. His gruesome little tale has much in common with witch hunts, a term we now frequently hear in connection with child abuse cases.

In the same vein, corporations need to be concerned about whistle-blowing. The greatest evil may lie not in the whistleblower's "betrayal" of the corporation but in the development of a climate of whistleblowing where employees make themselves into corporate watchdogs, eternally vigilant for the slightest sign of wrongdoing. More generally, we should be leery of any one who helps to create an atmosphere of suspicion. When labor and management exchange escalating allegations of ill will and dastardly deeds, we ought to wonder whether the imagination of the parties is manufacturing a portentous evil.

In these cases, the low self–control model does not fit. There is, in a certain sense, an excess of control. The individual's imagination has taken in the whole of the situation and is busy ordering and re–ordering it in light of whatever speculations it finds pleasing. As I have already noted, these speculations can make themselves immune to any objections. The agent sees what her imaginings have conditioned her to see. Any who do not see must be corrupt. Such logic displays a willful ruthlessness. Unlike the person with low self–control, the agent caught up in this logic is not in the least concerned as to whether she is doing some deed that will be punished. On the contrary, the agent is certain her cause is just. She believes herself to be on a divine mission to protect the organization, customers, and fellow employees from some unspecified but growing horror.

James' rendition of evil echoes the various phases of brainwashing–e.g., milieu control, the cult of confession, the brainwasher's belief

in ideology even at the expense of the welfare of the persons the brainwasher is trying to "save" or "purify," and the assertion by the brainwasher that she alone is the guarantor or preserver of other people's
existence (Lifton, 1990). The Jamesian view of evil is especially relevant to corporations and organizations insofar as all of them employ
milieu control and make employee welfare contingent upon "good"
service to the organization (an evaluative judgment rendered by the
powers that be, a group whose exact identity often is not clear). All
corporations attempt to get the employees to see themselves as part of a
larger team. That is *not* to say that all organizations engage in brainwashing. It *is* to say that sometimes the difference between brainwashing and corporate education and initiation practices  is not that great.
Since this education is carried out by individual people within the firm,
the whole issue of who qualifies as an "evil" person should not be separated from the question of how exactly the judges are arriving at such a
judgment. If the reasoning of these judges is not subject to many external checks and balances, we ought to be concerned that evil is afoot.

*Jim Thompson: Evil as Labeling That Impedes Development*

Jim Thompson's novel *The Killer Inside Me* is the first–person narrative of a serial killer. The killer Lou Ford slips into rages and strikes
out at his victims who, he contends, were "asking for it" (Thompson,
45). Like the criminals described in the criminological literature, Lou
acts on impulse. But not always. He plots some of his murders in detail and executes them cunningly. He does believe his crimes are low
risk. His belief, though, does not stem from his perception that the
crime is simple to execute but rather from his absolute certainty that he
can fool everyone (Thompson, 194). And in fact he has spent his
whole life doing so. Everyone in town is convinced that Deputy Lou
Ford is a good ol' boy. Although he has nothing but contempt for most
of the townfolks who live their lives thinking that everything is black
and white, he himself speaks in clichés. He has rigidly schooled himself in these banalities so no one will suspect who or what he really is.

Who is he–really? Lou has difficulty answering this question because he has spent his life spouting formulaic clichés (Thompson, 28).
His speech has become a way of not thinking, of never having to look
at what he is doing or what he truly wants. Moreover, he sometimes
talks as if he is convinced that no one else can understand his private
and unique pain. His story, however, is a narrative, and a narrative, by
definition, is available to others to interpret. While Lou's telling of his
murderous spree is disjointed, the parts of it do form of a pattern. As a
very young boy, he was accused of abusing a small girl. The details are
unclear, but apparently he was simply imitating some action he had

suffered at the hands of his father's housekeeper. Lou's older brother Mike takes the blame for the younger boy's "abuse." Lou's father subsequently adopts a policy of always watching over Lou. The father never forgets, nor does he ever allow the boy to forget, this abhorrent deed. On the one hand, Lou's past "abuse" becomes part of the boy's public character and identity. On the other hand, this identity paradoxically must always be shrouded in order not to contradict the official story that it was his brother Mike who abused the young girl. Lou finds himself driven to live in conformity with social expectations concerning who he is–the "good" brother as opposed to the "evil" brother. Yet he always knows he is living a lie. His brother took the rap for him, so his brother Mike actually must be the "good" child while Lou must really be the "evil" one. Anyone who sees any good whatsoever in Lou threatens the only identity he has *and has been permitted to forge* and, therefore, this party must die.

The social plays a large role in the formation of Lou's identity. For all of us, the social is the place where we achieve our identities. We learn who we are in part through the judgments our parents and teachers make about our actions and speech. Since the townspeople dwell in a world where everything is either black or white, Lou is given no language and no opportunity for exploring why he did what he did to the young girl and why it was not the type of behavior in which he should be engaging (Thompson, 215). This lack of opportunity is troubling, because these questions of motivation need to be explored. It is open to question whether the very young are guilty of "abuse," if the children are only repeating what they have seen the adults in their lives do. When Lou's father explodes and berates the boy for his evil deed, the housekeeper warns the father against making the act "to mean." Our social practice of making acts "to mean" may itself sometimes be the cause of evil, a possibility that communities do not see because they are convinced that various deeds simply "are" good or evil.

My point is not that there is no such thing as "abuse," "murder," or "evil." The point is rather that, when we locate evil entirely in the deed and ignore the process by which we individually and collectively bestow meaning upon our actions, we become a bit like Lou Ford. We slip into a formulaic, mechanical approach to life. This approach conceals us from ourselves every bit as much as Lou's clichés prevent him from probing too deeply into his own psyche. Having labeled some deed "evil," we move very quickly to the conclusion that, because person X did this evil deed Y, person X must be evil. The judgment that the person is evil reduces the person forever to that one deed. Lou Ford unquestionably is a killer. However, there are many ways to kill a man, and a reduction of the sort just described might also qualify as a kind of murder. Like murder, it destroys the other's personhood. It is not so surprising that at the end, Lou takes steps to force his fellow law officers to kill him. He has felt himself to be dead for years. This final blaze of bullets merely re–enacts the obliteration that occurred early in his life and that he visited upon himself daily every time he chose to speak in clichés and assumed the person of good ol' Lou (or evil child Lou).

To put the point still more simply: the act of labeling is morally freighted. On Thompson's view, labeling is the prime evil to the extent that, and because, it annihilates personhood by either reducing people to caricatures or by locking them into a mode of self–definition that relies upon language not subtle and fluid enough to permit their souls to develop. It may be no accident that violence erupts in these cases of the living dead. What do they have to lose if they kill others and then turn the gun upon themselves? It would be fanciful to think that Thompson has located the key to unlock the mystery of violence. Nevertheless, his account might prove useful in thinking about violence in the workplace, especially given that some of the most affected corporations (e.g., the U.S. Post Office) are highly regimented and rule–bound.

Businesses offer many other less dramatic examples of the dangers of labeling. Consider the ubiquitous distinction between "customer" and "employee." Customers are those external people the employee serves, whose good will the company needs in order to prosper. Employees then become, by way of contrast, beings who exist only to serve the external customer. Salespeople will do anything to please the customer, but will not lift a finger to help a colleague in strategic planning or operations.[6] The Total Quality Movement's introduction of the concept of an "internal customer" was designed to help avert this dynamic and to encourage employees to be more responsive to their fellow workers. If employees came to see their fellow employees as people whose voices and interests needed to be heeded, then all business was likely to run smoother and with less hostility. In order to accomplish this goal, a change in language was necessary. Employees required a more nuanced way of thinking about themselves if they were to avoid acting badly.

The employee–management distinction is another one that engenders a good deal of anger and frustrates development. In reality, both managers and employees are employees of the firm; and the contributions of all employees are needed in order for the business to function well. A corporate leader who is able to move people away from a fixation on status and misleading titles and to get them to consider what needs to be done for the firm as a whole to prosper is, in terms of the

Thompsonian framework developed above, less evil. Semco, a Brazilian firm managed by CEO Ricardo Semler, is a good illustration of a company that has introduced a more subtle and flexible language for use in employee self-definition. Semco asks a large number of its employees to choose their titles, define their jobs, and set their salary levels. While employees are given information regarding industry-wide salary figures, they may give themselves a salary higher or lower than the industry norm. Each person commits to performing specific tasks in order to merit this salary. Every year the firm's members are reviewed by all of those with whom they work (a 360° review) and a judgment is made as to whether they earned their salary (Semler, 1989).

The approach Semler initiated is virtuous, or at least less evil, on several scores. First, it shifts all employees' attention away from who has what title and toward the question of what exactly is being done by whom. Since it is these various activities that have to be coordinated in order for a firm to be successful in the long run, this shift in focus is appropriate. Second, the approach requires that all employees think about what it is they actually want to do to earn their pay. Employees must look inward and do some soul-searching instead of complaining about the big bucks somebody else is earning. Third, the employees become better educated as well as to what value the market places on different skills and competencies. This education curbs the fantasy that the employee's life would be much better if only he could work in some other higher-paying corporation. There is a reality check on high-flown fantasies. Finally, the approach encourages employee realism regarding their individual strengths and weaknesses. The employee commits to delivering certain products and to producing specific outcomes. This performance is what justifies the salary she has accorded herself. She becomes personally responsible for this performance. If she fails because she has overestimated her talents or underestimated the difficulty of the task, then she suffers a penalty. There is a direct connection between what she has done and her reward or penalty, a connection that exists in the eyes of all the employees. It becomes harder for employees to argue that they have been badly treated by the other–"evil" management–or for management to blame its poor performance on the company's "evil" or "untrustworthy" employees. In this scheme, all are *employees* of the firm with self-chosen tasks to perform; and all are *managers* of their own fate. Semco appears to have successfully broken down long-standing, rigid, and detrimental distinctions and replaced them with a vocabulary and some practices that encourage greater self-development, responsibility, and cooperation on the part of all members of the corporation.

*Martin Buber: Evil as Losing Oneself in Omni–possibility*

According to Martin Buber, evil produces effects and actions but it itself is neither effect nor action. Evil is the impulse born of the belief in omni–possibility. The soul is not evil but its imagining may be. The soul loses itself in omni–possibility when it does not take its bearings from reality but instead creates a reality for itself (Buber, 92). Buber insists that this impulse to create reality is necessary. In fact, this "play with possibility, play as self–temptation, from which ever and again violence springs" is even more necessary than the good impulse (also within man). "[W]ithout it man would woo no woman and beget no children, build no house and engage in no economic activity, for it is true that 'all travail and all skill in work is the rivalry of a man with his neighbor . . ." (Buber, 91, 94). Evil, then, is not something to be extirpated. Instead, we should avoid evil by loving God with a whole heart. To love God with a whole heart is to love him *with a heart in which the good and evil urges have been re–united*. This reunification requires self–knowledge and an acknowledgement of the evil impulse within. Cain's "sin" lay less in the murder of Abel than in Cain's unwillingness to acknowledge before God the impulse to create and refashion a new reality in which Abel ceased to be (Buber, 89)

Loving God and renouncing evil are not impossible: ". . . [s]traying and caprice are not innate in man, they are not of the nature of original sin; in spite of all the burdens of past generations, [man} always begins anew as a person [when] . . . the storm of adolescence first deluges him with the infinitude of the possible–greatest danger and greatest opportunity at once (Buber, 93)." "Finality does not rule here. Again and again, with the surge of its enticements, universal temptation emerges and overcomes the power of the human soul; again and again innate grace arises from out of its depths and promises the utterly incredible: you can become whole and one" (Buber, 127–128).

How does one achieve a whole heart? If evil "stems primarily from indecision" in the face of omni–possibility, then salvation comes through grace understood as a form of decisiveness. "[B]y decision we understand, not a partial, a pseudo–decision, but that of a whole soul . . . Evil cannot be done with the whole soul; good can only be done with the whole soul. It is done when the soul's rapture, proceeding from the highest forces, seizes upon all forces and plunges them into the purging and transmuting fire, as into the mightiness of decision. Evil is lack of direction and that which is done in it and out of it as the grasping, seizing, devouring, compelling, seducing, exploiting, humiliating, torturing and destroying of what offers itself' (Buber, 130).

What insights does this rather mystical account of evil give us into evil within the business world? The account warns us to be wary of at least three things: 1) moral exhibitionism; 2) decisions of a partial soul; and 3) a belief that all things are possible. I define "moral exhibitionism" as the flaunting of one's goodness. When leaders of companies proclaim their companies to be entirely ethical or socially responsible, we are witnessing corporate *moral exhibitionism*. This behavior is a form of will to power, a will that does not have any interest in learning what really is but instead wishes to impose its version of how things should be. The leader is typically intent upon making the company appear to be virtuous by forcing compliance with some code. In these cases, management typically puts little or no effort into talking with others to discover what might be good, what less so. In Buber's terms, nothing is allowed to "offer itself." Everything is simply by dint of executive decree.[7]

We can see the will to power at work, for example, at General Electric. Since 1946, GE has been writing various company policy codes. Staff appointed by the GE CEO drafts the code. Employees are given a copy of the statement. They must sign a statement saying that they have understood the code, will obey it and will report internally anyone who violates the code.[8] This type of top–down ethics enforcement does not give people the opportunity to learn from others' experiences or to re–evaluate possibly inappropriate governing values. In fact, it can encourage employees to simply follow authority (Nielsen, 1996). If the authority should decide, as GE executives did at one point, to ignore the promulgated code, employees may infer that this violation is permissible.[9] After all, the powers that be are responsible for establishing what is good and what evil. This example illustrates moral exhibitionism because those writing the code refused to be accountable to any external parties. The CEO and his appointed ethics panel simply assumed they knew exactly which policies were morally good and prided themselves on enforcing moral discipline.

*Decision by a partial soul* is a second warning sign. Partial soul is at work whenever a person proceeds as though he or she were completely beyond temptation. Buber would agree with Thompson that evil is present whenever a person identifies herself as a "good person" and either ignores any badness within herself or projects it onto others. In such cases, there is a "black–out" of part of the human soul. Executives at Dow Corning Corporation, which made silicon breast implants, engaged in a form of black–out when they refused to take phone calls from journalists who were trying to get information about the effects of the implants and from their women customers who were calling with concerns about the product. The executives decided that they need only talk with those whom they deemed "reasonable" (Byrne). This policy was an attempt to make these other "unreasonable" folks disappear. The company executives could reassure themselves they were completely in the right only by silencing any external critics who might raise inconvenient objections. In such a case, the evil impulse has not been reunited with the good. The company's actions and policies have merely been relegated to the shadows.

The third sign that evil is afoot is when employees adopt a belief that all things are possible. In a recent NPR interview, a marketing executive from Coke complained about the fact that people around the world consume 12 pints of fluid per day and only 1.5 pints are Coke. In effect, the marketing executive was saying that Coke is now in competition with water! He apparently desired to have everyone in the world drinking cola all the time. Such a diet would likely make people sick. This executive clearly was not concerned with any reality apart from the one he envisioned creating through successful marketing. Here we have a case of "grasping and seizing" at any and all opportunities.

*Common Threads*

Let me end by returning to the question: what is evil? We have seen how many different answers there are to this question. Each of the accounts I've examined appears somewhat plausible. Must we then conclude that evil is multiform and ultimately unknowable? Are there commonalities in these accounts? There appear to be at least three common threads:

1. Evil is a human phenomenon. All of the authors I've been discussing see evil as a mark or function of what is distinctively human— a capacity to narrate; an ability to generate speculations and then convert them into evidence of hypotheses, a desire to create reality. Cats do not see ghosts. Slugs do not live out their lives in accordance with an elaborate system of soul–deadening labels devised by the larger slug community. Monkeys do not believe that all things are possible.

2. Evil resides in the mode of representation more than in the act or the action's effects. Even the criminological model, which equivocates on this point, ultimately gets driven to locate evil in a defective self–narrative resulting in low self–control rather than in the criminal act *per se*.

3. What feature of the mode of representation is evil? Perhaps evil is identical with the certainty with which a person and/or the community clings to a false self–image–the embezzling clerk who is certain he is owed the world and equally sure he won't be caught; the governess who lets her imaginings become unshakeable convictions; Lou Ford's and the community's conviction that everyone

and everything falls into some black or white category; the sales-men's mantra proclaiming all things to be possible; the CEO's presumption that he knows exactly what behavior makes a company socially responsible. If evil and certainty are one, then we all share in evil. We are all prone to stake out positions and invest ourselves in them. What is more, we often reinforce one another's certainty. So, if evil is one with certainty, then evil is in individuals and in the community at large.

## References

Arendt., Hannah. "Personal Responsibility under Dictatorship," *The Listener*, August 6, 1964.

_____. *The Origins of Totalitarianism.* New York: Harcourt Brace & Company, 1979.

Aristotle. Translated by H. Rackham. *Nicomachean Ethics.* Cambridge: Harvard University Press, 1975.

Barber, B. *The Logic and Limits of Trust.* New Brunswick, NJ: Rutgers University Press, 1983.

Buber, Martin. *Good and Evil.* Upper Saddle River, New Jersey: Prentice Hall, 1953.

Byrne, John. *Informed Consent.* New York: McGraw–Hill, 1995.

Clinard, M. B. *Corporate Ethics and Crime.* Beverly Hills, CA: Sage Publications, 1983.

Foot, Phillipa. *Virtues and Vices and Other Essays in Moral Philosophy.* Berkeley: University of California Press, 1978.

Fukuyama, Francis. *Trust.* New York: Free Press, 1995.

Gottfredson, M.R. and T. Hirschi. *A General Theory of Crime.* Stanford, CA: Stanford University Press, 1990.

Herbig, K.L. "A History of Recent American Espionage." In Sarbin, T.R., R.M. Carney and C. Eoyang, *Citizen Espionage: Studies in Trust and Betrayal.* Westport, CT: Praeger, 1994.

Hosmer, L.T. "Trust: The Connecting Link Between Organizational Theory and Philosophical Ethics." *Academy of Management Review*, vol. 20: 379–403.

James, Henry. *The Aspern Papers and The Turn of the Screw.* New York: Penguin Books, 1986.

Koehn, Daryl. "Should We Trust in Trust?," *American Business Law Journal*, vol. 34, no. 2 (Winter 1996).

_____. "Whistleblowing and Trust: Some Lessons of the ADM Scandal," *ETHICS___Website Commentary*, September, 1995 at http://www.depaul.edu/ethics/.

Lewis, Michael. *Liars' Poker.* New York: Penguin, 1992.

Lifton, Robert Jay. *Thought Reform and the Psychology of Totalism.* Chapel Hill: University of North Carolina Press, 1989.

MacIntyre, Alasdair. *After Virtue*. Notre Dame, IN: University of Notre Dame Press, 1984,

Mitchell, T.R. and W.G. Scott. "America's Problems and Needed Reforms: Confronting the Ethic of Personal Advantage." *Academy of Management Executive*, vol. 4: 23–35.

Moberg, Dennis. "On Employee Vice." Forthcoming issue of *Business Ethics Quarterly*.

Ouspensky, P.D. *In Search of the Miraculous*. New York: Harcourt Brace & Co, 1949.

Nielsen, Richard P. *The Politics of Ethics*. Oxford: Oxford University Press, 1996.

Plato. Translated by Harold North Fowler. *Apology, Crito, Euthyphro, Phaedo, Phaedrus*. Cambridge: Harvard University Press, 1971.

Sarbin, T. R. "A Criminological Approach to Security Violations." In Sarbin, T.R., R.M. Carney and C. Eoyang, *Citizen Espionage: Studies in Trust and Betrayal*. Westport, CT: Praeger, 1994.

Sartre, Jean–Paul. *Being and Nothingness*. New York: Washington Square Books, 1993.

Semler, Ricardo. "Managing without Managers." *Harvard Business Review*, Sept–October 89, no. 5: 76–84.

Sereny, Gitta. *Albert Speer· His Battle with Truth*. New York: Vintage Books, 1995.

Staw, B.M and E. Szwajkowski. "The Scarcity–Munificence Component of Organizational Environments and the Commission of Illegal Acts." *Administrative Science Quarterly*, vol. 20: 345–354.

Thompson, Jim. *The Killer Inside Me*. New York: Vintage Books, 1952.

Unsworth, Barry. *The Rage of the Vulture*. New York: W.W. Norton & Co., 1982.

Young–Bruehl, Elisabeth. *The Anatomy of Prejudices*. Cambridge: Harvard University Press, 1996

# Notes

1. Moberg concedes that whistleblowing and other "betrayals" will sometimes be justified. But he does not seem to recognize that this concession means that there is a conceptual problem in associating "betrayal" with low self–control. Many so–called "betrayals" may be well considered and warranted. If so, the ethical problem is not one of betrayal but of figuring out how to distinguish between "true" and merely "apparent" betrayals.

2. Quote from Henry James appears in his introduction to Henry James, *The Aspern Papers and The Turn of the Screw*. New York: Penguin Books, 1986, p. 22.

3. "The 'Little Rascals' Ritual Abuse Case, Edenton, NC" at http://www.religioustolerance.org/ra_edent.htm.

4. Ibid.

5. "Little Rascals," op cit.

6. The customer–employee distinction has also hampered efforts to curb workplace violence. It was not until 1996 that OSHA issued guidelines urging management to endorse a policy that "places as much importance on employee safety and health as on serving the . . . client." "OSHA Issues Workplace Violence Guidelines" are at http://www.afscme.org/afscme/press/ 040896*5.htm.

7. Richard Nielsen does an excellent job of discussing the executive practice of imposing corporate codes. Richard P. Nielsen, *The Politics of Ethics* (Oxford: Oxford University Press, 1996), pp.39–54.

8. Nielsen, 40.

9. Nielsen, 52. "In the several G.E. examples, middle–level managers obeyed the orders of higher–level managers to violate G.E.'s own ethics code. The lower–level managers were so used to obeying orders that they did not think of questioning whether higher–level managers should be making exceptions to the ethics code. Since they had not participated in developing the ethics code, it was difficult for them to understand when an exception was being ordered for legitimate or illegitimate reasons" (52).

# 7

# Technology and Ethics: Privacy in the Workplace*

## Laura P. Hartman

## I. Introduction

I feel privileged to serve as the Second Annual Bell Atlantic Visiting Professor in Business Ethics and Information Technology; and I look forward to working with many of your during the week to come. I am honored to serve in a role previously held by one of my most esteemed colleagues, Richard De George, and fortunate to have been invited by one of the colleagues whom I admire most in my field and who has truly served as a guide and mentor to many in our profession, Michael Hoffman. Finally, I am grateful to the Center for Business Ethics here at Bentley, not only for its invitation, but also for its leadership in this field and for the impact that it has had on ethics institutes and practices around the world.

* Editor's note: Laura Hartman's chapter was originally delivered as a Wicklander Lecture. It was revised for a lecture at the Center for Business Ethics at Bentley College. The revised version has been reprinted in this collection by permission.

Privacy in the workplace is one of the more troubling personal and professional issues of our time. But privacy can not be adequately addressed without considering a basic foundation of "ethics." We can not reach a meaningful normative conclusion about workplace privacy rights and obligations without a fundamental and common understanding of the ethical basis of justice and a thorough understanding of the individual and organizational concerns and motivations.

I will then discuss the status of privacy in the workplace from a technological as well as a legal perspective. What was once considered as an inalienable right has now been reassessed as our society and the business world have grown ever more complex. Traditional ethical analysis offers some guidance on how to evaluate the balance between a worker's right to privacy and an employer's need for information with which to manage the workplace. But guidance is not the same as resolution: as concerns workplace privacy rights, there are many more questions than answers.

Finally, I will address the vexing issues of privacy, drawing on ethical theory to advance a means by which to identify the appropriate ethical balance for workplace privacy. The focus of my remarks is on employee privacy, in particular, because this is a critical area where technological advancement is spurred by our desire for information and the ease of its collection. We must ensure that our ethical analysis remains current with the possibilities created by innovations.

## A. Ethics as "Perception"

Individual views of appropriate bases for assessing the ethical nature of acts and consequences vary widely. If I were to ask any one of you for a definition of ethics, some of you may agree with that definition, while others may completely disagree or want to enhance it. For me, the concept of perception is critical for ethical assessment, since perception plays such a paramount role in framing issues. Our ethical decisions are influenced by our own perception of ourselves, by others' perception of our actions, and by our perception of "universal laws." Our final choices are determined by the perception that has the greatest impact or weight at the time.

For example, perhaps you have a certain hat that you love to wear; and it is simply the ugliest hat in the world. But it keeps you warm; and you're just going to wear it. You do not care what anyone thinks. You do not care if people stare at you walking down the block. All you care about is that you are comfortable. *Your* perception is all that matters. This same circumstance might exist for you in connection with an ethical dilemma. Sometimes you believe so strongly in what *you* think that, even if the entire universe believes what you are doing is wrong, you will go ahead and do it because you believe it is right. I assume you can imagine a few situations where the only opinion that concerns you is your own. You are following your own values. It is your particular perception that defines what is ethical.

Now contrast the influence of your personal perception in this situation to the origin of the second potential influence on our actions: what concerns you may be whether *society* perceives that what you are doing is right. You can define society any way you want: your mother, your particular colleagues tonight, people with whom you work, other family members, whatever you define as your society, including of course, the larger American or global society.

Ethicists often call this the *New York Times* or *CNN* test. Perhaps now we should call it the *web* test. When reaching a resolution to an ethical dilemma, you might test how you will feel if you saw what you did today all over the internet tomorrow. The question becomes, would you feel all right if everyone else (in your circle or society) knew about what you did? In fact, you might believe that what you did is absolutely right, but the world (or your mother) does not understand it, misunderstands it or misperceives it. You can probably imagine scenarios where you know what you are doing is right, but everyone is going to get the wrong impression so you simply choose not to do it. What matters to you in this decision is what other people think. There are certainly situations where all of us might be subject to that type of influence.

The third scenario is where one's determination of whether something is ethical is based on one's interpretation of some universal rule or rules (such as a religious guidance or the direction of universally–held principles). For some people, the question they ask themselves is "what would Buddha or Jesus or some other universalist do in this circumstance?" It is the "perception" of that religion, spiritual leader or other "omniscient" being that is critical to your decision. In the end, you believe that the rule is the word of God, or another being or force, and that is what is going to influence your decision, whether or not society or you independently agree with it.

So your determination of that which is ethical in any one circumstance truly depends on whose opinion is important to you. I will give you one example of the importance of perception in decision–making. When I first took my three and a half year old daughter on an airplane, about a year and a half ago, I was concerned about her comfort level since I am no fan of airline takeoffs or landings. I was trying to prepare Emma for the takeoff, so I said, "Emma, the plane is going to run, run, run and then jump in the air, and it's going to jump just like you do, but it's going to stay in the air, and it's going to be okay."

As we take off from the ground, of course, Emma looks out the window starts getting upset. But she is all upset about something to do with the *ground;* and I couldn't figure out what she meant until I realized that she perceived that *the ground was falling away* rather than the plane flying in the air. She could not see that we were in an airplane that was lifting up into the air. She saw that the ground was falling away; and it never would have occurred to me that she would perceive it that way. Yet that is what upset her to such a great extent.

Now maybe if I had considered how she might perceive the take-off, I might have addressed it differently. Do you ever go to sleep at night thinking that something that you did was just fine, but wake up the next morning with everyone angry at you? Or you hand in a memo to some manager, thinking it is perfectly clear; but she or he hands it back to you later saying, "I don't know what the heck you're talking about here, you've got to be more clear?" You thought you were so clear. In that regard it may be very helpful to engage in a bit of analysis to try to view things from the perspective of each of those individuals who might be impacted by your decision. We will see the importance of this type of analysis in just a moment.

I do not believe really that each of our ethics are fundamentally different; but we often care about different perspectives. Certain perspectives seem more valid, depending on the circumstances. Addressed this way, it is clear that businesses, in particular, generally care about what their primary stakeholders consider to be ethical because they are perceived to have the greatest impact on the business.

## B.  The Impact of Ethics as Perception in Business Decision–Making

There are a number of factors that influence businesses to care about how they are perceived by society. The law persuades us to be ethical using deterrents or punishments. The Federal Sentencing Guidelines prescribe hundreds of millions of dollars in fines or jail time for violations. Businesses are also influenced by pragmatic reasons. The Ethics Resource Center in DC found recently that firms with written codes of conduct are a better investment than those who do not have written codes. When firms engage in strong decentralization efforts, perhaps ethics is the only thing that creates a consistent link within the firm.

Society is also persuasive in its forms of chastisement or praise (consider the *New York Times* test, mentioned earlier). Consider, as well, the Johnson & Johnson case in connection with the tainted Tylenol containers. That situation arose decades ago; yet I still discuss it in my classes as a laudable way to respond to a situation. Wouldn't you like to believe that decades from now people in your firm say, "oh, you should always do that the way that _____ [input your name] did it in 2000?" Or would you rather that people decades from now say, "do it any way, but never do it the way that _____ did it back in 2000", such as the individual at Ford who recommended that they *not* recall the Ford Pinto?

There are also additional incentives for firms to engage in ethical behavior. First, it unethical behavior imposes terrible costs. Nestle continues to feel the backlash resulting from an insensitive marketing campaign for infant formula in developing economies that cost many children their lives. This happened over twenty years ago; yet I still discuss that case, as well. Texaco has paid out almost $200 million for their failure to pay attention to diversity. Mercury Finance, General ch, Bausch & Lomb, Microsoft: each of these firms has seen financial turmoil arise from ethical violations that were not originally anticipated.

## C. Our *Habitual* Business Decision–Making Process

Business decision making is not all that different from decision making by reasonably rational individuals. (Of course neither businesses nor people are completely rational.) So now that we have a more clear understanding of ethics and the impact of perception, as well as an awareness of the incentives toward ethical behavior, how do you *do* it? Usually, we make decisions *considering limited alternatives*. I may say to you, what do you do, choice a or choice b? You consider the options, feeling the pressure. You think, "oh my gosh, a or b, a or b . . . I'll take choice a!" But another option exists, does it not? One might say, "wait a minute, I need to think about this. There are other choices that you did not offer me–choices c, d, e, f." But usually, we consider only the limited alternatives.

We use *simplified decision rules*. You must make the choice to terminate someone. You choose to follow a rule of thumb such as firing the last one hired. "I'm sorry, there's nothing I can do." Rules of thumb relieve the decision–maker of the accountability for that decision. It feels better to say, " there is nothing I can do," than to explain that you have all the discretion in the world, but still firing the person.

Finally, we usually select alternatives that merely *satisfy minimum criteria*. I believe this normal habit is one of the most detrimental of our habitual decision–making practices. If all of us need to reach a compromise on something, we would naturally find a solution on which we all could agree, and then stop. It is often difficult to believe there is a better answer than the first possible solution on which there is no dispute. But, instead, it is seldom that one continues to seek alternative, *better* solutions at this point. Does anyone ever say, "wait, that might not be the best; let's keep trying?" It does not happen very often. You can imagine that one might miss out on the *best possible* decision instead of the *earliest or easiest* possible decision. This process is how we *usually* make decisions.

## D. The Ethical Process of –Decision–Making

What follows is a discussion of the *ethical* process of decision–making. It may appear to be awfully complicated. But let me tell you this: it becomes habitual, so habitual that it becomes *uncomfortable* when you are in circumstances where you cannot conduct an ethical decision making process.

If you have ever learned how to drive a stick shift car, you will understand the following metaphor. Consider the first time you sat in a stick shift car. You had eighty–five thousand, three hundred and thirteen things to remember. Stick shift driving is pretty complicated. You have to remember when to pop the clutch, when to put in the clutch, when to put the brake or the gas on, what to do with this hand over here, what gear you are in, and so on. You begin to drive and the car dies often, you stall, and you deal with it, and then you learn. However, once you become proficient at stick shift driving, you do not really think about when you have to put in the clutch anymore. I drive a stick shift car and I do not think about putting in the clutch. I do not think about which gear I should be in. I just drive. And, in fact, when I drive an automatic car, my left foot keeps going down to try to push the clutch in! I am uncomfortable driving an automatic car these days.

So, compare these circumstances to the ethical decision making process. It will be difficult or challenging or burdensome in the beginning; but later it will evolve into a habitual process–a process which, if you do not have the ability to follow it in a certain circumstances, you are still pushing that left foot in. You are trying to do it. It is uncomfortable that you cannot.

The ethical decision–making process is as follows:
1. **Issue(s):** Identify the dilemma.
2. **Facts:** Obtain all of the unbiased facts.
3. **Alternatives:** Identify the choices that you have (look not only to a and b, but also to y and z!)
4. **Stakeholders:** Identify those who have an interest? What are their motivations? How much power does each hold over you or your firm?
5. **Impact:** Identify the impact of each alternative on each stakeholder and the stakeholders' resulting impacts on you or your firm.

6. **Additional assistance/theoretical guidance:** Do theories uncover any hidden implications? Do they support one alternative over another?
7. **Action:** Decide how to respond and act.
8. **Monitor:** Monitor outcomes and make adjustments where necessary.

There are a few other questions that business practitioners might usually ask themselves that might offer a bit of guidance or direction.

1. How'd I get here in this dilemma in the first place?
2. Is my action legal? Where's the legal line?
3. Am I being fair and honest (is it "just")?
4. Am I acting in line with my personal integrity? The firm's core values? The character traits I endeavor to exhibit?
5. Am I being only self–serving or am I considering others?
6. Will it stand the test of time?
7. Is this a model of "right" behavior?
8. How will I feel afterwards? (Am I proud?)
9. Will someone get the wrong idea?
10. Is my loyalty in the "right" place?
11. Is this something a *leader* should do?
12. How do I never get here again? What should I have done a while ago to avoid getting to this horrible place?

The important factor in ethical decision–making is not necessarily arriving at a correct or right decision, but is instead to be conscious of the impact of the decision on one's self and others. It is practically impossible not to be affected by this consciousness in one's decision–making if one follows the process set forth above. The end result is a world of more conscious, considerate decisions rather than those based on rapid fire, gut–based instincts.

**Ethical Decision–Making with Regard to Employee Privacy.** Applying this ethical decision–making process to the complicated challenge of employee privacy, one must first identify the issue and understand the dilemma. Then one must obtain all of the facts, identify the variety of alternatives available to both employees and employers, and identify all of the stakeholders. The next step is to attempt to understand the impact of the different alternatives in terms of workplace monitoring, surveillance, etc. Perhaps ethical theories will provide some insight. The issue of whether a fundamental "right" exists in personal autonomy or, conversely, managing the workplace may be illuminated by ethical theories. Finally one needs to make a recommendation and monitor the outcomes. In the course of my research in this area, I am at the point of making a recommendation. I do not yet have evidence monitoring the outcomes.

## II.  Ethics in Information Technology and Workplace Privacy

### A.  Ethical Issues Unique to Information Technology

> "It appears to me that in ethics the difficulties are mainly due to the attempt to answer questions without first discovering precisely what question it is which you desire to answer."–George Edward Moore

Information technology provides us with a host of ethical challenges. New technology imposes new implications for the balance of power in the workplace. We now have in–home offices, allowing for greater invasions. Moreover, the line between personal and professional lives has become blurred as workers conduct personal business in the office and professional business at home. The office usually provides faster, cheaper and easier access to the internet, while some work must be done at home in order to be completed according to our modern, technologically–enhanced pace.

Faculty members, for instance, do not go home and become people other than faculty members. We often conduct work at home such as grading, class preparation and so on. Similarly, our profession affords us a great deal of autonomy in terms of how we spend our days. We do not punch a clock nor hand in a time sheet. All of my students have my home number. My professional and personal lives are awfully blurred. (Sometimes, I wish they were not so blurred!)

Technology allows employers to ask more of each employee because now we are now capable of greater production; we have greater abilities due to technology. We do not seem to know any longer when our work day is over. I used to be a lawyer and the understanding in that profession was, if you can work more hours, you do. This is because you will then be viewed as the preferred colleague. You will be the one who is going to get the plum assignments because you work so darn hard.

Other issues are raised by enhanced technology. For instance, should the technological ability to find something out make it relevant? With new employment testing technology, you can find out all sorts of personal information. Through genetic testing, hair follicle testing, drug testing, your employer can find out anything it wants to know about you. I will discuss the implications of these issues a bit more later this week as I discuss in the faculty workshop whether the ability to do something creates a responsibility to do that act.  Similarly, here, should the employer find out the information simply because it can?

In addition, new technology allows for a more faceless communication.[1]  If you have to fire someone, it is significantly easier to fire that person by e–mail than to walk into her or his office.  In the latter case, you see the individual, desperate, perhaps disappointed, frustrated with the fact that you've worked them so hard and now you are terminating them.  It is a lot easier to be nasty when you do not have to look your stakeholders in the face.

Finally, there is research that shows that the excessive exertion of power and authority may lead to what they call a "semi–schizoid response" including insecurity, "disruption of biographical continuity," feelings of being overwhelmed and powerless, and doubts about worthiness.  The implication is that, if someone questions you too much or takes away too much of your power, the ultimate cost may be your emotional security.  Somewhat prophetically, Lawrence Lessig writes in his new bestseller, *Code*, "We have been as welcoming and joyous about the net (and other technologies) as the earthlings were of the aliens in 'Independence Day.'  But at some point, we too will come to see a potential threat . . . and its extraordinary power for control."

## B.  Ethical Issues in The Privacy Arena

Specifically in connection with privacy, ethical issues arise with gathering information, assessing its accuracy, correcting it, and disclosure, as well as the substance of the information itself.  Simply knowing that someone knows personal information about you can feel invasive or violating.  For that amorphous reason, privacy is a slightly difficult concept to define.  Ethan Catch says it is "the ability to control what others can come to know about you."  Why do we care that someone knows our personal information?  We can imagine items of personal data that we simply do not want others knowing, whether or not they would actually do something with that information.  We do not like people knowing things about us; it comes down to one's ability to be autonomous in controlling one's personal information.

Do you, personally, care about the information others know about you?  Would you care if your boss knew of all of your off–work activities?  Consider Milton Hershey. Milton Hershey would tour Hershey, Pennsylvania, making note of workers' lawns that were not kept up, or homes that were not maintained.  He would even hire private detectives to find out who was throwing trash in Hershey Park.  Another business owner, Henry Ford, used to condition wages on workers' good behavior outside the factory.  He had a hundred and fifty inspectors in his "sociological department" to keep tabs on workers' hygiene habits and housekeeping.  Imagine!

Only recently did OSHA retract a statement that the occupational safety and health standards apply equally to workplaces and personal homes, when you work as a telecommuter.  Can you imagine if you had to maintain the same standards of safety in your home that your employer must maintain at the traditional workplace?

## C.  Status of New Technology with Regard to Workplace Privacy

A multitude of basic and inexpensive computer monitoring products allows managers to track web use, to observe downloaded files, to filter sites, to restrict your access to certain sites, and to know how much time you have spent on various sites, including products such as WebSense, Net Access Manager, WebTrack and Internet Watchdog.

One particular firm, SpyShop.com, claims to service one–third of the *Fortune* 500 firms.  This firm sells items such as a truth telling device that links to a telephone.  You are told that you can interview a job candidate on the phone and the device identifies those who lie. Another firm, Omnitracks, sells a satellite, that fastens to the top or inside of a truck.  The product allows trucking firms to locate trucks at all times. If a driver veers off the highway to get flowers for her or his partner on Valentine's Day, the firm will know what happened.

Spy Zone.com sells an executive investigator kit that includes the truth phone I mentioned earlier as well as a pocket recording pen. Other outlets sell pinhole lens camera pens, microphones that fit in your pocket.  The motto of one firm is "In God we trust.  All others we monitor."  That firm offers a beeper buster, a computer program that monitors calls placed to beepers within a certain vicinity.  A screen on your computer will show you all of the numbers so that you can determine whether the individual is being distracted during working hours.

## D.  Competing Interests

The predominant question that I have sought to answer by my recent research is whether a balance is possible between the employer's interest in managing the workplace and the employees' privacy interest. Do employees even have a right to privacy?  If one believes the answer is "no," then the entire issue becomes moot.  If the employee does have some, even limited, right to privacy, one must seek to find a balance of interest. While we will return to the consideration of "rights" as we apply ethical theories, below, it is helpful to identify the proposed rights in dispute.

The employer has a right to manage the workplace.   In more specificity, employers want to manage the workplace so that they can place workers in the appropriate positions. They want to ensure compliance with affirmative action, administer workplace benefits. They want to ensure effective or productive performance. They need to know what their workers are doing in their workplace. The employer's perspective is as follows: "I am paying them to be there working. If they are not working, I should know that and either pay them less, or hire different workers." It seems like a relatively understandable concern.

Employees, on the other hand, want to be treated as free, equal, capable and rational individuals who have the ability to make their own decisions about the way their lives will unfold. They are interested in their own personal development and valued performance (the lack of privacy may prevent "flow"); conducting *some* personal business at office; being free from monitoring for performance reasons (wary of increased stress/pressure from monitoring); being free from monitoring for privacy reasons; and in being able to review and to correct misinformation in data collected.

Consider the issue of personal work conducted at the office. I get to work some days at 7:00 a.m. and I do not leave until 7:00 p.m. on some days. Last I heard, many doctors' offices are not open before or after 7:00 in the morning or night. So when is one supposed to call and make an appointment, much less ever go to an appointment, if one is punching the clock with those hours? The employer has to understand that workers must be able to call the doctor and make an appointment. Workers need to be able to conduct *involuntary* personal matters at the office. Now, one might not need to e–mail their mother or chat on the phone with friends. Should workers still have the right to conduct that *voluntary* personal business, as well? Perhaps the resolution lies in the precise definition of voluntary or involuntary business.

## III. The Law, New Technology and Workplace Privacy

As dictated by the ethical decision–making process, one must obtain all the unbiased facts before responding to an ethical dilemma. Where new technology impacts the dilemma, the "facts" may be all the more difficult to ascertain since we are not yet completely equipped to obtain the necessary information. For example, some scholars contend that nearly everyone who has a computer (estimated to be about eighty percent of the people in the workforce in the United States) is subject to some form of information collection, no matter how much we protect ourselves.[2] Another source reports that more than 30 million workers were subject to workplace monitoring last year, up from only 8 million in 1991.[3]   We are not yet at a point where we can even determine whether this information is realistic.

We are relatively certain about the ways in which information is collected. As of 1999, two–thirds of mid–to large–size firms conduct some form of monitoring, whether it is computer–based monitoring, video monitoring, monitoring of personal investments or maybe simply monitoring key card access to the building or parking garage (up from 30% in 1993).[4] Our style of working, even of communicating, has created greater possibilities for monitoring. In connection with email, for instance, over 90 million American workers now send over 2.8 billion e–mail messages per day, an average of 190 emails per day per worker.[5] We might not be too concerned about some forms of monitoring, while others might feel particularly invasive.

## A.  Federal Legislation

Over one hundred bills on privacy protection have been introduced in Congress, but only one on the collection of personal information from kids on the Internet has been approved. Also, the White House right now is only supporting privacy protections related to medical information privacy because they believe that this type of uncertainty will dissolve as firms and employees become more comfortable with the medium.

## B.  Constitutional Protections

The Fourth Amendment to the U.S. Constitution protects the "right of the people to be secure in their persons, houses, papers and effects, against unreasonable searches and seizures." This protection implies a reasonable expectation of privacy against intrusions *by the State, only.*  As this provision of the Constitution does not apply to actions by private sector employers, their employees must rely instead on state–by–state laws and the common law made and accepted in the courts.   Similar limitation exists in connection with the First Amendment's protection of personal autonomy  and  the  Fifth  Amendment's  protection  against  self– incrimination–each of these only protects the individual from invasions by the State. Currently there is proposed employment–related privacy legislation  in  several  states  that  would  apply  to  private  sector employers, but those states fall in the distinct minority.

What the courts will generally consider in cases involving both the Fourth Amendment and common law privacy protections is (a) whether the employer has a legitimate business interest in obtaining the information and (b) whether the employee has a reasonable expectation of privacy. Several examples of common law actions by the courts are illustrative of the courts' attempts at creating this balance, but perhaps more significant are the settlements reached by firms concerned about the *prospect* of a judge's decision.

## C. Case Law

In one recent case, two McDonalds restaurant employees used voicemail to transmit love messages during an affair. They believed that these messages were private since the firm told them that only *they* had the access codes. The franchise owner monitored the voicemail messages and later played messages for the wife of one of the workers. The lovers sued for invasion of privacy. They settled for several million dollars, so we do not yet have any judge's decision in a situation like this.

In another case that never made it to the courts, the Minnesota Attorney General sued several banks for revealing personal information about clients to marketers in exchange for more than $4 million in fees. One bank eventually agreed to pay attorney fees plus $2.5 million to Habitat for Humanity.

While the law has not yet settled in connection with monitoring or the privacy of obtained information, hence the settlements, monitoring does seem justified by several cases where email was later used as evidence to encourage a settlement. Within the past several years several large firms, including R. R. Donnelly, Morgan Stanley, and Citicorp, have found that cases often hinged on e–mail transmissions that people originally thought were deleted. In one case this included an email containing 165 racial, ethnic and sexual jokes sent to the entire firm. In another, the email included sexual jokes about why beer is better than women. Had the firms enforced stringent policies about the use of email and monitored to enforce these policies, perhaps these emails would never have been sent.

A few short months ago, the *New York Times* also found itself in some problems. They fired twenty–four employees at a Virginia payroll processing center for sending "inappropriate and offensive email in violation of corporate policy." The public sector is not immune from similar challenges: The U.S. Navy reported that it had disciplined over five hundred employees at a supply depot for sending sexually explicit e–mail. It happens all the time, and it's continuing to happen. You would think that people would actually learn.

In cases where the courts have been able to address the issue, it seemed at first that notice of monitoring might emerge as the critical factor. Perhaps persuaded by early case law, of the 67% of mid– to large–size firms that monitor, 84% notify their employees of this activity. Notice might range from a one–line comment in the middle of an employee manual that someone receives on the first day of work to a dialogue box reminding you that email may be monitored that pops up each time you hit the "send" button to transmit an email.

In an early case addressing this topic, the court in *K–mart v. Trotti* held that the search of an employee's company–owned locker was not appropriate where the workers were told to use their own personal lock. The basis for the decision was that the employees were left with the legitimate, reasonable expectation of privacy because it was their own locks. On the other hand, an employer's search of employee lunch buckets was held reasonable by another court only two years earlier.[6]

In a later 1990 case, *Shoars v. Epson,* Epson won a suit filed by an employee who complained about e–mail monitoring .[7] In that case, the court distinguished the practice of *intercepting* an email transmission from *storing and reading* email transmissions once they had been sent, holding that the latter was acceptable. In a 1992 action, Northern Telecom settled a claim brought by employees who were allegedly secretly monitored over a thirteen–year period. In this case, Telecom agreed to pay $50,000 to individual plaintiffs and $125,000 for attorneys' fees.[8]

Similarly, an employee–plaintiff in a 1995 federal action won a case against his employer where the employer had monitored the worker's tele-phone for a period of 24 hours in order to determine whether the worker was planning a robbery. The court held that the company had gone too far and had insufficient evidence to support its claims.[9]

One might therefore conclude that, if an employer adequately noti-fies workers that it will conduct monitoring, it has effectively destroyed any reasonable expectation of privacy on the part of the workers. It would now be *unreasonable* to expect privacy since one is told not to expect it. However, in a case where the alternative extreme was true, where a firm notified workers that it would *not* monitor, the court did not follow congruent logic. It did not find a reasonable expectation of privacy based on a firm's a pledge not to read email.

In this case, *Smyth vs. Pillsbury*, Smyth sued the firm after a man-ager read his e–mail. At the time, Pillsbury had a policy saying that it would not read e–mail. One might presume that this policy should have created this reasonable expectation of privacy. But, instead, this was the first federal decision to hold that a private sector, at–will employee has no right of privacy in the contents of one's e–mail when one sends it over the employer's e–mail system. The court held, "We do not find a reasonable expectation of privacy in the contents of email communi-cations voluntarily made by an employee to his supervisor over the company email system, notwithstanding any assurances that such communications would not be intercepted by management."

## IV.  The Limitations of the Legal System: A Call for Ethics

The law offers little, if any, guidance in this area in connection with workplace monitoring, and technology as a whole.  In fact, "the development of our moral systems has not been able to keep pace with technological and medical developments, leaving us prey individually and societally to a host of dangers."[10] And does this not represent our current situation in terms of technological advances?  It never occurred to most workers that some of this information was available or that they could be monitored in various ways.  When it does not occur to them, they do not adequately protect themselves against it.  Failure to completely understand the new technology may prevent people from completely understanding their exposure or potential vulnerability.

In his State of Union address just a few weeks ago, Clinton said, "Technology has to be carefully directed to assure that its reach does not compromise societal values.  We have to safeguard our citizens' privacy."[11] The primary ethical issue for analysis is therefore whether the employee's fundamental right to privacy outweighs the employer's right to administer the workplace according to its desires.  If not, is there a way to satisfy both parties? As law does not yet provide the answers, we turn to ethics for guidance.

The strongest, most persuasive and most consistent guidance in this area is based in a theory called Integrative Social Contracts Theory (ISCT), promulgated by Tom Donaldson and Tom Dunfee, both faculty in Wharton's ethics program. ISCT seeks to differentiate between those values that are fundamental across culture and theory ("hypernorms"[12]) and those values which are culturally specific, determined within moral "free space" and which are not hypernorms. In identifying values as hypernorms, Donaldson and Dunfee propose that one look to the convergence of religious, cultural and philosophical beliefs around certain core principles.[13]  Included as examples of hypernorms are the freedom of speech, the right to personal freedom, the right to physical movement, and informed consent.[14]  In fact, individual privacy is at the core of many of these basic, minimal rights and is, arguably, a necessary prerequisite to many of them.[15]

Specifically, ISCT seeks evidence of the widespread recognition of ethical principles that support a hypernorm conclusion, such as:
1.  Widespread consensus that the principle is universal;
2.  Component of well–known industry standards;

3. Supported by prominent nongovernmental organizations such as the International Labour Organization or Transparency International;
4. Supported by regional government organizations such as the European Union, the OECD, or the Organization of American States;
5. Consistently referred to as a global ethical standard by international media;
6. Known to be consistent with precepts of major religions;
7. Supported by global business organizations such as the International Chamber of Commerce or the Caux Roundtable;
8. Known to be consistent with precepts of major philosophies;
9. Generally supported by a relevant international community of professionals, e.g. accountants or environmental engineers;
10. Known to be consistent with findings concerning universal human values;
11. Supported by the laws of many different countries [16]

With regard to privacy, a key finding of a recent survey of the status of privacy in fifty countries around the world included the following conclusion:

> Privacy is a fundamental human right recognized in all major international treaties and agreements on human rights. Nearly every country in the world recognizes privacy as a fundamental human right in their constitution, either explicitly or implicitly. Most recently drafted constitutions include specific rights to access and control one's personal information.[17]

Accordingly, it would appear that the value of privacy to civilized society is as great as the value of the various hypernorms to civilized existence. Ultimately, the failure to protect privacy may lead to an inability to protect personal freedom and autonomy.[18]

The application of ISCT, however, has limitations. ISCT does not quantify critical *boundaries* for rights. If employees have a right to privacy based on a hypernorm, how far does it extend and what should happen in a conflict? Does not the employer have certain hypernorm-based rights that might be infringed by the protection of the employees' privacy right? To quantify the boundaries of the universal rights, one must therefore look beyond ISCT to a more fairness-based methodology.

Ethicist John Rawls' theory of distributive economic justice provides fairness-based guidance for quantifying the boundary levels of fundamental rights. Distributive justice is a teleological approach to ethical decision-making that defines *ethical* acts as those that lead to an *equitable* distribution of goods and services.  To determine a fair method for distributing goods and services, Rawls suggests that one consider how we would distribute goods and services if we were under a "veil of ignorance" that prevented us from knowing our status in society (i.e. our intelligence, wealth, appearance).  He asks that we consider what rules we would impose on this society if we had no idea whether we would be princes or paupers.  Without knowing what role we might play in our society, would we devise a system of constant employee monitoring or complete privacy in all professional and personal endeavors?  Rawls contends that those engaged in the exercise would build a cooperative system that was sensitive to the interests of all stakeholders.  The reason Rawls believes that such a standard would emerge is that the members of the exercise do not know whether they would be among the employer population or employee population.  Actions consistent with a system devised under a veil of ignorance are deemed ethical because of the inherent fairness of the system.

Rawls' theory of distributive justice does not provide guidance for identifying the categories of fundamental rights.  What Rawls does provide is a method for establishing distribution rules that avoid market transgressions of the boundaries of ethical actions.

Conjoining ISCT and Rawlsian methods enables the identification of basic human rights and boundaries, and provides for a reasonable balance between economic and ethical consequences of privacy protection for both employees and employers.  ISCT establishes the underlying or foundational hypernorms within a society, while distributive justice offers guidance on the extent of those hypernorms and the means by which to implement them.

Scholars are not in complete agreement as to whether a right to privacy is a hypernorm, though most would agree that some form of personal autonomy must be protected.  As mentioned above, evidence of a hypernorm such as freedom from slavery unequivocally supports this conclusion–personal autonomy serves as a cornerstone of this protection.  On the other hand, the *quantification* of one's right to privacy, in particular workplace privacy, is better identified using a Rawlsian analysis.  A proposal for such a fairness–based balance follows.

**The Implementation of An Ethical Resolution.**  Assuming for the purposes of this argument that privacy is a hypernorm, but one that may be limited by the employer's congruent right to managerial autonomy, how should the matter be resolved?  I suggest a fairness–based decision based on two values: integrity and accountability.

Integrity, meaning consistency in values, would require that the decision–maker define her or his values, as well as create a prioritization of those values.  This effort is often accomplished by a firm's mission statement or statement of values.  Then, when faced with a dilemma or conflict between two or more of these values, the decision–maker will have internal as well as external guidance regarding the direction her or his decision should take.  Second, no matter which direction is taken, the decision–maker must be accountable to anyone who is impacted by this decision.  That would require a consideration of the impact of alternatives on each stakeholder; a balancing of that impact with the personal values addressed in the first step; and actions that represent the accountability to the stakeholders impacted by the decision.

Applying this process to a firm's response to monitoring and its impact on employee privacy, the firm may obtain guidance from its mission statement or alternative statement of values. Does monitoring satisfy or further the mission or values of the firm? Assuming monitoring satisfies or furthers the values of the firm, does (since a negative relationship here would end the discussion and resolve the dilemma), the employer must impose monitoring in a manner that is accountable to those affected by the decision to monitor.

To be accountable to the impacted employees, the employer must respect their privacy rights and their right to make informed decisions about their actions.  Accordingly, this model would require that the employer should give adequate notice of the intent to monitor, including the form of monitoring, its frequency, and the purpose of the monitoring.  In addition, in order to balance the employer's interests with those of the work force, the employer should offer a means by which the employee can control the monitoring in order to create personal boundaries.  In other words, if the employer is randomly monitoring telephone calls, there should be a notification device such as a beep whenever monitoring is taking place *or* the employee should have the ability to block any monitoring during personal calls.  This latter option would address an oft–cited challenge to notification: if employees have notice of monitoring, there is no possibility of random performance checks.  However, if employees can merely block personal calls, they remain unaware of which *business–related* calls are being monitored.

**If it feels wrong, it probably is.**  Ethicist Gary Marks suggests that we look to a number of questions about monitoring, and he proposes that if you answer "yes" to these questions, your monitoring is more likely to be unethical.

- Does the *collection* of the data involve physical or psychological harm?
- Does the technique cross a personal boundary without permission?
- Could the collection produce invalid results?
- Are you being more intrusive than necessary?

- Is the data subject prohibited from appealing or changing the information recorded?
- Are there negative effects on those beyond the data subject?
- Is the link between the information collected and the goal sought unclear?
- Is the data being used in such a way as to cause a disadvantage to the subject?

As a manager, you are not without additional guidance on these issues. Kevin Conlon, District Counsel for the Communication Workers of America, suggests additional guidelines that may be considered in formulating an accountable process for employee monitoring:

- There should be no monitoring in highly private areas, such as restrooms.
- Monitoring should be limited to the workplace.
- Employees should have full access to any information gathered through monitoring.
- Continuous monitoring should be banned.
- All forms of *secret* monitoring should be banned.
- Advance notice should be given.
- Only information relevant to the job should be collected.
- Monitoring should result in the attainment of some business interest.[19]

Moreover, in its bargaining demands for last year, the Union of the United Auto Workers demanded concessions with regard to monitoring, including:

- Monitoring only under mutual prior agreement
- No secret monitoring–advance notice required of how, when and for what purpose employees will be monitored
- Employees should have access to information gathered through monitoring
- Strict limitations regarding disclosure of information gained through monitoring
- Prohibition of discrimination by employers based on off–work activities

# V.  Resolution?

I am emphatic in much of what I have presented here this afternoon because I passionately believe that there is a balance possible between workers and employers–not simply in the privacy/monitoring debate, but in many of the ethical challenges presented by new technological advances. Ultimately, employees and employers share a common vision with regard to the purpose of work and of the market in general. When the personal interests of both sides are considered, viable alternatives emerge.

Extreme opinions exist. An employer may believe that employees should simply quit if they don't want to be monitored, while certain employees may believe that they should have the ultimate control over their personal communications and other information. Two extremes. Yet, there is an absolute middle. One can absolutely respect the interest of the employee while also protecting the interest of the employer. A monitoring program that is developed according to and guided by the mission of the firm, then implemented in a manner that is accountable to the employees, follows the integrity/accountability approach I explored earlier.

From the employees' perspective, this type of resolution would respect their personal autonomy by providing for personal space, by giving notice of where that space ends, by giving them access to and the right to change or correct the information gathered, and by providing for monitoring that is directed toward the personal development of the employee and not merely to catch wrongdoers.

From the employer's perspective, this balance offers a way to effectively but ethically supervise the work done by their employees. It protects the misuse of resources, while also allowing them to better evaluate their workers and to encourage their workers to be more effective. I contend that any program that fails to satisfy these basic elements has the potential not only for ethical lapses, but also for serious economic problems.

Vice President and current presidential candidate Gore, who of course is an appropriate person to quote since he *invented* the Internet, claims that "new technology must not reopen the oldest threats to our basic rights: liberty and privacy. But government should not simply block or regulate all that electronic progress. If we are to move at full speed ahead into the information age, government must do more to protect your rights—in a way that empowers you more, not less. We need an electronic bill of rights for this electronic age."

## VI.  Concluding Thoughts

Before I conclude my remarks, I ask that you consider the following questions not only with regard to information technology and the impact that that technology has on your particular workplace, but also with regard to the ethical issues that arise in other areas of your work. Consider what you might be willing to quit over. What would be so damaging, so intrusive, so much of a violation of your personal space that you would simple quit right then and there? What could be so bad?

Second, and perhaps it seems extreme in this particular circumstance, what would you be willing to give your life for? You may not believe right now that information technology is going to present life and death ethical dilemmas, and yet when we consider the ultimate usage of some of that technology, it really does have a life–and–death impact. If you knew that it would have a fatal, negative impact, would you quit if your firm or client failed to ameliorate it? Monitoring probably does not fall within this range, but you can imagine situations where technology does allow such an extreme unethical and certainly illegal act.

The reason why I want to conclude with this query is because this is really the purpose of the past hour. The world is a better place because you have thought about these questions now, rather than when you are first faced with these challenges in the workplace.

Have you ever had a situation where you act impulsively in the face of some dilemma, and you realize hours later that, if you'd only thought about it, there were other alternatives or there were other ways to look at it? It did not occur to you at the time. The best solution is to consider these situations now, in advance, so that your gut tells you more information when you need to know it. In speaking of inventor Charles Lindbergh, it is said that, "of all the man's accomplishments, and they were very impressive, the most significant is that he spent most of his life considering and weighing the values by which you should live."

If I ask you what your personal mission statement was so that you could actually implement the integrity and then accountability steps, would you know what it would be right now? Could you recite to me what you think are your critical values? Maybe not, but now is the time to think about them and not when those values are ultimately challenged.

I'll leave you with this. Stanley Milgram conducted an experiment in the 1960s. In that experiment he called in two people. We'll take Megan and Jim. Megan and Jim come into my laboratory at Yale University, and I am wearing a white lab coat. I give to Jim fifty cards that have printed on them fifty pairs of symbols, i.e. a square and a heart, a diamond and a star, etc. Jim has a few minutes to memorize these. "Okay, Megan," the laboratory technician explains, "you are going to come into another room and test Jim. You're going to read off one of these symbols and, if he gets it correct, you'll continue. If he doesn't, you'll shock him with this electric shock machine, and then continue higher and higher voltages each time. It's just a little uncomfortable." Megan says that she understands.

Minutes later, the experiment begins. Jim remembers a few pairs in the beginning, but on the fourth card, he makes a mistake. He gets shocked and Jim says, "ah, that really hurt!" Megan says, "well, sorry." They keep going. They continue through a few more and Jim's saying, "wait a minute. This really hurts. Let me out of here! Let me out of here!" Later we hear, "I have a heart condition! Please let me out of here. This is horrible! I can't bear this any longer!" Megan's asking the experimenter, "what should I do?" The technician responds, "the experiment requires that you continue. You're being paid to participate in the experiment. There is no permanent tissue damage."

Continuing, Megan gets to number forty–eight, and she hears no sound from Jim's chamber. She looks to the technician who informs her that "no response is the same as a negative response." So she swallows, takes a deep breath and she zaps him. Forty–nine, no response. Fifty, no response. She stands up, gets out of the chair and says, "go, go, see if he's okay!"

And, of course, Jim is okay. He's reading from a script. He's not hooked up to a machine. He's part of the experiment. What is being tested is whether Megan will do what she has been told to do by an authority figure in a business or medical environment, against what she believes to be this person's best interest. One can now understand how this might be relevant to ethics and business ethics in particular.

Would you do something you knew was wrong because your boss tells you to do it? Oftentimes people say, "well if I didn't, I'd be fired." Well, so is it worth being fired? Should you do it or not do it? You still have a choice. You have a choice in everything.

How many of you sitting here this afternoon believe that you might actually continue the whole experiment and go through number fifty. Probably very few and certainly significantly fewer than the more than 60% that completed the experiment for Milgram.

Now, the essential question: what is the difference between those of you in this room and those tested? Are those of you listening today unique? Well actually yes, because you sat here for the past hour listening to a discussion about ethics and you have had the opportunity to consider the issues for a moment. It creates a bit of skepticism. Moreover, you have the opportunity under these circumstances to observe the ethical dilemma and to have a slightly more objective opinion as to what you might do.

I believe that if any of you went into a psychological experiment tomorrow in real life, you would still challenge that experiment early in its process. Why? Because you have actually thought about what you might do in that circumstance. You have thought about the power or lack of power that this lab person would have over you. I am hoping that, as we consider ethics more and more on a regular basis, when ethical dilemmas come up, perhaps you will already have considered your response or at least your values with regard to the dilemma.

Simply by virtue of considering a dilemma beforehand, considering how you would act or what is important to you, you are going to make a different decision. The process cannot help but modify how you act. And so that's why I appreciate you caring about and listening to this subject. Thanks very much.

## Notes

1. For additional insight in this area  (and perhaps foresight, given the original date of publication), *see* William S. Brown, "Ontological Security, Existential Anxiety and Workplace Privacy," *Journal of Business Ethics,* v. 23, no. 1, p. 61 (Jan. 2000), citing in addition R D. Laing, *The Divided Self* (New York, NY: Penguin Books, 1965).

2. "More   us   firms   checking   email,   says   AMA" http://www.amanet.org/research/specials/monit.htm.

3. Julie Cook, "Big Brother Goes to Work," *Office Systems* (Aug. 1999), pp. 43–45; John MacIntyre, "Figuratively Speaking," *Across the Board* (Jan. 1999) p. 17.

4. Id.

5. Id.

6. *Simpson v. Commonwealth of Pa., Unemployment Compensation Bd. of Review*, 450 A.2d 305 (Pa. Comm. St. 1982), *cert. den'd*, 464 U.S. 822.

7. No. SCW112749 Cal. Sup. Ct., L.A. Cty., 1989, *appeal den'd*, Sup. Ct. Ca., 994 Cal. LEXIS 3670 (6/29/94); James McNair, "When You Use Email at Work,  Your  Boss  may  Be  Looking  In,"  *Telecom  Digest*, http://icg.stwing.upenn.edu/cis500/reading.062.htm, reprinted from *The Miami Herald.*

8. Bureau of National Affairs, "Northern Telecom Settles with CWA on Monitoring," Individual Employment Rights (Mar. 10, 1992) p. 1.

9. Winn Schwartau, "Who Controls Network Usage Anyway?" *Network World* (May 22, 1995) p. 71.

10. John Haas, "Thinking Ethically About Technology," http://www.nd.edu/~rbarger/haas.ethic.

11. http//www.whitehouse.gov/WH/SOTU00/sotu–text.html  (Jan.  27, 2000).

12. Thomas Donaldson & Thomas Dunfee, "Toward A Unified Conception of Business Ethics: Integrative Social Contracts Theory," *Academy of Management Review*, v. 19 (1994) p. 252, 264 (hereinafter "Donaldson & Dunfee") (defining hypernorms as those principles that would limit moral free space, analogizing hypernorms to "hypergoods," "goods sufficiently fundamental as to serve as a source of evaluation and criticism of community-generated norms [within moral free space]." Id.)

13. Thomas Donaldson & Thomas Dunfee, "Toward A Unified Conception of Business Ethics: Integrative Social Contracts Theory," *Academy of Management Review*, v. 19 (1994) p. 252, 265.

14. Id.

15. Donaldson and Dunfee suggest that one look to international rights documents and statements of human rights for evidence of or support for certain hypernorms. Donaldson & Dunfee, at 265–267. Evidence of privacy and data protection as a hypernorm may be found in the Organization for Economic Co–operation and Development's "Recommendation of the Council Concerning Guidelines Governing the Protection of Privacy and Transborder Flows of Personal Data" [O.E.C.D. Doc. C(80) 58 final (Oct. 1, 1980), *reprinted in* 20 I L.M. 422 (1981)], the Council of Europe's "Council of Europe, Convention for the Protection of Individuals with Regard to Automatic Processing of Personal Data" [Jan. 28, 1981, EUR. T.S. NO. 108, *reprinted in* 20 I.L.M. 317 (1981)], or the Commission of the European Community's Council Directive on the Protection of individuals with Regard to the Processing of Personal Data and on the Free Movement of Such Data [COM(92)422 final 1992], European Commission Press Release IP/95/822 (7/25/95), "Council Definitively Adopts Directive on Protection of Personal Data." In support of the claim that privacy is either a hypernorm or a prerequisite to fundamental human rights, Charles Fried contends that privacy is necessary to other values such as love and trust. *See, e.g.,* CHARLES FRIED, AN ANATOMY OF VALUES: PROBLEMS OF PERSONAL AND SOCIAL CHOICE, 142 (1970).

16. Thomas Donaldson and Thomas Dunfee, Ties that Bind (Boston, MA: Harvard University Press 1999) p. 60.

17. Global Internet Liberty Campaign, "Privacy and Human Rights: An International Survey of Privacy Laws and Practice," http://www.gilc.org/privacy/survey/exec–summary.html (1998)

18. For a discussion on identifying Donaldson's and Dunfee's Integrative Social Contracts Theory–relevant ethical attitudes and the establishment of hypernorms, see Donaldson & Dunfee, *supra* note 103, at 274–275, 276–277.

19. Kevin Conlon, "Privacy in the Workplace," *Labor Law Journal* (Aug. 1997) p. 444, 447. *See also,* Organization for Economic Cooperation and Development (OECD), "Guidelines on the Protection of Privacy and Transborder Flows of Personal Data," available from the OECD at 202/785–6323.

# 8

# The Ethics of Everyday Life: Social Class and Moral Character in Women's Narratives

## Frida Kerner Furman

### Section 1. A Project is Born

In February of 1997, I returned, both exhilarated and terrified, from an American Academy of Religion committee meeting in Atlanta. I immediately called my colleague and friend, Beth Kelly, to set up an urgent coffee date. A day or two later, in this very building, I told her about my intense dinner conversation in Atlanta with two women, one an ethicist, the other a theologian–virtual strangers–who insisted I had to write about the many border crossings that have characterized my life and that of my family of origin. Beth had also heard about these stories of migration, dislocation, and the fluidity of identity that describe my life, and she, too, had urged me to put pen to paper for some time. This seemed to be the right time: I had just finished writing a book and was ready to start a new project; and I wanted to turn to a topic dealing with identity and difference. The only glitch was that writing about my life for public consumption seemed too risky, too lonely an enterprise.

Over the course of an hour and more than one cup of coffee, Beth and I decided we would invite her long–term friend, Linda Nelson, to join us in a collaborative project, one we came to call "Three Lives: Women Speaking Across Difference." And we have done a lot of speaking in the past two years, meeting for week–long marathons, taping our autobiographical conversations, intensely exploring issues of difference and socio–cultural location that both separate us and bring us together. These conversations have been transcribed, coded, and organized along thematic categories. We are now at the stage of analysis and writing.

I begin with a brief introduction of the collaborators of this project. Beth is an Irish–Catholic lesbian who is a feminist political theorist and Director of Women's Studies at DePaul. Linda is an African–American linguistic anthropologist with a background in writing pedagogy and literary studies; she teaches at Stockton State College in N. J. I am a Jewish social ethicist whose family emigrated from Chile when I was a child. We have a great deal in common–as feminist scholars, as women who have chosen (and often struggled) to shape careers in higher education while meeting complex family responsibilities, and as individuals who entered academic life from working–class or poor backgrounds–yet our differences remain profound.

Long before we imagined this project, we shared a commitment to interdisciplinary scholarship and teaching that is multivocal and multicultural, respectful of work that takes place within and against the traditional parameters of disciplinary domains. Long before we embarked on this project we all believed in the power and value of storytelling as a cultural genre. Whether told across a kitchen table or in the university lecture hall, stories bring people together. Storytelling has enormous potential for traversing boundaries and building bridges between seemingly disparate communities and cultures. It was precisely this view that propelled us to move forward, as we are keenly aware that one of the thorniest ethical problems in the U.S. today is the reality of diversity, and the enormous difficulties, at all levels of society, of dealing with it in productive ways. Situated as we are in highly divergent socio–cultural locations, our goal in our project is to find points of understanding through an ongoing process of in–depth conversations. Our commitment, in effect, is to develop a vision of human possibility that locates profound commonality, while simultaneously respecting cultural, ethnic, religious, and social diversity.

## Section 2. The "Ethics of Everyday Life": Narrative, Ethics, and Moral Character

I have always been suspicious of certain kinds of abstractions in the study of ethics, even when I could not have expressed it in this manner. However hard I tried during graduate school, for example, I could not warm up to philosophical ethics. Years later, I would write in my two published books that I like to work with living, ordinary people from whom I can learn about personal and cultural values and about the moral dimensions of their experience–what I came to call the "ethics of everyday life."

I have recently turned to some of the works of the late philosopher, Philip Hallie, whose book, *Lest Innocent Blood be Shed*, is well-known to many. In the years that I have taught that book, I have been attracted to Hallie's analysis of moral character. Hallie does not speculate about abstract ethical ideas, nor does he begin with principles against which he measures human achievement. Rather, he explores the moral character of the inhabitants of Le Chambon, a mountain village in southern France that rescued some 5000 Jewish refugees during WWII. Hallie focuses especially on Andre Trocme, the Huguenot pastor of the village. He grounds his analysis in the narratives of Trocme's life, in his actions, and in the actions of his community.

Hallie seems to be saying that it is in the concrete experience of living, and through the narratives that organize that experience for oneself and for others, that we can locate some of the living and breathing sources of moral character, moral predisposition, and moral action. Though he does not say so, I think he is arguing for attention to "embodiment." As feminist ethicists have especially noted, moral action generally is not derived wholesale from intellectual analysis and reflection, but more holistically from our entire embodied experience—mind, body, feelings, cultural and social experience, and so on.

"Now here's a good way to do concrete ethics," Hallie counsels. "Don't just tell stories interpreted in the old words of ethical theories. Show the intimate feelings of the storyteller . . . ." Rather than locating ethical oughts in abstract principles, Hallie continues, "find their force in the feelings, thoughts, and actions of particular human beings with their particular stories, or you find that force nowhere."[1] As an ethicist on this joint project, my job is to turn to the concrete, embodied experience of three women, expressed in autobiographical narratives–those written by each of us, and those emerging out of shared conversations. In the narratives I look for moral character–its grounding, its formation, its evolving vision. Hallie argues that narratives are revealing because "they *show* you something, something particular, and yet something of large significance."[2] In my view, the point is not *only* to reveal a person's life, or aspects of that life, as an end in itself, but also as a prism that opens up topics of contemporary socio–cultural importance, since personal experience is situated within a social matrix of power relations and cultural meanings.

Autobiographical narratives raise special questions about subjectivity, since stories about our own lives are clearly selective and especially given to revisionism. But beginning with the premise that "there is no such thing as 'unbiased' knowledge," I support Camilla Stivers' view that "personal narrative models a way of knowing . . . by blending the subjective with the system–wide."[3]

At this particular moment in history, of course, women's telling their stories is a political as well as a therapeutic or literary enterprise. It is potentially both a personally liberatory act and a socially transformative one. By telling our stories we define ourselves and hence claim agency over our lives, a possibility granted to women only recently, largely through the auspices of feminism.

In examining the narratives of my own life, and those of my colleagues, I hope to locate some of the ethical oughts that emerge from our family histories and coming–of–age stories, from our educational journeys and work experiences. I am interested in identifying, as well, those moments, sometimes seen in retrospect like photographic snapshots, that shaped in significant ways our moral character, which contributed to our becoming the moral agents we are today. In the next section I move to a discussion of social class and its shaping influences, recognizing, of course, that social class does not exist in isolation, but alongside other markers of our respective identities.

## Section 3.  Social Class

When I was a child growing up in Chile, the word "roto," or its diminutive, "rotito," was used to refer to a poor person. It denoted that person's clothing, as "roto" means torn, and the poor in those days often wore rags. Poor children also frequently went barefoot. I have vivid memories about that, memories poignantly captured for me even now, almost 40 years later, by Nobel Prize winning Chilean poet, Gabriela Mistral, in the first words of one of her most beloved poems: "Piecesitos de ninos, azulados del frio . . . ." (Children's little feet, blue from the cold...). Roto has a second meaning in Spanish. It also means "broken." I doubt very much whether the designation "rotito" was used with this meaning in mind, that is, with the conscious awareness

that the poor are often broken, in body as well as in spirit. That meaning, I suspect, remained hidden, and hence safely out of sight.

I have recently returned from my first visit to Chile since my departure in 1961. I saw no "rotitos" this time around, even when my
friend Sergio Topaz drove me through some of the poorest housing
developments of Valparaiso, the port city of my birth. I saw no one in
tatters, and everyone wore shoes. But to conclude that there is no poverty left in Chile would be a mistake. As Sergio explained, there is a
serious problem with *hidden* poverty in that picturesque city of hills.
Used clothing from the U.S. is now sold in Chile; such sales evidently
were not allowed in my days. So today everyone can buy jeans and t–
shirts, homogenizing clothing and hence self–presentation, much like
in the U.S. My friend, who used to be a member of Valparaiso's city
council, argues that poverty remains, and it is quite intractable. But
now it is also invisible.

As a social ethicist, I am interested in how societies name social
problems and identify moral dilemmas. Equally important from a
moral point of view, I have discovered, is what remains culturally hidden, out of sight, and hence beyond the reach of social and ethical
analysis, criticism, and potential redress.

Class is a frequently ignored dimension of social experience in the
U.S. As a sociological category, it is conceptually messy and highly
contested. And as Janet Zandy suggests, class is "the missing identifying principle . . . mentioned but not really welcomed into the multicultural conversation."[4] Indeed, class is invisible even in the academy,
where middle–class discourse and assumptions frequently dominate the
curriculum and interpersonal relations among faculty, students, and
staff. Our public celebration of freedom, opportunity, and social mo-
bility occludes the fiscal insolvency, insecurity, and instability endured
by those scarcely noted in the pages of *The New York Times Magazine*
or in our weekly TV programming.

Why social class is made invisible in American society is a complicated issue, deeply informed by ideology. In the first place, this
nation was conceived in opposition to the European *ancien regime*, a
system variously organized around rigid class distinctions. Ours was to
be a classless society, where all citizens were to be measured by their
own efforts, not by their group locations. The Puritan ethic, followed
by the Horatio Alger myth, undoubtedly trained Americans to "read"
social location in terms of personal success or failure: given the presumed equality of opportunity for all, financial success would accrue to
those who worked hard, poverty or fiscal marginality, to the lazy.

According to Barbara Ehrenreich, the working class as we think of
it today was *discovered* in the 1960s, "an imaginative product of mid-

dle–class anxiety and prejudice." She argues that this was not the working class that was involved in important labor militancy in this country. Rather, middle–class observers, she notes, "discovered a working class more suited to their mood: dumb, reactionary, and bigoted."[5] Picked up by the popular media, such characterizations of the working class may explain why the vast majority of Americans–irrespective of income–call themselves middle–class. Class refers to far more than income or wealth; it has profound cultural meanings that serve to inform personal and group identity and shape people's lives in critical ways. If the middle–class is the norm, with the upper or affluent class a rarity and the poor morally unacceptable, working–class folk are frequently conceptually constructed and represented as middle–class want–to–be's who have somehow failed. Jane Vanderbosch puts it rather pointedly when, referring to her own experience, she writes,

> The essence of what it means to be "working class" . . . is to *be* inferior, to be everyone else's "bottom line." So that those in the classes "above" me can feel better about themselves because they are—at the very least—superior to me, to my family, to my neighbors. To those who inhabit my class.[6]

Social ethicists have of course regarded poverty as a significant problem. Important studies and arguments have attempted to awaken the American people to the egregious gap in income and wealth in a nation that proclaims "equality and justice for all" as its guiding moral goal. In public discourse, Americans applaud the ideology of equal opportunity, but they seldom publicly acknowledge the country's failure to provide equal access. And extreme inequalities in outcome are rarely taken seriously by politicians, the media, or the educational system. Exposes regarding these matters have not been limited to the work of professional ethicists–witness the impressive impact of books like sociologist Michael Harrington's *The Other America* in the 1960s, or, more recently, journalist Jonathan Kozol's *Savage Inequalities*.

On the other hand, very little scholarship has been focused on an issue that interests me greatly, namely, the role of moral experience and the development of moral character linked to the particularities of social class. Assumptions about working class or poor folks are rife in American society, but, as I have suggested, these assumptions are largely produced by the middle–class and do not reflect the actual experience of working–class or poor people themselves. In fact, academics who write about social class all too often do so in highly abstract terms, "as a social system and a function of institutions," but "with little attention paid to its actual effect on individual lives and individual methods of survival and interpretation."[7] These are precisely the issues that interest me, for they engage embodied experience, what bell hooks calls the "passion of experience" and the "passion of remembrance," "ways of knowing that [are] often known through the body, what it knows, what has been deeply inscribed on it through experience."[8]

It would be inaccurate to claim that Beth, Linda, and I emerged from identical socio–economic locations. Indeed, our childhood followed distinctive paths marked not only by how our parents made their living, but also by conditions dictated by race, nationality, and educational opportunities. And yet, we were all positioned outside the middle–class, and hence outside the mainstream. That location imbued us with a kind of "local knowledge," from the ground up, as it were, that made possible at many points the poignant identification with each other's experiences.

As three women separated by ethnicity, religion, sexual orientation and nationality, we find most commonality around  that most submerged of analytic categories in our cultural lexicon.  Our narratives explore how social location shaped our childhood, educational choices and experiences, our work commitments, and our life within and outside communities of meaning and support.  In doing so they reveal the power of social class to shape moral character, to advance or impede life opportunities, to sustain or weaken family ties.  They call me to probe the social–ethical dimensions of social class, including the injustices inherent in social relations and cultural conventions that obscure its existence and diminish its significance.

## Class Longings and Humiliations

I was already in my 40s when I first I came to interpret some formative experiences in my life through the lens of social class.  Until then, my experiences of socio–cultural marginalization had seemed more directly tied to my identity as an immigrant and as a Jew.  A number of Eureka! moments  in the course of intense conversations with Beth and Linda suggested that class had indeed played a significant role in my life experience, even if I had not so identified it until the present.  While for them class consciousness has been a part of their intellectual apparatus for many years, my situation was complicated by the fact that I was born and raised in a different culture.  In Chile my family and I thought of ourselves as middle–class; everyone  who was not very rich or very poor did so.  That self–understanding continued, unquestioned, in the U.S., even though my father worked as a traveling salesman and my mother as a stenographer once we arrived here.

I share with you now several stories that capture class–based experiences and insights from our childhood and educational journeys.

## Of Coal Bins and Boiler Rooms
Linda remembers:

> There was almost no place where I felt a safe belonging. The family home was always in flux, always temporary, it seemed at this point, now looking back. We were always going somewhere, always "here" for just a little while longer, until things got better. We stayed a few months, some times longer, but never achieving any authentic sense of home. Perhaps this was due to the circumstances of our occupancy. We were never rent–paying tenants, but "supers."
>
> Superintendents and their families were granted an apartment in these N.Y. City tenements as the major part of their salary for the upkeep of the building. The apartment designation was no more than a euphemism for subterranean rooms, adjacent to the coal bin and the boiler room, which once a week yielded heavy cans of ashes. These "ash cans" had to be somehow hoisted by sheer muscle power up the concrete stairs that led down to the area of their joint living and fuel storage quarters for the building. I can recall my father, who was by this time close to sixty years old, literally rolling each of these cans once a week up the stairs in preparation for the sanitation truck's arrival. In retrospect, I draw a vaguely defined connection between the challenges of this work, the frequency and likelihood of error, and the consequent landlord or tenant dissatisfaction with the super's performance and our frequent moves.
>
> As I recollect now, through the benefits of age and academic training, I can mark these as moments that began to shape my class consciousness. These were the times that defined the boundaries and constructed the class hierarchy in frightfully stark terms. Those who occupied the uppermost strata were those who lived above ground, those who were secure in upstairs apartments from whence their angry hammering of the pipes would signal to the super below

*that he'd better hurry back to the rear of the base-
ment, to the boiler room, to see what was preventing
them from getting sufficient heat, their unquestioned
entitlement. Those who slept in the warmth of the
"steamheat," away from the steady roar of the fur-
nace, could not know of the constant, low–droning
fear we felt sleeping less than twenty yards from the
power of that heat, which my mother believed could
blow up at any time and "reduce us all to ashes."*

*The physical and spatial arrangement of our
lives in relation to the tenants was a concrete mani-
festation of our social location. "Us and them," was
indelibly impressed upon me by the thick concrete
stairs that led down to our rooms by the coal bin and
the bleached marble hallway stairs, ritually washed
by my father on Saturdays, that led up to what I
imagined to be the splendor of the apartments of the
tenants. They lived in clean spaces, they were
warmed by my father's labors, and they were White.
We were unseen, unwelcome, scrutinized, and Black,
and if anything went wrong in the building, there was
only one person held accountable, my father, the su-
per. In this way, no place could be fully home until
several years later, when we actually passed into the
hands of the City and went to live in the projects.*

## "My Refrigerator is Always Full"

It is my turn to tell a story:

*I must have been ten years old when Auntie Lily
left Chile for the U.S. Her departure was a painful
one for me and for my family–separations and good
byes seemed destined to go on and on. I remember
going to the airport, crying as I clung to my aunt,
who had been like a second mother to me.*

*We corresponded frequently. I have forgotten
most of her newsy letters, but I remember this. She is
enticing us to consider emigrating, too. She reports,
in words that remain indelibly imprinted in my mind,
"My refrigerator is always full." This from the
woman who lived for some years in my home, worked
as a secretary and had an independent life, and once
in a while would treat my brother and me to a hot*

*dog and a soda; or would bring home a large candy
bar, which my mother would distribute, one square at
a time, keeping the remainder under lock and key; or
who under exceptional circumstances—I do not know
how many times–would arrive home with bags of
groceries, to carry us over until normalcy was rees-
tablished. My parents had a small women's wear
store at that time, and they could not always count on
a steady flow of cash.*

*I cannot say we felt deprived, though by U.S.
standards we certainly were. I used to steal stray pe-
sos from my mother's empty purses to join my friends
at the candy store—there was no such thing as an allowance in my home, and I expected none. But today
my eyes spout tears and my throat constricts when I
think of Auntie Lily's words, which to us, still using
an ice–box and, I suppose, not a full one at that, must
have sounded like music to our ears. For though I
don't recall any particulars, I do know that the refrigerator and its promises became a vivid topic of
conversation around the dinner table for quite some
time to come.*

Experiences of exclusion and deprivation–relative, to be sure–
mark these and other childhood memories. I cannot fathom Linda's
daily deprivations, told to Beth and me, sometimes in passing, sometimes in sober and anguished tones. How her father, a barely literate
man, would sometimes leave the house with bucket and rags, hoping to
get a job cleaning something, anything, so he could bring some food
home for his children. How at times there was virtually nothing to eat,
save for a small glass of juice and half a doughnut. And sometimes in
despair, Linda's father would mix some flour and water and try to
"make something happen" on a dry frying pan, since there was no fat to
be had. Clearly Beth and I were located higher up in the hierarchy of
social class–neither of us ever went hungry, though Beth recalls peri-
ods in which her mother rationed milk, and I remember my parents'
constant worries about money while we lived in Chile, and, in retrospect, doing without what is taken for granted by middle–class Americans: a family home, an automobile, plenty of shoes and clothes, travel,
vacations, and eating out.

<u>Educational Journeys: Application to College</u>

I spent several days this summer taking my daughter, Daniella, on a brief college tour on the East Coast. The months leading up to this experience were difficult ones for me. Perusing school catalogues and guides to colleges, I found myself salivating at the plethora of possibilities open to my daughter that had been outside my radar screen when I was her age. Coming from a working–class, immigrant background, I did not have access to the conceptual maps, role models, school counseling, parental involvement, or financial wherewithal that would allow me to consider leaving the state to attend a college of my choice, or, short of that, a university outside Los Angeles. It simply never occurred to me.

All the so–called "egghead" students in my high school applied to UCLA, the public and very fine university in town; so did I. But I soon switched my application, when I discovered quite by accident from a classmate that the virtually full four–year scholarship I had received from the State of California to attend UCLA could be transferred to USC, the very expensive private university located much closer to my family's home. This serendipitous development allowed me to live at home and commute to campus, an arrangement that saved my parents the cost of university housing, which would have been quite a stretch. It also permitted me to stay within the ambit of the family, a choice that seemed appropriate for me at the time, having arrived only a few years earlier from a traditional family–based culture.

In this way, at age 17, I came to join the hoards of commuters clogging the congested freeways of Los Angeles, in my case, to pursue an education that would open up my world and allow me to do fulfilling work. My parents rejoiced with me in having this opportunity, one they themselves had deeply craved as young people, but which had been denied them due to the financial exigencies in their families.

Linda's college search, such as it was, was not so different from mine. Also an excellent student, she reports that she always knew she was going to college. Though her parents supported her collegiate ambitions, she says, "there was nobody at home who helped me with anything, who knew how to help me. . . . There was nobody to say, 'Go to this school.' To me, going to college was almost like you go to whichever one you pointed toward." With the help of some teachers, she applied to two local universities and enrolled at Long Island University as a New York City Mayor's Scholastic Achievement Scholar, one of three students selected in 1965 out of a pool of one thousand. Appearing in the *New York Times* and on the six o'clock news, Linda was "the kid from the projects who'd become this local celebrity, featured shaking Mayor Wagner's hand. Though also admitted to Hunter College, a public institution, she attended Long Island University because, with a full scholarship to a private school, "You don't go to the free school, where I wouldn't have to pay anything. It would be disloyal, it would be ungrateful for me not to take the money and say, 'Thank you.'" It did not occur to her to go to Columbia University, which evidently would have accepted her scholarship. Nobody suggested she apply there.

In high school Beth had been tracked into a secretarial program. When, as a sophomore, she confessed to her guidance counselor her secret dreams of going to Mount Holyoke College and studying French so that some day she could become an interpreter at the U.N., "the guidance counselor seemed surprised. She coughed gently and then suggested that perhaps I was 'aiming too high.' 'Girls like me' should be thinking about getting married. Typing and shorthand would be more 'realistic' for me than college, 'given where I come from.' She did not say 'the wrong side of the tracks.' She did not need to."

There was no encouragement from her parents, either, about Beth going to college; in fact, "college was not part of the family vocabulary," nor was there the money to finance it. So she spent five years following graduation working as a secretary in various offices. Then one evening in October of 1972, she and her friend Vicky decided college would be their ticket to "some kind of independence and security," an answer to a series of "dead–end jobs."

Within a month Beth drove to get an application to Stockton State College. But she did not make it past the parking lot: "I pulled into the parking lot and immediately had the mother of all anxiety attacks. I sat there for about an hour and fifteen minutes, unable to get out of the car, so I drove away." In retrospect Beth recognizes that this paralytic moment was shaped by multiple factors, many pertaining to class position. For one, college represented a completely foreign world for her. Indeed, it has been noted that a common experience for working–class students in college is to feel like they are "immigrants," for they encounter "different notions about money, privacy, creativity, family, work, play, security." Valerie Miner has coined the term "cultural agoraphobia" to characterize that experience, for "the landscape seems dotted with land mines that might blow up in our faces at any time."[9] Within a month of this event it occurred to Beth that she could request a college application by phone. She then proceeded to enroll.

But there was one other issue to address, for Beth also feared telling her parents about her plans, a well–warranted concern since her father reacted to this information by walking out on the conversation, while her mother attempted to dissuade her, wanting to know "why I wanted to do this." At age 22 she intuitively knew that a college education had a great potential to separate her from her family, something she did not want. Working–class writers have validated this intuition in accounts of their own lived experience, suggesting, as does Suzanne Sowinska, for example, that her parents offered her no support, moral or financial, because they "did not want to participate in my separation from them."[10]    Without her parents' support, Beth managed to complete an illustrious college career in three years.

Despite our many differences, Linda, Beth, and I shared some key features in our transition to college. The most pointed similarity among us was the absence of advice at home regarding college. To put it simply, none of our parents knew anything about higher education, consequently they could not provide us with any maps as to what college entailed, from the application process to graduation. In a real sense, we had to fend for ourselves.[11] In this regard, our experience has much in common with that of other students from working–class backgrounds.[12] Donna Langston, for instance, tells about her application process in a way that resonates very much with our own: "It never occurred to me when I won scholarships to attend institutions of higher learning, that it made a difference which school I went to. A B.A. was a B.A., right?"[13] The discourse of the academy is such, however, that it often assumes incoming students' familiarity with a university education, from soup to nuts.[14] This came home to me during my recent college visits with my daughter. In one information session after the next, presentors alluded to "liberal studies requirements," "internships," and "tutorials" without defining what these were or how they fit into the overall academic goals of the institution. They simply assumed their audience was initiated into the ins and outs of the college scene.

University education has become available to a much broader segment of American society since our days as students. Yet based on my admittedly limited sample, it appears that the university all too often fails to note that an increasing number of its applicants arrive without roadmaps to negotiate its mazes or unpack its coded discourses. Many students first encounter the university as a site of fear and mystification, not because they are intellectually deficient or emotionally immature, but because the institution remains encased in unexamined middle–class assumptions that privilege some as they marginalize others.

## On to Graduate School

Graduate school is a time when students become socialized into the canons of their discipline. It is also a time when outsiders to the middle class often experience the "hidden injuries of class."[15] Beth calls her experience of class otherness "the Great Wall of China." Having completed a master's degree in education at Harvard, she was living in

Cambridge, "buying time" before continuing her education. One evening a group of close friends involved in grass roots politics gathered in Beth's kitchen. This is how she tells it:

> *Photographs littered the kitchen table, family pictures taken at holiday gatherings in my childhood and recently gleaned while I was visiting my parents in South Jersey. A friend shrilled, "Beth! You weren't kidding about being working class!" as she riffled through the pile of photos. Some showed my grandfather and my uncles in their undershirts, the overflowing ashtrays and quart bottles of Schlitz on my grandmother's kitchen table in the 1950s. Others showed me as a toddler on the fire escape of the row house where we had lived in West Philadelphia, or my grandparents wearing their "Sunday Best" on the boardwalk at the shore. My friend's words stunned me; I had been attempting, to no avail, to get a discussion of class issues on our group's agenda for months. Why would I kid about being working class? Why would I kid about where I come from? I had loved the people in these photographs; sometimes, they had loved me back. I stared back at my friend in mute wonder, hearing her laugh along with the others, looking from their faces to the photographs and back. Then she exclaimed, through the laughter, "I always thought you were born with a silver bookmark in your mouth!" The laughter rose around me, but I could not join in. I did not take the joke; I did not want to. To this day, I refuse to see the humor in her words.*

Her friends' levity around class issues silenced Beth. She could not find the courage "to spoil a good party," to use Patricia Williams' expression.[16]

Linda does not know how she survived graduate school. The main breadwinner of a family of four, her life of deprivation and sacrifice is at a complete remove from that of most grad students. Broken–down cars and stoves, kerosene heaters to save on the gas bill, impossibly long commutes to class, sick children. "I was in foreclosure court four times in five years. It was hard, and you can't tell those stories because the bottom line is, 'Where is your paper? Did you do the reading? Do you understand? Are you ready to discuss the issues critically?"

Looked at from this vantage point, the level playing field does not look so level after all.

Linda and I had troubling dreams surrounding crucial graduate–school rites of passage. During the time I prepared for doctoral exams, for example, I repeatedly dreamt of accidentally killing my parents. Linda had nightmares about abandoning her family of origin while she worked on her dissertation. Both types of dreams point to the threat shared by many who are outside the middle class: the threat of ultimate separation from one's family as one scales the social hierarchy into the higher reaches–the stratospheric and privileged world–of academe.

## Section 4.  Sensibility, Moral Character, and Work Commitments

More could be said about our experiences of deprivation and exclusion and the consequent insight deriving from our class backgrounds, and especially about how we have experienced our class differences in the academy. There is a growing literature that chronicles the experiences of academics from the working class, and our accounts are supported by those of others.[17] Due to time constraints, however, I move now to a brief consideration of how the class backgrounds you have heard about have shaped our sensibilities, moral characters, and work commitments.

In our book project, my colleagues and I plan to draw on narratives where the speaker attempts to understand the nature of identity construction as a process more fluid than static, more contingent than essential, more inclusive than exclusionary. That is, we will assume that identity is not permanent, but changes given the experiences of one's life; in our case, we will focus on the many boundaries we have crossed along different social locations to develop a sense of who we are. But we will also try to identify elements of who we are that appear enduring and typical, aspects of ourselves that have been sustained and that are consequently somewhat predictable. In this latter effort, we will be dealing with character.

Character refers to ways in which people most commonly tend to think and act, based on the kinds of choices they tend to make. When we think about character, we assume that our lives have some kind of internal coherence, that our character can provide "the threads that bind together the various episodes and commitments" of our lives.[18]

It would be a mistake to assume one–on–one correlations between social class of origin, on the one hand, and moral sensibilities and char-

acter, on the other. Based on our conversations, I could trace a variety
of factors that account for the kind of moral agents we are today–they
include parents, family, friends, role models and mentors, religious and
communal values, and the variety of marginalities we collectively have
occupied. Class background, then, is one variable among others, and I
hope the finished book will take a more comprehensive account of all
these factors. For now I will simply suggest some lines of connection
that identify class as provisionally central. I begin by identifying some
enduring moral sensibilities that characterize each of us.

It is a cold Friday in December, and we are sitting around my
kitchen table. We are talking about money and displays of status and
affluence, themes all three of us have strong feelings about and which
often crop up in our conversations. I tell my colleagues that as long as
I can remember I have experienced a tremendous tension when I've
been invited to a beautiful and well–appointed home. "I feel real am-
bivalence," I say. "On the one hand it is gorgeous and aesthetic and
magnificent, and I drool over the hardwood floors and the high ceilings. And a piece of me wants it, right? But another piece of me feels
repulsed. I know this is a crude type of Marxism, yet I can't help but
think of the folks around the corner who are not getting enough nutri-
tion."

Linda ventures a clarifying interpretation. "You have a class consciousness," she tells me, "that does not align neatly with where you
are now [financially]. And with that consciousness comes empathy."
That might explain, too, why I virtually never wear the diamond ring I
inherited from my grandmother. And it might clarify why, along with
my husband, I have chosen to live a lifestyle more modest than our
income could support. But class consciousness assumes an intellectual
awareness, and for much of my life it was my gut, not my intellect, that
dictated these decisions. This is an example of feelings informing morality, of the heart leading the head in moral sensibility.

Linda, in contrast to me, enjoys displaying some outward signs of
prosperity. "It was important for me to get a Coach bag," she says,
having to explain to me what that is. Tellingly, Linda also tends to
overbuy at the supermarket, so that her refrigerator is now *always* full,
to the point of routine waste. To my mind the Coach bag and the over-
stuffed refrigerator are compensatory symbolic gestures by someone
who experienced extreme deprivation while growing up and who, having entered the middle class, uses such symbolic moves to counter her
continuing inner experience of financial insecurity. Linda herself supports this interpretation when she describes her embarrassment regarding her home, which is more modest than that of her professional colleagues. She says, "Rather than look objectively at the reasons why my

home may look different from others,' I use it as another emblem of the way in which I'm an outsider." We all laugh when she adds, "So the least I could do is carry my Coach bag."

I have asked Linda how the prestige of her educational accomplishments–her doctorate, her academic appointment, her publications–have affected her sense of self. "Class has been primal for me," she replies. "I can name all kinds of marginalizations that have had to do with color and gender, but they don't have the awful, awful pain for me as class." Evidently her earned prestige has not supplanted the pain of her early poverty. That poverty, as she puts it, "has made everything hard–won and tentative . . . it's never an uncontested achievement or talent or gift; it's always clouded at least a little bit by the poverty." In other words, there is always for Linda the residual fear of losing all, the persistent vulnerability of the economically marginal. But she is an optimist. She quickly adds, "It's such a mixed bag, because in many ways I feel that [that history of poverty] has given me a sensitivity and an awareness and actually a compassion–without romanticizing it."

Beth also refuses to adopt a romantic attitude. She resents the rhetoric frequently attached to class that "has a lot to do with 'plucky victim of class surmounts all obstacles and makes it.' Well, I am neither plucky nor a victim." Linda and I tease her, claiming some people might very well call her 'plucky.' "No, not plucky," she argues. "Stubborn and tenacious, I will accept. I am uncomfortable with those rhetorical tropes. I as a working–class woman remain defined by middle–class experience, ethics, and values, and I don't want to do that. I want to have the right to claim my own ethic, my own experience, my own values, on my own terms." Here Beth alludes to the middle–class tendency to assume that anyone lower on the class scale must unquestioningly wish to join the middle class and entirely abandon their former class position. It is Beth's loyalty to her class of origin that informs one of her important professional inclinations–her deep well of empathy for students who are outsiders to the academy.

Linda, Beth, and I share a history of marginalizations that includes the marginalization of social class. As has already been suggested, this history has also given rise in each of us to an empathetic sensibility, that is, the ability to understand and share someone else's feelings. Empathy, from the Greek *empatheia*, "feeling into," has many sources. I am inclined to think that a significant source resides in personal experiences of pain coupled with "sympathetic identification"[19] with others. Linda says, "Feeling my own pain and the pain of my experiences really allows me to recognize how people who are vastly differently situated are also deeply hurting." In some cases this pain–inspired empathy leads to compassion, the capacity to "suffer with" that moves from the *feelings* of empathy to *action* on behalf of others. This is a move into the heart of ethics, that is, into moral behavior.[20]

Beth, Linda, and I reveal compassion in several areas of our lives. The tendency to do something to alleviate the pain of others is consistent enough that a compassionate orientation might be considered part of our moral characters. Here I will focus on some of the compassionate commitments we have made in our work as educators. Some of these commitments involve our concern and action on behalf of particular individuals, namely our students, in the classroom or in our offices. Other actions reveal our commitment to persons we have never met, representatives of groups that are marginalized or oppressed in some fashion, which we address through the pedagogical and content choices we make in our teaching. These commitments to social justice are not purely abstract and ideological. They are also grounded on the embodied, formative experiences of our own lives.[21] In my remaining comments, I will limit myself to these.

All three of us have felt infused by a commitment to social justice for much of our lives. I switched from sociology to social ethics as a field of study because my impetus to "change the world" was frustrated by the positivistic perspective of my undergraduate sociology department. By the time I entered graduate school, I knew I needed to integrate my passion for justice with what was becoming increasingly clear—that I had an academic kind of temperament. The first half of Linda's career consisted of what she calls "outlaw teaching," advocating for kids in group homes, so–called "problem kids"; it was an environment of service, as she puts it, to the "excluded, the under–represented, the unspoken for." Beth had what she terms "a sense of social justice that was tuned to run on overdrive." When she looks deeper at the wellsprings of why she does what she does, how she sees her work, she concludes, "I see my work as an educator as a praxis, because I don't want any young person to have to live the way I have lived."

All three of us have been involved in one or another sort of social activism in the course of our lives. The demands of academic life and other obligations are such, however, that we currently engage our passion for justice in the work of the classroom and research, not in the trenches. At times, we have all felt some guilt about these choices. But, as I tell my colleagues, "I've come around to recognize that it is in the university that I make a difference; it is in the teaching, in the texts that I select, it's how I teach, it's the mission I have, it's the value–laden education. I have come to recognize that this is a form of activism, that we in fact are social change agents." For me this means an ongoing effort in the classroom: to bring about a transformation in students from a sense of entitlement to social engagement. I confess that I feel agitated by those who take their privilege for granted. I detest complacency and smugness everywhere. They bespeak of the unreflected life. My job as a teacher is to contest these, to challenge students to step outside their "comfort zones" and hold up a mirror to their lives. And that often involves "teaching what you are not."[22] "I take a philosophical position," I tell Beth and Linda, "that you reach across differences in order to alleviate suffering, no matter what. I probably fail at times to do that. I am sure I do. But I believe that when I fail to do it, I've been irresponsible."

Linda agrees with this attitude. She has told us some of the texts she assigns her students to engage them in empathetic learning. She now turns to a key pedagogical concern. This is how she puts it: "It is because I've come from particularly fragile places vis–a–vis the academy that there is absolutely no way for me to ever do what I do without passion, because this would be to deny my whole experience of reality and my construction of reality . . . . The choices that I make in teaching always return to who I am, the tension that I've felt, the pain that I've experienced. And it also reminds me that in some way or other, we chose to be scholars to study ourselves."

The three of us have talked about how we repeatedly place ourselves at risk in the classroom, when we all teach about women to men or about the poor to the comfortable; Linda teaches about African–Americans to largely white classes, I teach about Jews to Christians, and Beth about gays and lesbians to straight folks because of our commitments to multiculturalism and inclusion. We talk about how vulnerable we feel when students assume we are engaged in special pleading, when in fact we are concerned about justice. And of course we risk offending members of any of these groups when we, as outsiders, teach them about themselves. Beth inspires us when she quotes Gertrude Stein, "Considering how dangerous everything is, nothing really is very frightening." Beth then parses the quote this way, "If you take teaching seriously, you're always going to be at risk, so you might as well take your risks with ethical integrity. You might as well, because otherwise, how do you look in the mirror at the end of the day?"

## Conclusion

In this collaborative work, three women academics have taken a mirror and looked deeply into it. We have seen our images in a fresh light, refracted, this time, by the gaze of the two others. We have seen ourselves anew through the penetrating and challenging questions we have posed one another, from each of our social locations, regarding who we have been, who we are now, and where we are going.

"An unexamined life is not worth living," said the ancient philosopher. I thank the Wicklander family for the gift of time to engage in this work of examination.

## Postscript

In the time since I presented this lecture, Beth, Linda, and I have completed our work on this project and have welcomed the publication of *Telling Our Lives: Conversations on Solidarity and Difference.*[23] I reiterate my appreciation to the Wicklander family and acknowledge, as well, the University Research Council and the College of Liberal Arts and Sciences at DePaul University for their support, which has made this project–and its outcome–possible.

## Notes

1. Philip Hallie, *Tales of Good and Evil, Help and Harm* (New York: HarperPerennial, 1997), pp. 85, 175.

2. Philip Hallie, "Scepticism, Narrative, and Holocaust Ethics," *The Philosophical Forum* XVI, nos. 1–2 (Fall–Winter 1984–85), p. 45.

3. Camilla Stivers, "Reflections on the Role of Personal Narrative in Social Science," *Signs* 18, no. 2 (Winter 1993), (408–425), pp. 410, 424.

4. Janet Zandy, "Introduction," in *Liberating Memory: Our Work and Our Working–Class Consciousness*, ed. Janet Zandy (New Brunswick, NJ: Rutgers University Press, 1995), p. 10.

5. Barbara Ehrenreich, *Fear of Falling. The Inner Life of the Middle Class* (New York: HarperPerennial, 1989), p. 101.

6. Jane Vanderbosch, "Notes from the Working Class," in *Queerly Classed: Gay Men & Lesbians Write about Class*, ed. Susan Raffo (Boston: South End Press, 1997) (83–94), p. 91.

7 Susan Raffo, "Introduction," in *Queerly Classed: Gay Men & Lesbians Write about Class*, ed. Susan Raffo (Boston: South End Press, 1997), p. 3.

8. Bell hooks, *Teaching to Transgress: Education as the Practice of Freedom (New York: Routledge, 1994), p. 91.*

9. Pam Annas, "Pass the Cake: The Politics of Gender, Class, and Text in the Academic Workplace," pp. 165–178 in Michelle M. Tokarczyk and Elizabeth A. Fay, eds., *Working–Class Women in the Academy: Laborers in the Knowledge Factory* (Amherst: The University of Massachusetts Press, 1993), p. 171.

10. Suzanne Sowinska, "Yer Own Motha Wouldna Reckanized Ya: Surviving an Apprenticeship in the 'Knowedge Factory," pp. 148–161 in To-

karczyk and Fay, p. 156. See also Richard Rodriguez, *Hunger of Memory: The Education of Richard Rodriguez* (New York: Bantam, 1982) for a typically male working–class account of the tension between higher education and familial ties. Valerie Miner writes, "In becoming a writer, the working–class person makes an irrevocable shift, moving beyond the family's imagination." In Tokarczyk and Fay, p. 77.

11. I did receive assistance, however, from my parents in filling out financial aid forms; as I recall, my father's accountant completed these for me every year of college.

12. See, for example, Elizabeth A. Fay and Michelle M. Tokarczyck, "Introduction," pp. 3–22 in Tokarczyk and Fay, pp. 9, 12.

13. Donna Langston, "Who Am I Now? The Politics of Class Identity," pp. 60–72 in Tokarczyk and Fay, p. 68.

14. See contributors to *This Fine Place So Far From Home. Voices of Academics From the Working Class*, ed. C.L. Barney Dews and Carolyn Leste Law (Philadelphia: Temple University Press, 1995), for testimonials that support this point.

15. The phrase is the taken from Richard Sennett and Jonathan Cobb's classic book, *The Hidden Injuries of Class* (New York: Alfred A. Knopf, 1973).

16. The metaphor of "spoiling a good party" is developed by Patricia J. Williams, *The Alchemy of Race and Rights* (Cambridge: Harvard University Press, 1991), 129–130.

17. See, for example, Zandy; Raffo; Dews and Law; Tokarczyk and Fay; and contributors to *This Bridge We Call Home· Radical Visions for Transformation*, ed. Gloria C. Anzaldua and Analuise Keating (New York: Routledge, 2002).

18. Joel J. Kupperman, *Character* (New York: Oxford University Press, 1991), p. 12.

19. The term is Mary Watkins', cited in Laurent A. Parks Daloz, Cheryl H. Keen, James P. Keen, and Sharon Daloz Parks, *Common Fire: Leading Lives of Commitment in a Complex World* (Boston: Beacon Press, 1996), p. 67.

20. Daloz, p. 69.

21. Certainly not all people who have endured pain turn into compassionate beings; there is some evidence that those who do, experience their work on behalf of others as healing of their own pain. See Daloz, pp. 186–188.

22. The expression is borrowed from the book title of *Teaching What You're Not: Identity Politics in Higher Education*, ed. Katherine J. Mayberry (New York: New York University Press, 1996).

23. Feminist Constructions Series (Lanham, MD: Rowman & Littlefield, Publishers, 2005).

# 9

# Lying and Lawyering: an Honest Perspective

## Steven H. Resnicoff

### Salutation

Thank you, Dean Lewis, for your kind introduction. First, I would like to express my sincere gratitude to Mrs. Callista Wicklander, the wife of the late Raymond Wicklander, and to the entire Wicklander family, for their generous support of DePaul University and, of course, for establishing the Wicklander Chair for Business and Professional Ethics. It is only through such benevolent philanthropy that DePaul is able to so effectively promote its educational and ethical objectives.

Of course, I also thank all those (such as Father Minogue, Executive Vice President Richard Meister and former College of Law Dean Teree Foster) who were instrumental in affording me the opportunity to occupy the Wicklander Chair during the 2000–2001 academic year along with the people (including Kelly Johnson and Grace Cichomska–and others whose names I do not all know) who helped with all of the administrative details that occupying the Chair entailed, including all of the practical arrangements for this Colloquium.

Finally, I thank all of you–friends and colleagues–for taking time from your overburdened schedules, and weathering this rainy day, to attend this Colloquium.

Today's topic is "Lying and Lawyering: An Honest Perspective."
Yes, I know that some of you have already complained that the phrase
"Lying and Lawyering" is a bit redundant. Of course, this attitude implicitly acknowledges how daunting a task I have today. If lying so
pervasively affects the practice of law, how can I possibly cover this
truly comprehensive topic in just the one hour that I've been given? In
any event, to the extent that time permits, I would like to discuss the
following six propositions:

1.  As a general rule, lying is morally wrong.
2.  Nevertheless, there are times when lying may not only be
    morally correct but may be morally mandated.
3.  Some legal ethics rules seem morally wrong. They allow
    some deceptions that are arguably NOT justified while forbid-
    ding others that ARE justified.
4.  The actual practices of attorneys are in many ways even worse
    than those prescribed by the rules.
5.  What explains the nature of the rules and actual attorney prac-
    tices?
6.  What, if anything, ought to be done?

**1.  As a general rule, lying is morally wrong.**

What do I mean by "lying"? For purposes of today's discussion, I
am going to use an expansive definition which includes any verbal action, or inaction, that is intended either to make it more likely that
someone *believe* something that is *not* true or more likely that someone
*disbelieve* something that *is* true.

By the way, many of you have heard the following:

QUESTION:     How do you know when a lawyer is lying?
ANSWER:       His lips move.

Well, according to my definition, which includes verbal inaction, the
answer, "His lips move," is *underinclusive*

How does one establish that, as a general proposition, lying is
morally wrong? My personal predilection would be to rely, first, on
religious sources. Although many superlative attributes are ascribed to
G–d,[1] He is said to have created the world through the attribute of
Truth.[2] The *Mishnah,*[3] a literary source of Jewish law compiled a little
over 1,800 years ago, reports in the name of Rabbi Shimon the son of
Gamliel that truth is one of the three pillars that support the world.[4]
Subsequent authorities, citing Scriptural sources, declare that G–d is
called "Truth," that the throne upon which He sits is Truth, that all of
His words are Truth, and that all of His judgments are Truth.[5]

We are commanded to emulate G–d as much as we can, as the verse says, "And you shall walk in His ways." [*Deuteronomy* 28:9] This commandment is repeated and we are told "to walk in all of His ways." [*Deuteronomy* 10:12, 11:22]. Thus, just as G–d is truthful, we must endeavor to be truthful and, hence, lying is wrongful. Many of the world's religions, including, of course, Christianity, agree.

But not everyone is persuaded by religious sources. Americans, however, hold certain "truths" to be self–evident, and, although un- armed with empirical evidence, I would venture to say that the proposi- tion that lying is generally opprobrious is one such proposition. In- deed, throughout world history, most, albeit not all, philosophers and ethicists have criticized dishonesty.

Lying has many negative consequences. Jewish law says that defrauding someone is like stealing from his mind. It is an intimate, disingenuous intrusion into a person's inner consciousness, his very being–and it is far worse than stealing his wealth.

Lying has a morally corrosive effect on the soul of the liar himself. As Maimonides, a leading 12th–century Jewish authority, writes:

> It is forbidden to accustom oneself to smooth speech and flatteries. One must not say one thing and mean another. Inward and outward self should correspond; only what we have in mind should we utter with the mouth. We must deceive no one . . . . A person should al- ways cherish truthful speech, an upright spirit, and a pure heart freed of all pretense and cunning.[6]

Thus, false speech is a peril to the very spirit and heart of the speaker. And, as each person has an effect on the community in which he dwells, one man's moral decay deleteriously affects the whole.

Moreover, as a practical matter, specific forms of lying are often linked with other types of morally indefensible conduct that produce yet additional harms.

**2.  Nevertheless, there are times when lying may not only be mor- ally correct but morally mandated.**

Some religious authorities, such as Church Father Augustine, Bishop of Hippo, and some secular philosophers, such as Immanuel Kant, have contended that it is wrong to lie even if the lie is necessary to save human life. According to this view, if an armed terrorist bear- ing a bomb stops you on the street and asks you which way to get to the Sears Tower, you could not lie and give him directions to the nearest police station instead.

The vast majority of religious and secular thinkers, however, would disagree. It is said, for instance, that the Papal envoy in Istanbul, Angelo Guiseppe Ronacalli, who was later chosen to be Pope John XXIII, agreed to a plan whereby the Catholic church issued false baptismal certificates to Jews in Budapest to protect them from capture by the Nazis during World War II.[7] In fact, most commentators maintain that in many instances lying would be permitted –or even affirmatively required–to accomplish purposes far less important than the saving of human life.

3.  **Some legal ethics rules seem morally wrong. They allow some deceptions that are arguably unjustified while proscribing others that are justified.**

Let's consider some of the types of the arguably wrongful deceptions that are allowed.

**EXAMPLE 1:    ARGUING A FACTUALLY "FALSE" ALTER-NATIVE**

A.    **Facts**
1.    Suppose the defendant is accused of robbery
2.    Suppose also that the defendant tells you he did it, and you believe beyond a reasonable doubt that he's telling you the truth.
3.    You also believe the evidence in the case shows that someone else, X, had both a motive to commit the robbery and the opportunity to do so.

B.    **Questions**
1.    **Question One:**
You do not believe that the defendant will commit robbery again.   Should you try to get the jury to try to believe that X may have done it in order that the jury may acquit the defendant?
*    Is there something "dishonest" about trying to get the jury to believe in a story that you know is false?
*    On the one hand, you are not really lying.   Instead, the "effect" of your statement is simply showing that the prosecution has not carried its burden of providing the defendant's guilt beyond a reasonable doubt.
*    Yet if you do not present the argument this way but, instead, try to persuade the jury that the factually fallacious alternative is what happened, isn't this deceitful?   Some

people, but not I, might even take a more aggressive position and contend that if you "know" that the defendant is
guilty, why does it matter whether the prosecution has
theoretically discharged its burden of proof? Why should
a guilty defendant go free? Aren't trials and presump-
tions of truth designed to protect the potentially innocent?
Here, you "know" that the defendant is guilty!

 *      On the other hand, isn't it true that the defendant is not
        guilty until he is held to be so by a court or jury?

**NO!**

This last argument, i.e., that the defendant is not guilty until he is held
to be so by a court or jury, is really a "red herring." In a seminal article
on the purported "right" to present a false case, Prof. Harry Subin
writes:

> The argument that the attorney cannot know the truth until
> a court decides it fails. Either it is sophistry, designed to
> simplify the moral life of the attorney, or it rests on a con-
> fusion between "factual truth" and "legal truth." The for-
> mer relates to historical fact [i.e., either the defendant
> committed the offense or he did not; no judicial judgment
> can affect this historic fact]. The latter ["legal truth"] re-
> lates to the principle that a fact cannot be acted upon by the
> legal system until it is proven in accordance with legal rules
> . . .[8]

The fact that the legal system does not formally act upon "legal guilt"
until it is determined through litigation does not mean that a particular
person's moral decisions cannot–or should not–be based on his knowledge regarding factual truth. A person confronts many moral questions
and must act on them based on the degree of knowledge that he or she
has at the time the decision must be made. If a person has the type or
degree of knowledge that he would use to act on similarly important
decisions in his personal life, then he should be able to act on such
knowledge in deciding moral questions in his professional life as well.

 *      But even if one recognizes the distinction between "fac-
        tual guilt" and "legal guilt," doesn't an attorney owe her
        entire allegiance to her client? Isn't she supposed to do
        everything that the law allows in order to serve her cli-
        ent's best interests? It isn't her job, is it, to determine, or
        to act upon, her client's actual guilt?

To these questions, there are at least three answers:

One:      The view that an attorney owes her entire allegiance to her
          client appear inconsistent with the position taken by early
          American authorities.

          For example, David Hoffman's Baltimore "Resolutions" of
          1836 is regarded as the first American attempt to establish le-
          gal ethics rules. Resolution 15 provides that:

          When employed to defend those charged with crimes of the
          deepest dye, and the evidence against them, whether legal, or
          moral, be such as to leave no just doubt of their guilt, I shall
          not hold myself privileged, much less obliged, to use my en-
          deavors to arrest, or to impede the course of justice, by special
          resorts to ingenuity–to the artifices of eloquence–to appeals to
          the morbid and fleeting sympathies of weak juries, or of tem-
          porizing courts–to my own personal weight of character–nor
          finally, to any of the overweening influences I may posses,
          from popular manners, eminent talents, exalted learning, etc.
          Persons of atrocious character, who have violated the laws of
          G–d and man, are entitled to no such special exertions from
          any member of our pure and honourable profession; and in-
          deed, to no intervention beyond securing to them a fair and
          dispassionate investigation of the *facts* of their cause, and the
          due application of the law: all that goes beyond this, either in
          manner or substance, is unprofessional, and proceeds, either
          from a mistaken view of the relation of client and counsel, or
          from some unworthy and selfish motive, which sets a higher
          value on professional display and success, than on truth and
          justice, and the substantial interests of the community. Such
          an inordinate ambition, I shall ever regard as a most dangerous
          perversion of talents, and a shameful abuse of an exalted sta-
          tion. The parricide, the gratuitous murderer, or other perpetra-
          tor of like revolting crimes, has surely no such claim on the
          commanding talents of a profession, whose object and pride
          should be the suppression of all vice, by the vindication and
          enforcement of the laws. Those, therefore, who wrest their
          proud knowledge from its legitimate purposes, to pollute the
          streams of justice, and to screen such foul offenders from mer-
          ited penalties, should be regarded by all, (and certainly shall
          by me,) as ministers at a holy altar, full of high pretention, and
          apparent sanctity, but inwardly base, unworthy, and hypocriti-
          cal–dangerous in the precise ratio of their commanding talents,
          and exalted learning."

> The notion that the aggressive version of the adversary system–as we know it today–is the only system that works or is the only system that we have every had–is a myth.

Two:   Even now, most ethics rules do not assert that the attorney's moral decision–making apparatus are totally subordinated to those of the client.

Let me take a minute to very briefly identify some of the overlapping systems of rules that regulate attorneys:

1. They are subject to specific federal or state statutes, such as the Federal Fair Debt Collection Practices Act, to anti-money–laundering laws, and the like.
2. They are subject to tort law for malpractice, breach of fiduciary duty, etc.
3. They are subject to the ethics rules applicable to the bars of which they are members.   The ethics rules vary from state to state and, on occasion, it may be difficult to determine which f two or more competing rules should prevail.
4. They may also have agreed to abide by the ethics rules promulgated by bar associations or other organizations of which they arc mcmbers.

From time to time the American Bar Association has promulgated ethics rules.  These do not per se have any binding force upon lawyers, but most states have looked for guidance to the approaches taken, from time to time, by the ABA.

The most recent American Bar Association approach constitutes the Model Rules of Professional Responsibility, adopted in 1983.  Rule 3.3(c) states that "A lawyer may refuse to offer evidence that the lawyer reasonable believes is false."  Thus, even if the lawyer does not know the evidence is false, he has the ethical right to resist his client's insistence that the evidence be used.

Ironically, this very example, however, is problematic, in that Rule 3.3(c) clearly permits the lawyer to use evidence even though he reasonably believes it is false–and it allows him to do so without making any further inquiry as to the whether the

evidence is false.    If the attorney actually knows that the evidence is false, Rule 3.3(a)(4) would not allow him to use the
evidence.  But the Rules provide no adequate explanation as to
when a lawyer would be said to actually know evidence is
false.

Three:    What are the benefits to the justice system of having an attorney advocate what she knows to be a factually untrue story on
behalf of a client the attorney knows is guilty?

As Professor David Luban points out:

> [I]t is unsurprising to discover that the arguments purport-
> ing to show the advantages of the adversary system as a
> fact–finder have mostly been nonempirical, a mix of a pri-
> ori theories of inquiry and armchair psychology.[9]

And as Professors Roy Simon and Murray Schwartz put the
question,

> [H]ow can advocacy of something that the lawyer knows is
> untruthful serve the ends of truth?  How can a lawyer claim
> to be helping the search for truth by making a guilty client
> appear not guilty . . . or by making an unlikely story seem
> true?  If the version of the facts being argued by the defense
> is not true, how can that foster truth?[10]

## 2.    Question Two:
Suppose you believe that the defendant   WILL commit
robbery again.   Should you try to get the jury to try to believe that X may have done it in order that the jury may
acquit the defendant?

*    Is it wrong to try to help a guilty person escape punishment when doing so will enable him to victimize other innocent people?

*    Does this concern in anyway interact with any uneasiness
you anyway have about convincing the jury to believe in a
story about X that is untrue?

## 3.    Question Three:
Suppose the defendant is accused of gruesome rape, murder or child abuse. [By the way, I do not mean to imply

that there is such as a thing as a non–gruesome case of rape, murder or child abuse.] You do not believe that the defendant will do it again. Should you try to get the jury to try to believe that X may have done it in order that the jury may acquit the defendant?

\* Does the fact that the defendant is guilty of such a heinous offense make things worse?

4. **Question Four:**
   Suppose you believe that the defendant WILL commit another gruesome rape or murder or WILL gruesomely abuse another child. Should you try to get the jury to try to believe that X may have done it in order that the jury may acquit the defendant?

\* Does the seriousness of the likely repeated offense raise the (ethical) ante at all?

5. **Question Five:**
   In any of these cases, SHOULD you have THE RIGHT NOT TO TRY TO GET THE JURY TO BELIEVE THAT X, INSTEAD OF A, COMMITTED THE OFFENSE?

   In other words, even if a defense attorney might be morally justified in engaging in any of these actions, should our legal system REQUIRE that she do so? Or, in the alternative, is there room in our system of legal ethics to at least permit a person of conscience to refrain from such actions?

**EXAMPLE 2:     DISCREDITING AN INNOCENT VICTIM**
**A.     Facts**
   1. The defendant is accused of a gruesome rape. The defendant tells you that he is guilty of the rape. He even tells you factual details that corroborate his confession and that only the real rapist should know.
   2. Nevertheless, you think that you might be able to successfully convince the jury that the rape victim was really a prostitute who filed a complaint against the defendant because he failed to pay her all of the money that she demanded.

3.       Suppose, further, that in order to succeed, you will
         have to subject the innocent rape victim to a wither-
         ing cross–examination which will undoubtedly cause
         her to experience substantial emotional distress.
         Nevertheless, for a variety of reasons, you believe
         that this tactic is likely to work.

Even if an attorney might otherwise be permitted to argue a factually
fallacious alternative, should he be forced to do so when this
will further disparage an innocent victim?  Should he have the
RIGHT NOT TO DISCREDIT THE INNOCENT VICTIM?

By the way, although this makes the reading a little less dramatic, I use "MF" and "N–word" instead of particularly offensive epithets.

Consider the following episode related by attorney Seymour
Wishman:

> My client's sister and I joined the parade of wounded and
> mutilated bodies staggering through the swinging doors.
> Across the lobby, a heavy but not unattractive woman in a
> nurse's uniform suddenly shrieked, "Get that MF out of
> here!" Two woman rushed forward to restrain her. "That's
> the lawyer, that's the MF lawyer!" she shouted.
> I looked around me.  No one else resembled a lawyer.  Still
> screaming she dragged her two restrainers toward me.  I
> was baffled. . . .
> "That's the son of a bitch that did it to me!" she screamed.
> I didn't know what she was talking about.
> "Kill him and that N–word Horton!"
> Larry Horton. . . . of course.  Larry Horton was a client of
> mine.  Six months before, I had represented him at his trial
> for sodomy and rape.  At last I recognized the woman's
> face.  She had testified as the "complaining witness"
> against Horton.
> WISHMAN:  Isn't it a fact that after you met the defen-
>           dant at a bar, you asked if he wanted to
>           have a good time?
> LEWIS:    No! That's a lie!
> WISHMAN:  Isn't it true that you took him and his
>           three friends back to your apartment and
>           had that good time?
> LEWIS:    No!

WISHMAN:       And, after you had that good time, didn't
               you ask for money?
LEWIS:         No such way!
WISHMAN:       Isn't it a fact that the only reason you
               made a complaint was because you were
               furious for not getting paid?
LEWIS:         No! No! That's a lie!
WISHMAN:       You claim to have been raped and sodom-
               ized. As a nurse, you surely have an idea
               of the effect of such an assault on a
               woman's body. Are you aware, Mrs.
               Lewis, that the police doctor found no
               evidence of force or trauma?
LEWIS:         I don't know what the doctors found . . .
Weighing on me more heavily than the possibility that I
had helped a guilty man escape punishment was the unde-
niable fact that I had humiliated the victim–alleged victim–
in my cross–examination of her. But, as all criminal lawyers know, to be effective in court I had to act forcefully,
even brutally, at times. I had been trained in law school to
regard the "cross" as an art form. In the course of my career
I had frequently discredited witnesses. My defense of myself had always been that there was nothing personal in
what I was doing. This woman was obviously unwilling to
dismiss my behavior as merely an aspect of my professional responsibility; instead of an effective counsel, she
saw me simply as a . . . ["MF."][11]

Let's assume Wishman had known that his client was guilty of the
rape. If so, Wishman's concept of being an effective attorney not only
wrongfully accused an innocent victim of being a prostitute, but, pre-
sumably, of adultery. This accusation may well have been in the presence of her husband, family and friends. Why do I use the word *accusations* even though Wishman only asked *questions*? Because I believe
that a listener–at least a listener who is not trained as an attorney–hears
Wishman's questions as factual accusations. Indeed, they are worded
so that they should be understood as such.

Moreover, Wishman's summation would undoubtedly appear to all
present as an indictment against the victim. Indeed, one can almost
hear Wishman conclude, "Based on all of the evidence, as I have re-
counted it for you, I submit that Mrs. Lewis not only had sex with the
defendant voluntarily." Although use of the phrase "I submit" would
technically prevent Wishman from being sanctioned for improperly
expressing his personal opinion,[12] I doubt that a listener would be sensitive to such a nuance. [When I mentioned this idea to a friend of
mine, he said it reminded him of the game show "jeopardy." The rules

194 Steven H. Resnicoff

of the game require people to give answers in the form of a question, but everyone knows that they are really giving answers. Similarly, everyone knows that the lawyer must put his statements in the form of questions, but they understand them to be accusations.]

The ethics rules, as I understand them, in virtually all jurisdictions would allow—and might require—Wishman to do precisely what he did.

Indeed, in the past, rape victims were often pilloried by defense counsel who investigated their past sexual histories in intimate detail, and with the victim under oath on the witness stand, in order to discredit the witness. While such practices were permitted, a number of attorneys worried that their refusal to utilize them on moral ground might expose them to disciplinary sanction or civil liability to their clients.

Interestingly, using the victim's sexual histories has since been banned by the enactment of laws protecting victims' privacy. This is another example of how, when we choose to do so, we, as a community, have the right to modify the extent of zealous advocacy which is provided.

Time does not allow examination of all of the other ways in which a litigating attorney is allowed to actively or passively mislead others, but after my prepared remarks, I would be happy to give additional examples in response to any questions you have.

As I mentioned, before, however, the ethics rules also err in the opposite direction, i.e., they proscribe certain conduct that may be morally mandated. American Bar Association Model Rule 8.4 states, in part, "It is professional misconduct for a lawyer to: . . . . engage in conduct involving dishonesty, fraud, deceit or misrepresentation." Note that this Rule is not limited to misrepresentations by the lawyer to a client, a court, an adversary or an adversary's client. In fact, it is not even limited to a misrepresentation made by the attorney in his role as an attorney. Instead, it applies to any misrepresentation—dishonesty, fraud or deceit—even in the attorney's private life.

Contrast this rule regarding dishonesty with ABA Model Rule 1.6 as to confidentiality. That rule provides[13] that a lawyer cannot generally disclose information that would be harmful or embarrassing to her client. Nevertheless, it sets forth several explicit exceptions, one of which is when the lawyer believes disclosure is reasonably necessary "to prevent the client from committing a criminal act that the lawyer believes is likely to result in imminent death or substantial bodily harm."

Thus, although Rule 1.6 specifies exceptions, Rule 8.4 regarding misrepresentation has no exceptions. As a result, it seems that Rule 8.4 forbids resort to misrepresentation even if it is necessary, for instance, "to prevent a client from committing a criminal act that the lawyer believes is likely to result in imminent death." Indeed, courts in Colorado and Oregon have construed their state versions of Rule 8.4 as being unconditional. The Colorado case involved a government attorney who lied to an armed fugitive in order to trick him into surrendering to authorities. By the time the attorney spoke to him, the fugitive had confessed to 3 brutal murders and a rape. The attorney testified that he was concerned that there was a significant risk that this fugitive would perpetrate additional violent crimes were he not swiftly apprehended.[14]

Rule 8.4 similarly precludes other forms of lying that might otherwise be deemed justifiable.[15]

### 4. The actual practices of attorneys are in many ways even worse than those prescribed by the rules.

*The Moral Compass of the American Lawyer*, written by Professors Zitrin and Langford in 1999, states:

> According to noted University of Pennsylvania ethics professor Geoffrey Hazard, lawyers, imbued with the adversary theorem, often seem like willing co–conspirators in their clients' lies. "Shading the truth and telling lies occurs in almost every case, I am sure," says Professor Hazard. "But we have created this adversarial system that encourages it." Judges agree as well; the president of the National Judicial College says that perjury–and not "a little white lie here or there"–occurs "in almost every case."[16]

My own observations when I practiced convinced me that one of the more important reasons why many attorneys were unhappy in the profession was the dishonesty of their professional colleagues.

### 5. What explains the current state of the rules and the current state of attorney practice?

Let's begin by trying to understand why lawyers lie. Myriad factors are at work; we will look only at the most salient. First, and perhaps foremost, is the fact that regular people become lawyers, and many–probably most–regular people lie.

The most recent annual survey of teens conducted by the Joseph & Edna Josephson Institute of Ethics, for instance, reports that 7 out of every 10 high school students questioned admitted to cheating on a test at least once in the preceding 12 months and almost 5 out of 10 said they did so more than once. But it's not just students who cheat. Principals, other administrators and teachers have also been accused of cheating–of giving students copies of exams in advance, of telling students the right answers during tests, and of allowing them to change incorrect answers. Student cheaters benefit from higher grades (and, possibly, from scholarships awarded by schools or rewards given by parents), while teachers and administrators receive positive job performance evaluations, thereby earning retention, promotion and raises. The symbiotic nature of this student–educator relationship decreases the likelihood of detection and punishment–and encourages the process to fester. Even educators who actively discourage cheating may be reluctant to report infractions, because of fears over endless administrative hassles or lawsuits–or even fears about their physical safety.

It is not clear how early on cheating begins, but once it begins, it soon becomes ingrained. The Talmud explains that a person who commits a sin and repeats it no longer feels the same degree of reluctance to engage in the conduct again. It becomes as if the act were "permitted."[17] In this way, a person is a product of his actions.[18] Similarly, Aristotle states, "The man, then, must be a perfect fool who is unaware that people's characters take their bias from the stead direction of their activities." Hamlet apparently acknowledges this process when speaking to his mother:

> Good night; but go not to my uncle's bed;
> Assume a virtue, if you have it not.
> That monster, custom, who all sense doth eat
> Of habits evil, is angel yet in this,
> That aptly is put on. Refrain tonight,
> And that shall lend a kind of easiness
> To the next abstinence; the next more easy;
> For use almost can change the stamp of nature
> And either [tame] the devil or through him out.[19]

The social psychology theory of cognitive dissonance suggests this phenomenon when it describes the "induced–compliance paradigm." Essentially, when a person is engaged in activities that he believes is wrong, he develops unpleasant feelings of guilt. If he cannot change his conduct, then, in order to relieve his guilt, he changes his attitudes and no longer considers the activities to be wrongful.[20] Thus, even if someone initially believes that lying is wrong, once he does it, he alters his attitude to alleviate his sense of guilt.

Second, the law school admissions process does not weed out such people who have developed such habits. A relatively recent scandal at one of Canada's top law schools, for instance, brings this message home. About 30 of the school's first year students were accused of lying about the grades they received on their midterm exams, grades that, under school policy, are not recorded on student transcripts.

A third group of problems arises from the fact that the law school education process blurs the distinction between truth and falsehood. In class, students are routinely asked, at the drop of a hat, to argue any side of any issue. They are taught to avoid developing an attachment to one side or the other, but, rather, to expand the range of their intellectual power, their ability to create imaginative arguments that could plausibly be asserted on behalf of even the most dismal of positions. The point, they are told, is not which argument is "right" but rather whether one can formulate an argument which is plausible and, therefore, which may persuade the judge or jury. This approach is pursued in extracurricular competitions as well. Moot court, negotiation and client counseling competitions routinely require competitors to switch from arguing one position to the other. These academic exercises are critical to develop analytic skills. Nevertheless, students can become confused and miss the difference between creatively developing useful "arguments" with which to respond to difficult questions from a judge and creatively making up useful "facts" to answer such questions.

Perhaps this confusion is exacerbated by the fact that law school casebooks, and sometimes exams, often provide ambiguous facts, requiring students to make and state their assumptions. Students must be made to realize that when real life transactions involve factual ambiguity, they must go and find out what the real facts are.

Similarly, just as law school teaches students that few arguments are unambiguously right or wrong, it teaches students that few words have unambiguous meanings. Thus, former President William Clinton, a brilliant graduate of the Yale Law School, can unabashedly respond in a discovery proceeding that the answer to a question put to him depends on the definition of the word "is." If words, even the simplest ones, have no fixed meanings, then surely there can be no truths and no lies.

Furthermore, law schools do not do a particularly good job at emphasizing the difference, mentioned earlier, between "factual guilt" and "legal guilt." Consequently, students feel that just as certain costs–such as humiliating truthful witnesses–may be morally justified in representing someone whose factual guilt is at question, it is also morally justified to incur such costs when representing someone whose factual guilt is clear but whose "legal guilt" is as yet undetermined.

In addition, legal education's emphasis on the adversarial nature of the judicial system frees students from feeling morally accountable for their actions. In fact, they are worried that should they refrain from a form of zealous advocacy on moral grounds, they may be prosecuted by applicable attorney disciplinary commissions or sued by disgruntled clients.

In an article published about 10 years ago, my colleague, Steve Landsman, cites the work of Dr. Stanley Milgram and the writings of Prof. Robert Cover in providing another reason why lawyers (and judges, by the way) may tend to ignore the moral implications of their conduct. Let me quote from the Landsman article:

> The subjects of Milgram's work were told that as part of a study concerning the effects of punishment on learning they were to administer increasingly severe electric shocks to others apparently participating in the exercises. Milgram found that despite the ever more agonized protests of the person seemingly suffering the shocks, about two–thirds of his subjects would continually increase voltage at the direction of a gray–coated experimenter [read: three–piece suited partner]. Milgram concluded that:
>
>> [O]rdinary people, simply doing their jobs, and without any particular hostility on their part, can become agents in a terrible destructive process. Moreover, even when the destructive effects of their work become patently clear, and they are asked to carry out actions incompatible with fundamental standards of morality, relatively few people have the resources needed to resist authority.[21]

Cover points outs that while the legal process is one that imposes pain on litigants, the lawyers often do not see this pain. This is perhaps particularly true as to the pain experienced by their adversary's clients. As Landsman says:

> Like the subjects in Milgram's experiments, lawyers feel insulated from the injuries they cause and may "act violently without experiencing the normal inhibitions." In any such setting the risk of doing unwarranted harm is greatly magnified.[22]

The feeble efforts that most law schools take to improve ethics are generally unsuccessful. While law schools often have "honor codes," from the students' perspective at least, these just represent more rules. I attended Princeton as an undergraduate. It had an Honor Code requiring at the end of each exam that we sign that we had neither given nor received assistance. In exchange, however, the University demonstrated that it believed and trusted us by not having any proctors present to police us. This seems to be the rare exception and not the rule.

When, in the wake of Watergate, the bar became concerned about legal ethics, law schools began requiring courses in legal ethics. Yet for the most part these courses do not train people to be honest, they just teach them the extent to which the law says they must be honest. Indeed, it is even possible that during the same term that a student takes a legal ethics course, she may be participating in a trial advocacy or skills class, taught by practicing attorneys, which promotes morally dubious tactics.

A fourth type of problem arises from the post–graduate experience. Part of the problem is financial and part arises from their inability to cope with many types of legal issues. Because students leave law school with overwhelming financial burdens, they must succeed in their jobs. But their jobs are difficult and challenging–often calling for knowledge of legal subjects with which they are unfamiliar. Relatively few graduates may have relatives who are experienced attorneys, able to provide the assistance they need. Once these young graduates make mistakes, lying and engaging in sharp practices may appear their only means of defense against adverse consequences.

Finally, a fifth problem arises from the lack of a perceived consensus as to which ethics rules are appropriate and from a sense of alienation from the process that produces ethics rules. While there is a myth of self–regulation, the truth is that few if any rank and file attorneys have any meaningful role in creating rules. Given this alienation, the rules may have no morally compelling claim of authority.

By the way, what about the other question–why are the ethics rules drafted as they are? It is in the selfish best–interests of lawyers to win their cases. It is also in the selfish best–interest of lawyers to minimize any feelings of guilt for the ethical decisions that are made. Rules rule calling for the zealous representation of a client, and for minimal attorney autonomy, serves both of these interests.

### 6.  What, if anything, ought to be done?

Frankly, I'm not sure (and, if I've been successful, I've used up all my time by now and don't really have to give an answer). Nevertheless, I am just going to mention a few possibilities, without examining any of them in detail.

We have identified two types of problems. One concerns the content of the secular ethics rules themselves. I think that certain sleazy tactics ought to be prohibited. At the very least, however, it should be

even clearer that an individual attorney need not employ techniques
that he or she considers unethical.

Second, as to how attorneys act, we have identified five types of
problems, namely:

> (1) that many attorneys are habituated to lying and cheating
>     even before law school;
> (2) that the law school admissions process does not weed
>     such people out;
> (3) that legal education, in a number of ways, encourages de-
>     ceitful conduct;
> (4) that the post–graduate experience often involves pressures
>     that may drive young attorneys to lie and cheat;
> (5) that there seems to be an inadequate moral consensus re-
>     garding the which ethics rules are appropriate, and alien-
>     ation from the rule–making process reduces the perceived
>     duty to abide by the official rules.

There are three basic ways to proceed. The first would be to make
a number of individual proposals designed to address each of these five
categories. The second would be to try to propose a more global solution. The third would involve a combination of the first two.

One combination approach might include some of the following
types of elements:

> (1) An educational component designed to develop a stu-
>     dent's ethical sensitivities at a much earlier point in time–
>     whether as a pre–law requirement or in the first year of
>     law school;
> (2) An admissions requirement component that requires law
>     school applicants to demonstrate a substantial, personal
>     involvement in altruistic endeavors;
> (3) Legal education changes that might include, for instance:
>     (a) Active coordination between legal ethics classes and
>         skills classes to ensure, among other things, that con-
>         sistent messages are communicated as to how seri-
>         ously to consider ethical issues in selecting tactics;
>     (b) A much smaller faculty–student ratio in legal ethics
>         classes, which would permit a greater variety of pro-
>         jects and much more interaction between faculty and
>         students;
>     (c) An emphasis on:
>         i. the distinction the need for creativity as to argu-
>            ment but accuracy as to facts;

ii.   the difference between "factual guilt" and "moral guilt";

(d)  Less of an emphasis on "zealous representation" and more on the need for the lawyer to act an accountable moral agent;

(4)  Improved post–petition financial support; a more developed alumni mentoring network for recent graduate; continuing legal education requirements; a mandatory apprenticeship period; required mandatory malpractice insurance;

(5)  A restructuring of the rule–making process for the purpose of re–enfranchising rank and file attorneys. The rules should be revamped to provide clearly for consid erably more attorney moral autonomy.

More global aspects of this suggestion might include:

(6)  Eliminating the undergraduate degree prerequisite and replacing it with a 5 or 6 year law school program. Such a item would make it more likely that students could take a series of classes designed to raise students' ethical sensitivities and could minimize post–graduate impressions by providing students with a much broader base of legal training; and

(7)  A radical reduction as to the expectation of publications from faculty with a commensurate increase in the number of teaching hours faculty would have to provide. This sort of a change might be necessary if students are seriously going to take small group legal ethics classes.

Alternatively, even more ambitious approaches might include:

(8)  Congressional or state legislative enactment of ethics rules to be enforced by courts other than ones in which the accused regularly appears; To the extent that the people who make the laws are not *practicing attorneys*, perhaps there will less of a conflict of interests in the moral decisions reflected in the Codes. Alas, however, a high percentage of legislators are attorneys, and many are aware that they may be required to return to active practice;

(9)  Socialization of legal services, which could dramatically affect the types of financial and other pressures within

which lawyers would work. But consideration of such a proposal is surely beyond the scope of today's talk.

## Conclusion

Richard Cohen remarks:

> Erich Segal, author of the goopy novel Love Story, wrote that being in love means never having to say you're sorry. Wrong. People in love are forever apologizing. Having a code of ethics means never having to say you're sorry.[24]

But having to say one is sorry is a function of having moral autonomy, and it is moral autonomy that really allows us the opportunity to emulate the Divine. May we be blessed to use this opportunity successfully.

## Notes

1. See, e.g., Encyclopaedia Judaica CD–ROM Version 1.0, entry "G–d"; Aryeh Kaplan, The Handbook of Jewish Thought (New York: Moznaim Publishing Corporation, 1979), at 7–20; R. Avraham Chaim Feuer, Tashlich and The Thirteen Attributes (New York: Mesorah Publications, Inc., 1979).

2. See, e.g., Abraham ben Eliezer ha–Levi Berukhim (c. 1515–1593)(compiler), *Tikunei Zohar, Tikun* 63; Avraham Tuvulski (contemporary), *Medevvar Shekker Tirkhak* at 13 (citing Israel Meir ha–Kohen (*Hafetz Hayyim*; 1853–1933)). This is supposedly hinted at by the fact that the final letters of the first three words and the final letters of the last three words of the Biblical description of creation each spell the Hebrew word for "truth." Id., at 10 (citing R. Yisroel ben Yosef Al–Nakawa (d. 1391), *Menorat ha–Ma'or, perek* 35).

3. The *Mishnah* was compiled approximately in the year 188 of the common era (year 3948 according to the Jewish calendar). See, generally, *Encyclopaedia Judaica*, entry *"Mishnah."* The Babylonian and Jerusalem Talmuds are organized in accordance with the format of the Mishnah.

4. *Mishnah, Avot* 1:1: "Rabban Shimon ben Gamliel says: 'The world stands on three things: on truth, on justice, and on peace . . . .'" See also *Babylonian Talmud, Shabbat* 104a (contends that the fact the world is supported by truth and destroyed by falsehood is hinted at by the form of the Hebrew letters making up the words for truth and falsehood). Cf. R. Shimon ben Tzemah Duran (*Rashbatz*; (1361–1444)), *Magen Avot, Pirkei Avot* 1:18 (citing other hints of the positive traits of truth and the negative nuances of falsehood from various aspects of the relevant Hebrew letters, including the numbers that such letters represent).

5. *Ohtiot de–Rabbi Akiva* 1, cited by Tuvulski, supra n. 4, at 11.

6. See Maimonides, *Mishneh Torah, Hilkhot De'ot* 2:6; Eliezer Waldenburg, *Tzitz Eliezer* XV:12 (citing Rebbenu Yonah).

7. See L. Elliott, *I will be called John, a Biography of Pope John XXIII* 166 (1973). Interestingly, it is possible that Jewish law might not have permitted Jews to make use of such certificates. See, e.g., Irving J. Rosenbaum, *The Holocaust and Halakhah* (1976), pp. 44–46.

8. Robert F. Cochran, Jr., and Teresa S. Collett, *Cases and Materials on The Rules of the Legal Profession* (1996), at 35 (citing Monroe Freedman).

9. David Luban, *The Ethics of Lawyers* at 149–150.

10 Roy D. Simon, Jr. and Murray L. Schwartz, *Lawyers and the Legal Profession: Cases and Materials* (3d ed. 1994), at 153.

11. Seymour Wishman, *Confessions of a Criminal Lawyer*, in Cochran and Collett, supra n. 8, at 166–167.

12. See, e.g., *Goutis v. Express Transport, Inc., Division of F.V. Miranda Inc.*, 699 So.2d 757, 764 (Fla. 4th DCA 1997); *State v Lane*, 119 N.C. App. 197, 458 S.E.2d 19 (1995); *State v Asbury*, 415 S.E.2d 891 (W.Va. 1992); *People v Sheridan*, 57 Ill.App. 3d 765, 15 Ill. Dec. 323, 373 N.E.2d 669 (5th Dist. 1978); *United States v Stulga*, 584 F.2d 142 (6th Cir. 1978); *Hill v State*, 1977 Ok.Cr. 42, 560 P.2d 213 (Okla.Crim.App.1977). See, generally, 75A *Am Jur. 2d Trial* §§ 566, 635, 699 (1991); *Florida Civil Trial Practice, CIVTP FL–CLE* 16–1.

13. (a) A lawyer shall not reveal information relating to representation of a client unless the client consents after consultation, except for disclosures that are impliedly authorized in order to carry out the representation, and except as stated in paragraph (b).

(b) A lawyer may reveal such information to the extent the lawyer reasonably believes necessary:

(1) to prevent the client from committing a criminal act that the lawyer believes is likely to result in imminent death or substantial bodily harm; or

(2) to establish a claim or defense on behalf of the lawyer in a controversy between the lawyer and the client, to establish a defense to a criminal charge or civil claim against the lawyer based upon conduct in which the client was involved, or to respond to allegations in any proceeding concerning the lawyer's representation of the client.

14. *People v. Pautler,* _ P.3d _, 2001 WL 1162015, 4, 8 (Colo.O.P.D.J.).

15. Such purposes might include, for instance, preventing a person from wrongfully oppressing innocent people in other ways.

16. Richard Zitrin and Carol M. Langford, *The Moral Compass of the American Lawyer* (1999), at 163. Similarly, Prof. Charles Craver, an expert on negotiation and settlement is quoted as saying: "I've never been involved in legal negotiations where both sides didn't lie." Id., at 161. See also Joseph C. Sommer, Letter to *National Law Journal* (January 18, 1999).

17. See, e.g., R. Shlomo Yitzhaki (*Rashi*; 11th century), *Babylonian Talmud, Avodah Zarah* 6a, *Nazir* 23b.

18. R. Aharon ha–Levi (13th century), *Sefer Ha–Hinukh, Commandment* 16.

19. William Shakespeare, *Hamlet,* act 3, sc. 4, lines 176–87.

20. Davida H. Isaacs, *"It's Nothing Personal"–But Should it Be?: Finding Agent Liability of Violations of the Federal Employment Discrimination Statutes,* 22 *N.Y.U Rev. L. & Soc. Change* 505, 528 (1996):

> In this paradigm, a person is persuaded to have in a way (acting "not–X") that is contrary to her attitudes ("I believe X"). Since the action–cognition ("I acted not–X") cannot be changed, the individual will reduce the dissonance by changing the original attitude to "I believe not–X."

21. Stephan A. Landsman, "Satantic Cases:  A Means of Confronting the Law's Immorality," 66 *Notre Dame L. Rev.* 785, 786 (1991).

22. Id , at 786–787.

23. Richard Cohen, *A Rolling Ethic Gathers No Moss, Washington Post Magazine* (May 1, 1988), in Zitrin, pp  15–16.

# 10

# Spirituality in the Workplace: Individual and Organizational Transformation

## Michael F. Skelley

I would like to express my deepest gratitude to Mrs. Callista Wicklander, the wife of the late Raymond Wicklander, and to the entire Wicklander family for establishing the Wicklander Chair and for their great generosity to DePaul University. Such support is vital to the great work being done throughout this university.

I would also like to thank our president, Fr. Minogue, Executive Vice President Dick Meister, and my Dean, Susanne Dumbleton for making it possible for me to hold the Wicklander Chair during the 2001–2002 academic year. And I would like thank Assistant Vice President for Academic Affairs Kelly Johnson and all of her colleagues for managing all the practical details associated with this position so smoothly.

And finally I would like to thank all of you for taking time away from your work and other commitments to be here for this conversation today.

# Introduction

The topic I have chosen for our gathering today is the relationship between spirituality and the workplace. There has been rapidly growing popular interest in and activity about this subject in recent years.[1] Unfortunately, most of the popular approaches to workplace spirituality do not include enough ethical analysis to invite any substantive change in the status quo.[2] They do little more than help workers cope better with business as usual. While that may be a small and important step in the right direction, it does not begin to tap the potential of spirituality to transform our individual, organizational and social experience of work.[3]

There is a new and expanding field of academic study about spirituality and the workplace that is opening up deeper dimensions of this topic.[4] Many scholars of business management, organizational development, and organizational behavior have contributed to this field.[5] They are typically limited, however, by their lack of expertise in the field of spirituality. Unfortunately, the philosophers and theologians who have this expertise have paid surprisingly little attention to the contemporary workplace and are equally limited by their lack of experience in the study of work.[6] Those theologians who do address the workplace usually do so in such explicitly and narrowly faith–based terms that their approaches cannot find much public support in our culturally and religiously diverse workplaces.[7] Consequently, there is still much to be done to develop spiritualities that are appropriate to our workplaces and that can support genuine transformation.

In a few moments I will explain what I mean by spirituality. But before I do there are two important premises behind my approach to the topic of spirituality and work that I want to acknowledge. My first premise is that we desperately need to learn how to make major changes at the individual, organizational and social levels of work and that these changes are interrelated and interdependent. Specifically, we need to radically transform the individual and organizational ways we work in the developed world if we are to have more peaceful, just and sustainable societies. I believe spirituality can and should increase the satisfaction that individuals take in their work. But the spirituality of work is not simply about helping us cope better with business as usual.[8] Ultimately it should nurture the kinds of social change envisioned by pioneers such as St. Vincent de Paul.

We are witnessing a wide and deep crisis of work today. Work has always been at best an ambivalent part of human experience. But the negative aspects of work have taken on new and more serious dimensions in the information age. Many people today have great difficulty finding meaning or satisfaction in their work and consequently are unable to do great work. Much more seriously, many other workers toil away in situations where they are terribly misused or exploited. Still others are unable to find sufficient decent work through which they can earn a living wage.[9] Granted, many of us here today are fortunate enough to enjoy our work and take pride in the positive contributions we make to society.[10] But even those of us who find our work rewarding and meaningful cannot escape the ways in which our work is deeply rooted in very problematic historical and social contexts.[11] The work we do in the developed world takes place within technological, organizational, economic and social systems that enable us to accomplish things that were scarcely imaginable a century ago. But these structures also perpetuate desperate new levels of injustice, violence and environmental destruction locally, nationally, and globally.[12] Even though we do not intend it, the work we do directly contributes to and perpetuates our most serious social crises. Individuals, communities and the earth itself are being devastated by the ways work is organized and done today. So we cannot advance toward greater social justice unless we help businesses learn more socially responsible ways to produce their products and provide their services. Not–for–profit and public organizations are also implicated in these problems and have as much to learn as for–profit companies.

The second premise behind my approach to spirituality and the workplace is that the changes that are necessary in our workplaces are only possible if they are rooted in spirituality. The crises we must address today at the individual, organizational and social levels of work all have solutions within reach. What we find ourselves desperately short of are the individual and collective intrapersonal and interpersonal resources to initiate and sustain those solutions. The task of transforming the ways we work requires that we access depths of wisdom, courage, hospitality, forgiveness, hope and creativity that we have great difficulty tapping into either individually or collectively. The only adequate and lasting responses to these crises will have significant spiritual components to them. Our efforts to change our workplaces, therefore, need to be nourished by, and lived out in, spirituality.

I will try to explain today where these two premises lead me. First, I will explain what I mean by "spirituality." I will define spirituality at the most abstract level as the way we live out the freedom that makes us human. At the practical level, I will propose that one concrete way to define spirituality today is as a way of living that is grounded in a balanced worldview, that is supported by practice, and that helps us find and make peace. I will then briefly explore three different ways in which spirituality and the workplace are related. My intention is to highlight some of the challenges and opportunities we have to more authentically express our deepest potential as human beings and to do great work together.

# I. Spirituality

The word "spirituality" has become tremendously popular in recent years.[13] In the process, it has taken on so many new and disparate connotations that it is rarely clear what any particular person means by it.[14] Fifty years ago, the word "spirituality" was heard only infrequently within, and rarely outside of, anglican, orthodox, and roman catholic christian communities.[15] But spirituality has long since ceased to be the concern exclusively of people committed to a religious tradition.[16] Millions of people with and without connections to formal religion now seek personal development and offer guidance in what sociologist of religion Wade Clark Roof calls the "spiritual marketplace."[17] This recent explosion of interest in new expressions of spirituality has unquestionably enriched our understanding and appreciation for the life of the spirit. But spirituality is in danger of being so inclusive that it becomes meaningless. The challenge is, as feminist christian theologian and peace activist Dorothee Soelle says, to democratize spirituality without trivializing it.[18]

Spirituality is primarily a matter of what we do with the capacity for freedom that makes us distinctively human. Religious interpretations or expressions of spirituality are important, but ultimately they are secondary to the universal human capacity for self–transcendence.[19] Spirituality is what we do with our capacity to determine the meaning and value of our lives by the commitments we make. That freedom can be lived out in all kinds of authentic and inauthentic ways. Authentic spirituality is any way of living out our freedom that deepens that freedom and that expands the conditions of freedom for others.[20] Saying that authentic spirituality is a matter of how we live out our freedom only defines this aspect of human experience in a very general and abstract way. We cannot, however, live out our freedom at an abstract level. Every religious tradition, therefore, has inspired a variety of spiritualities to help guide and sustain the life of freedom. Many other spiritualities have also developed over the course of human history without a connection to religion. There can be no one concrete, universally valid way to articulate what spirituality is at the level of real life.[21] We are challenged to find the best possible ways we can to integrate and practice spirituality in the concrete circumstances of our lives.

The best way I can define authentic spirituality in our social context today is as *a way of living that is grounded in a balanced worldview, that is supported by practice, and that helps us find and make peace.* What does this mean? First of all, spirituality is a way of living. Spirituality is not primarily about profound emotional experiences, and certainly not primarily about our religious activities. It is essentially the way we integrate and orient all the disparate elements of our lives. Spirituality involves everything we do including how we take care of our bodies, where we spend our money, whether we vote, when we talk with one another, and why we work. Consequently spirituality is closely related to ethics and should always be accompanied by critical and comprehensive moral reflection on the choices we make.[22] Spirituality helps us make choices about the ultimate values that shape the priorities of daily living. It challenges us to construct our lives in ways that awaken us to our full potential and inspire us to concretely transform patterns of suffering, deprivation and injustice in the world around us. Sulak Sivaraksa, one of the leading voices of engaged buddhism[23], says:

> Spiritual considerations and social change cannot be separated. Forces in our social environment, such as consumerism, with its emphasis on craving and dissatisfaction, can hinder our spiritual development. People seeking to live spiritually must be concerned with their social and physical environment.[24]

The second part of my definition says that authentic spirituality is a way of living that is grounded in a balanced worldview. A worldview is a comprehensive way of seeing and interpreting reality; a set of fundamental values and basic assumptions about the meaning of human life. Our worldviews are often unbalanced and emphasize some insights and values at the expense of others.[25] We can only move toward a more balanced worldview if we think critically about the basic assumptions we have about life. Such reflection should draw us away from our preoccupation with our private joys and concerns and into a deeper engagement with what is ultimately important in the world.[26] Those of us who live at the upper levels of the developed world's economies have the most comfortable and indulgent lives of any people in human history. The danger of spirituality today is that it only makes us more self–absorbed and irresponsible. Far too much of contemporary spirituality affirms a futile pursuit of a happiness that will allow us to protect our privileges and ignore the rest of the world's suffering.[27] Our worldviews need to be worked out in the context of what cultural historian and "geologian" Thomas Berry calls the Great Work of moving from human devastation of the Earth to being present to the Earth in a mutually beneficial manner. Berry says this is the basic call addressed to all people today.[28]

The third part of my definition says spirituality is a way of life that is supported by practice. Spiritual practices are the deliberate ways in which we try to cultivate and express our way of life and our worldview. They develop our capacity to live out our spiritual commitments consistently and authentically. Without practices that engage our depths and help us change, spirituality is a superficial and self–serving affair.[29] Reading the Bible, reciting prayers, focusing on one's breath, enjoying nature, serving the poor, exercising our bodies, advocating about social issues, and restoring wild places can all be spiritual practices, depending on the meaning these activities have for us when we engage in them. Spiritual practices help us wake up to a depth dimension in our world that usually eludes us.

There is a profound paradox to spiritual practice. If we try to use spiritual practices for the benefits they might bring, we typically gain little. But if we commit ourselves to them for their own sakes, not trying to gain anything, we will in fact gain a great deal. This paradox about spiritual practice explains why so much of the advice commonly given about workplace spirituality is ultimately misguided. Too much of it attempts to market spiritual practices by promising specific results. In the process, the intrinsic values of the practices are lost as they are reduced to techniques for growth and development.[30]

The fourth part of my definition of spirituality is that it is about finding and making peace. By "peace" I do not mean necessarily the absence of stress, conflict, or violence, but rather the full presence of harmony, justice and freedom. Peace very often is, in fact, difficult and painful work. By focusing on peace as the symbol of ultimate value I mean to highlight the ethical challenges that are an essential part of spirituality. The symbol of peace is a provocative and compelling symbol of that which is most sacred and transformative in our world. Peace is not quite as subject to the pre–conceived ideas that have robbed the symbol of God of its ability to challenge us to transcend the individual and social arrangements that we allow to limit the full expression of our humanity. In Soelle's words, the symbol of peace can democratize spirituality without trivializing it. I fully agree, therefore, with the scholar of world religions Raimon Panikkar when he says,

> Peace today constitutes one of the few positive symbols having meaning for the whole of humanity. Peace is the most universal unifying symbol possible . . . . The symbol of "God" has ceased to be universal–if it ever was—not only because of the wars that have been

waged in the divine name, but also because, rightly or wrongly, a considerable part of human consciousness sees in the theisms the last residue of a monarchical conception of reality fated to disappear.[31]

I think, then, that one way to understand what spirituality means for us in our cultural situation today is as a way of living that is grounded in a balanced worldview, that is supported by practice and that helps us find and make peace. One of the critical areas in which we must live out our spirituality is in the workplace. So what does this approach to spirituality mean for work? I will attempt to indicate this through three different models: spiritualities *of* the workplace, spiritualities *for* the workplace, and spiritualities *in* the workplace.

## II. Three Models for Relating Spirituality and Work

### Spiritualities *of* the workplace

Many proponents and most opponents of integrating spirituality and work share one important assumption. They both tend to assume a very dualistic view of the world in which the realm of spirituality and other concerns about the sacred are completely separated from the realm of work and other secular concerns. They both, therefore, assume that any explicit association of spirituality and work would be introducing spirituality into a foreign territory where it is not already present. The proponents of this move applaud such initiatives while the opponents resist them.

There are, however, very good theoretical and experiential reasons to question this assumption that work does not already involve spirituality. If we accept that spirituality is a matter of how we interpret and live out the basic freedom that makes us human, then work and the workplace are deeply and unavoidably connected to spirituality. No matter how alienated we may be from our work, the way we go about that work shapes and expresses the fundamental commitments that form us as human persons. Each of us interprets the meaning of our work in the light of our worldview, our basic assumptions and ultimate values about life. How we do that work constitutes a set of practices that directly express and reinforce that worldview. Because work is a thoroughly human activity, it is unavoidably a deeply spiritual experience. The question is not whether there is already a spiritual dimension to our work, but what sort of spirituality it is. Each of us, even if we ignore or suppress it, already has a spirituality of work.

The issue I want to highlight here, however, is that the organizations in which we work have spiritualities as well. This is what I mean by spiritualities *of* the workplace. Spiritualities *of* the workplace are those aspects of our organizations and their cultures that attempt to interpret and shape the ways in which we exercise our freedom.[32] Every organization has fundamental assumptions deeply embedded within it about what work ultimately means in the context of human life.[33] Every organization implicitly and explicitly attempts to shape the commitments its members make to it and to its goals. The spiritual dimension of an organization is not just the aggregate values and behaviors of its members. It is a cohesive system, or set of systems, for interpreting and shaping who we are. One line of evidence I would use to support this claim is provided by the scholarship on organizations as learning systems. Scholars such as Peter Senge, Chris Argyris and Donald Schön and many others have demonstrated that organizations as organizations, and not just as groups of individuals, are capable of learning.[34] Now there is a long history of thought in many religious and philosophical traditions that identify learning as an inherently spiritual activity.[35] Assuming this is so, organizations that learn are realizing and demonstrating their capacity for spirituality.[36]

Some of these same prominent organizational learning scholars also connect the great difficulties most work organizations have at engaging in transformative learning directly to issues of spirituality.[37] This is evidence that not only do our organizations have spiritualities of work, but also that the ones they have are deeply flawed. If an organization's culture fundamentally frustrates its ability to learn how to learn, which most organizational cultures do, then that culture is simultaneously frustrating its members' potential to more and more fully integrate their freedom. Helping organizations and the individuals within in them learn how to learn more deeply and comprehensively is one of the essential spiritual challenges of our day.

The spiritualities *of* work that are in place in most organizations, then, are surrogate or inauthentic spiritualities. They are spiritualities because they do interpret and shape the expression of our freedom. They are inauthentic, however, because they fail to expand that freedom and the conditions of freedom for others. Their efforts to channel their members' commitments usually end up diminishing freedom rather than enhancing it.

Most of the reasons that spiritualities *of* the workplace are so often inauthentic has to do with the unbalanced worldviews they assume. It is important to remember here that the values we espouse in our workplaces are rarely the values that we actually put into practice in our everyday work. The values we act on at work are usually shaped by our dominant culture's materialism, individualism, and consumerism. That is how our work organizations become the local congregations of the religion of the marketplace.[38] The fact that these spiritualities are inauthentic does not necessarily mean they are unsuccessful or unpopular. On the contrary, their values are espoused so persuasively and their core behaviors are practiced so skillfully, that we completely forget how dehumanizing, socially irresponsible and environmentally destructive these surrogate spiritualities ultimately are.[39]

**Spiritualities *for* the workplace**
The second way in which spirituality and work can be related is through what I call spiritualities *for* the workplace.[40] These are spiritualities that are explicitly faith–based and that apply the worldview and practices of a particular religious tradition to the workplace. Their goal is to help believers interpret and conduct their work in light of their faith commitments. Such approaches encourage believers to bring religious beliefs and practices into the workplace. This is the kind of spirituality, for example, that might encourage believers to participate in shared prayer or discussion of the Bible in the workplace. This approach might also be called religion for the workplace.[41]

The strengths and limits of this way of integrating spirituality and work can be seen by reflecting on the close relationship between spirituality and religion. On the positive side, the world's religions have generally proven to be more effective than any philosophy, ideology or value system in cultivating the universal spiritual dimension of human life.[42] Involvement with more than one religious tradition can be especially enriching[43]. Everyone interested in genuinely integrating spirituality and work would be wise to investigate the wisdom the world's major religious traditions have to offer.

The most effective faith–based spiritualities for the workplace help individual believers draw on the wisdom and practices of their religious traditions to develop their gifts and contribute to the common good.[44] At their best, these traditions see the sacred and the secular dimensions of life as interpenetrating. Then the task of these faith–based spiritualities for work is to use their religious resources to enhance the potential for individual, organizational and social transformation that is already present in the experience of work. If, as the catholic theologian and philosopher Karl Rahner said, our world is completely permeated with the presence of God, then we can experience God and achieve our fullest human potential even in the most ordinary kinds of work.[45] Such faith–based spiritualities are important and helpful, therefore, because of the great potential they have to support transformation.

But even at their best, these spiritualities are also seriously limited by their explicit ties to religious traditions. Because of these close ties to religion, they are not universally accessible and sustainable in the vast majority of workplaces. Given the diverse nature of our work-places, promoting any form of religion to foster individual and organizational transformation is almost always inappropriate. Such an approach presumes a consensus about religion that does not exist, should not be expected, and can never be imposed, in our work organizations.[46] Faith–based spiritualities are generally unable to support inclusive and collaborative efforts at the individual and organizational transformation of work.

Faith–based spiritualities of work are not only inadequate; they can also be counter–productive. This is because the relationship between spirituality and religion is not always positive. Organized religions often become pre–occupied with institutional concerns and leave their members hungry for the substantive spiritual nourishment they deserve and the world needs. The result is that religions are frequently tempted to become fundamentalistic and intolerant, believing that theirs is the only true path to salvation.[47] They end up minimizing the prophetic and transformative challenges of spirituality. Poet, essayist and activist Wendell Berry speaks to this when he says, "The organized church makes peace with a destructive economy and divorces itself from economic issues because it is economically compelled to do so."[48] Their dualistic thinking blinds them to the sacred dimension already inherent in secular activities such as work.[49] These faith–based spiritualities *for* work then attempt to make work explicitly religious. Spirituality becomes the intrusion of beliefs and practices that do little more than help believers cope with the status quo. Unfortunately, much of what is popularly touted today as workplace spirituality suffers from this dualistic thinking.[50]

### Spiritualities *in* the workplace

What I call spiritualities *in* the workplace arise from the spiritual potential hidden within the work that is already being done in our organizations. It takes a certain kind of vision to be able to see the spiritual potential of work. That sort of vision comes from a worldview that encompasses the wider social context of work and invites transformation in the status quo. Such a worldview might draw some of its inspiration from explicitly religious traditions, but it needs to find publicly accessible and inclusive language to articulate those insights in the workplace. The concept of peace, for example, is one symbol that can provide the foundation for such a worldview.

Even though such inclusive, accessible and transformative worldviews are critically important for spiritualities *in* the workplace, this is not their focus. Their main focus is on the dimension of practice. I explained earlier the critical role practices have in any spirituality.

Spiritualities *in* the workplace can focus on practices that significantly expand our individual and organizational capacities for learning. In the information age, such learning is central to the work we do each day. Practices that enhance our learning skills, therefore, are not only appropriate for the workplace, they are vital. But the process of learning is also a particularly powerful way of engaging and developing that capacity for freedom that makes us distinctively human.[51] Work practices that support and enhance deep individual and organizational learning, therefore, can form the core of a powerful spirituality in the workplace.[52] I think that there are two main areas in which spiritualities in the workplace can be most effective: individual and collaborative practices.

Individual practices are practices that help people discover and engage deeper and deeper levels of their interior lives. Such practices help individuals develop a wide variety of interior resources and strengths. No matter how little independence and discretion we may have in our work, at one level work always remains an essentially individual activity. Ultimately, my work comes forth from all my complexities as a human being and contributes to who I am as a person. Individual spiritual practices can help develop how my work expresses and creates me. There are many appropriate ways in which work organizations can provide opportunities to learn about and support such individual practices. But because there is great potential for organizations to be intrusive and manipulative here, the responsibility and control of such practices must always remain with the individual.

One of the strengths of the contemporary "spiritual marketplace" is that there are many opportunities available to us to learn spiritual practices that can help us more deeply integrate our interior lives. One type of such activities that I think is particularly powerful and easily integrated into the workplace can be broadly called "mindfulness" practices.[53] These are meditation or contemplative practices that expand our capacities to pay attention to what is going on within us and around us. The Vietnamese zen buddhist master Thich Naht Hanh is one of many who use the term "mindfulness" to refer to keeping one's consciousness alive to the present reality.[54] There are comparable practices in western religious traditions as well. Jesuit theologian Walter Burghardt called such practices a matter of taking a "long, loving look at the real."[55] But these are practices that can be taught and used without any religious content. Thich Naht Hanh, for example, encourages a kind of meditation practice that focuses on paying attention to the most basic activities of life such as our breathing. Such a practice is easily adapted to paying attention to aspects of our work. Howard Gardner

and his colleagues are among the scholars researching how contemplative practices can be incorporated into the professional workplace.[56]

We do not have time in this context to explore specific directions
for such mindfulness practices. With any spiritual practice, it is always
a good idea to get guidance from those who have experience with the
challenges and opportunities of the practice. I just want to suggest that
practices that help us slow down and pay deeper attention to the work
we are doing as we are doing it have great potential to transform us and
our work. I am not suggesting that we adopt religious practices that
would interrupt work. I am suggesting that we find ways to practice
paying a much more personal and profound kind of attention to our
work.[57] These practices are particularly useful in shaping how we respond to the constant pace of change that faces us in the workplace.
Such practices can help us work with much greater integrity and authenticity and discover a new capacity to do great work with our colleagues. In the words of Wendell Berry, through such individual practices

> One's inner voices become audible. One feels the attraction of one's
> most intimate sources. In consequence, one responds more clearly to
> other lives. The more coherent one becomes within oneself as a crea-
> ture, the more fully one enters into the communion of all creatures.[58]

In addition to such individual practices, collaborative practices are
essential for spiritualities *in* the workplace. If individual practices are
those activities that help us more authentically integrate our interior
lives, collaborative practices are those activities that help us more authentically work together with our colleagues. This means finding
ways to work together that greatly expand our capacities to learn from
and with each other about what truly matters. Such practices can
greatly expand our capacity to benefit from the diversity and plurality
of our workplaces. Fortunately, many such practices are readily available to us. The work that Peter Senge and colleagues have done on the
five disciplines of the learning organization is quite relevant here.[59]
Edgar Schein's process consultation is a philosophy that lends itself to
developing effective and appropriate collaborative relationships.[60]

The work that David Bohm, Bill Isaacs and others have done on
articulating the practice of dialogue is another extremely useful avenue
for nurturing collaborative relationships that help organizations learn
how to transform their work.[61] Again, we do not have time today to
discuss the specific dynamics of this practice. Guidelines for dialogue,
however, are readily available.[62] The point here is to note that fostering
dialogue is not only an essential part of developing transformative or-

ganizational learning.  It is also an essential spiritual activity that need not have any explicitly religious content to it.  But as Raimon Panikkar says, such dialogue is an absolutely revolutionary activity:

> It challenges, in point of fact, many of the commonly accepted foundations of modern culture.  To restore or install . . . dialogue in human relations among individuals, families, groups, societies, nations, and cultures may be one of the most urgent things to do in our times threatened by a fragmentation of interests that threatens all life on the planet.[63]

Mindfulness practices and dialogue practices are just two examples of the ways ordinary work activities can be integrated into highly effective spiritualities *in* the workplace.  Such practices complement and reinforce each other quite effectively.[64]  But we need to remember here the fundamental paradox of spiritual practice that I mentioned earlier.  That is that practices are only effective when we do them for their own sakes and not with the expectation of a specific gain.  This is a fundamental difference between spiritual practice and management fads.

In conclusion, this has been a very rapid and broad overview of the relationship between spirituality and work.  Finding new ways to acknowledge and integrate the spiritual dimension of work is no easy challenge.  But it is an essential part of the Great Work that we are each called to do.

# Notes

1. One small but significant indicator of this is the cover story that Fortune magazine, the standard bearer for corporate life, ran in the summer of 2001. The article was entitled "God and Business: The Surprising Quest for Spiritual Renewal in the American Workplace" and it explored a number of different spiritual paths managers and executives are taking to break what Fortune calls "the last taboo in corporate America." Fortune, Vol. 144, No. 1, July 9, 2001, pp. 59–80.

2. Despite the genuine insights many of the following authors have, their spiritualities are deficient in the ethical analysis of the social context of work: Michael Novak, *Business as a Calling: Work and the Examined Life* (New York: The Free Press, 1996); Alan Briskin, *The Stirring of Soul in the Workplace* (San Francisco: Jossey–Bass, 1996); C. Michael Thompson, *The Congruent Life: Following the Inward Path to Fulfilling Work and Inspired Leadership* (San Francisco: Jossey–Bass, 2000); Lewis Richmond, *Work as a Spiritual Practice: A Practical Buddhist Approach to Inner Growth and Satisfaction on the Job* (New York: Broadway Books, 1999); and, Parker Palmer, *The Active*

*Life. Wisdom for Work, Creativity, and Caring* (San Francisco: Jossey Bass, 1999).

3. When I speak of "transformation" in this paper, I am thinking of the kinds of deep and broad changes that are represented by notions of transformative learning. See Jack Mezirow, *Transformative Dimensions of Adult Learning* (San Francisco: Jossey–Bass, 1991).

4. This emerging field has benefited from and depends upon many of the advances made by the field of business and professional ethics. But this new field approaches the study of the conditions, conduct, and consequences of our work from different perspectives and with different resources. Like any new academic field, there are many important questions of method and scope in it that are far from settled. See Paul Gibbons, "Spirituality at Work: Definitions, Measures, Assumptions and Validity Claims," *Work and Spirit: A Reader of New Spiritual Paradigms for Organizations,* Jerry Biberman and Michael D. Whitty, eds., (Scranton: The University of Scranton Press, 2000), pp. 111–131.

5. Margaret Benefiel provides an excellent survey of the field in her paper, "Mapping the Terrain of Spirituality in Organizations: Goals, Conceptual Frames, and Research Methods," which was presented at the Academy of Management Annual Meeting in Washington, D.C., 2001. See also, Sandra King, Jerry Biberman, Lee Robbins, and David M. Nicol. "Integrating Spirituality into Management Education in Academia and Organizations: Origins, a Conceptual Framework, and Current Practices," *Work and Spirit· A Reader of New Spiritual Paradigms for Organizations,* Jerry Biberman and Michael D. Whitty, eds., (Scranton: The University of Scranton Press, 2000), pp. 281–293.

6. Some of the few exceptions to this are Dorothee Soelle, *To Work and to Love: A Theology of Creation* (Philadelphia: Fortress Press, 1984); Matthew Fox, *The Reinvention of Work: A New Vision of Livelihood for Our Time* (San Francisco: HarperSanFrancisco, 1994); Al Gini, *My Job, My Self: Work and the Creation of the Modern Individual* (New York: Routledge, 2000); and, Joanne B. Ciulla, *The Working Life: The Promise and Betrayal of Modern Work* (New York: Crown Business, 2000).

7. Despite the strengths of the following, they are all limited in this way: John C. Haughey, *Converting 9 to 5. A Spirituality of Daily Work* (New York: Crossroad, 1989); Miroslav Volf, *Work in the Spirit: Toward a Theology of Work* (New York: Oxford University Press, 1991); and, Michael J. Naughton and Helen J. Alford, *Managing as if Faith Mattered: Christian Social Principles in the Modern Organization* (Notre Dame: University of Notre Dame Press, 2001).

8. As Peter Block observes: "For several years now books on soul, poetry, and spirituality have sold well into the organization marketplace. These books and ideas, however, have stayed on the periphery; they have been used more as coping strategies to make outcome–and control–driven organizations more tolerable. What has not happened, though, is any real shift in the basic context of our organizations, which would be to believe that philosophic insights are essential to the survival of an institution and provide a basis for governance." Peter Koestenbaum and Peter Block, *Freedom and Accountability at Work· Applying Philosophic Insight to the Real World* (San Francisco: Jossey–Bass, 2001), p. 121.

9. Just a few accounts of these issues are: Max Stackhouse, Dennis McCann, Shirley Roels and Preston Williams, eds., *On Moral Business: Classical and Contemporary Resources for Ethics in Economic Life* (Grand Rapids: William B. Eerdmans, 1995); Charles Handy, *The Hungry Spirit: Beyond Capitalism: A Quest for Purpose in the Modern World* (New York: Broadway Books, 1998); Barbara Hilkert Andolsen, *The New Job Contract: Economic Justice in an Age of Insecurity.* (Cleveland: Pilgrim Press, 1998); and, Richard Sennett, *The Corrosion of Character: The Personal Consequences of Work in the New Capitalism* (W. W. Norton, 1998).

10. Accounts of some of the ways people are working well are: Howard Gardner, Mihaly Csikszentmihalyi, and William Damon, *Good Work: When Excellence and Ethics Meet* (New York: Basic Books, 2001); Peter Block, *The Answer to How is Yes: Acting on What Matters* (San Francisco: Berrett–Koehler, 2002); Donald Hall, *Life Work* (Boston: Beacon Press, 1993); John Cowan, *Small Decencies. Reflections and Meditations on Being Human at Work* (New York: HarperBusiness, 1992); and, D. M. Dooling, ed., *A Way of Working: The Spiritual Dimension of Craft* (New York: Parabola Books, 1979).

11. Joanne B. Ciulla, *The Working Life: The Promise and Betrayal of Modern Work* (New York: Crown Business, 2000), pp. 225–226: "It would be wrong, in fact morally dangerous, to assume that meaningful work is purely subjective. Meaningful work, like a meaningful life, is morally worthy work undertaken in a morally worthy organization. Work has meaning *because* there is some good in it. The most meaningful jobs are those in which people directly help others or create products that make life better for people. Work makes life better if it helps others; alleviates suffering; eliminates difficult, dangerous, or tedious toil; makes someone healthier and happier; or aesthetically or intellectually enriches people and improves the environment in which we live. All work that is worthy does at least one of these things in some small or large way."

12. For some analyses of these issues, see: Thomas Berry, *The Great Work: Our Way into the Future* (New York: Bell Tower, 1999), Herman E. Daly and John B. Cobb, Jr., *For the Common Good: Redirecting the Economy Toward Community, the Environment, and a Sustainable Future*, 2nd edition (Boston: Beacon Press, 1994); Sallie McFague, *Life Abundant: Rethinking Theology and Economy for a Planet in Peril* (Minneapolis: Fortress Press, 2001); Joerg Rieger, ed., *Liberating the Future: God, Mammon and Theology* (Minneapolis: Fortress Press, 1998); Leonardo Boff, *Cry of the Earth, Cry of the Poor* (Maryknoll: Orbis Books, 1998); Rita M. Gross and Rosemary Radford Ruether, *Religious Feminism and the Future of the Planet: A Buddhist–Christian Conversation* (New York: Continuum, 2001); Sulak Sivaraksa, *Seeds of Peace: A Buddhist Vision for Renewing Society* (Berkeley: Parallax Press, 1992); and, R. Edward Freeman, Jessica Pierce and Richard H. Dodd, *Environmentalism and the New Logic of Business: How Firms can be Profitable and Leave our Children a Living Planet* (Oxford: Oxford University Press, 2000).

13. See Robert Wuthnow, *After Heaven: Spirituality in America since the 1950s* (Berkeley: University of California Press, 2000). For a critical view of these developments, see L. Gregory Jones, "A Thirst for God or Consumer

Spirituality: Cultivating Disciplined Practices of Being Engaged by God,"
*Spirituality and Social Embodiment*, L. Gregory Jones and James J. Buckley,
eds., (Oxford: Blackwell Publishers, 1997), pp. 3–28.

14. For a survey of the contemporary scene in spirituality, see Michael
Downey, *Understanding Christian Spirituality* (New York: Paulist Press,
1997), 5–30.

15. The word "spirituality" originally developed in the Christian tradition.
For an overview of the history of the term, see Philip Sheldrake, *Spirituality
and Theology: Christian Living and the Doctrine of God* (Maryknoll: Orbis
Books, 1998), 36–47; and Walter Principe, "Christian Spirituality," *The New
Dictionary of Catholic Spirituality*, ed. Michael Downey (Collegeville: The
Liturgical Press, 1993), 931–938.

16. Sandra Schneiders, "Theology and Spirituality: Strangers, Rivals, or
Partners?" *Horizons* 13 (1983), 266; Joann Wolski Conn, "Toward Spiritual
Maturity," *Freeing Theology: The Essentials of Theology in Feminist Perpsec-
tive*, ed. C. M. LaCunga (San Francisco: HarperSanFrancisco, 1993), 236–7;
and Leonardo Boff, *Cry of the Earth, Cry of the Poor* (Maryknoll: Orbis
Books, 1997), 187–196.

17. Wade Clark Roof, *Spiritual Marketplace: Baby Boomers and the Re-
making of American Religion* ( Princeton: Princeton University Press, 1999).

18. Dorothee Soelle, *The Silent Cry: Mysticism and Resistance* ( Minneapolis: Fortress Press, 2001), 97. Many scholars of spirituality are seeking more
inclusive definitions of spirituality that do not trivialize it. Michael Downey
(*Understanding Christian Spirituality*, p. 14), for example, sees spirituality as
the way we live out our ultimate commitments. For Downey, spirituality is
specifically characterized by the awareness that there are levels of reality not
immediately apparent to us, and the quest for personal integration in the face of
forces of fragmentation and depersonalization. Walter Principe ("Toward Defining Spirituality," *Studies in Religion* 12 (1983) 136.), a prominent scholar of
the history of western spirituality, thought that a universally applicable definition of spirituality might be the way in which people understand and live the
loftiest aspect of their religion, philosophy or ethic. Christian feminist theologian Sandra Schneiders (Spirituality in the Academy." *Theological Studies* 50
(1989) 684) defines spirituality as "the experience of consciously striving to
integrate one's life in terms not of isolation and self–absorption but of self–
transcendence toward the ultimate value one perceives." Schneiders believes
that this definition excludes the organizing of one's life in dysfunctional or
narcissistic ways and potentially includes any spirituality, whether religious or
secular. For other definitions of spirituality, see Wayne Teasdale, *The Mystic
Heart: Discovering a Universal Spirituality in the World's Religions* (Novato:
New World Library, 1999), 15–30; Kenneth J. Collins, ed., *Exploring Christian
Spirituality: An Ecumenical Reader* (Grand Rapids: Baker Books, 2000); and,
Bradley C. Hanson, ed., *Modern Christian Spirituality: Methodological and
Historical Essays* (Atlanta: Scholars Press, 1990).

19. Raimon Panikkar, *A Dwelling Place for Wisdom* (Louisville: Westminster, 1993), 35–36.

20. The fundamental role of freedom in my understanding of spirituality
provides a natural and powerful link to the economic and philosophical work of

Nobel prize winner Amartya Sen. See, for example, his *Development as Freedom* (New York: Knopf, 1999).

21. See Ignacio Goetz, "On the Impossibility of a General Spirituality," *Journal of Humanism and Ethical Religion* 4 (1991) 26–40.

22. It is not always easy to distinguish ethics and spirituality since both terms are used in so many different ways. But in general I would say that ethics is concerned with what we should do (the normative), while spirituality is concerned with what we could do (our potential). Ethics focuses on how we should use our freedom responsibly. Spirituality focuses on how we can use our freedom to its full potential.

23. The movement known as "engaged Buddhism" highlights active engagement in addressing pain, suffering and evil in the world. It is a good example of spirituality that integrates a comprehensive understanding of ethics. See Christopher S. Queen, ed.., *Engaged Buddhism in the West* (Boston: Wisdom Publications, 2000); Arnold Kotler, ed., *Engaged Buddhist Reader: Ten Years of Engaged Buddhist Publishing* (Berkeley: Parallax Press, 1996); and Fred Eppsteiner, ed., *The Path of Compassion: Writings on Socially Engaged Buddhism* (Berkeley: Parallax Press, 1988). Various movements within chrisitianity have also integrated spirituality and ethics comprehensively. Liberation, feminist, ecofeminist and black theologies are examples. A particularly good overview of some of these theologies in connection with the themes of this book is Joerg Rieger, ed., *Liberating the Future: God, Mammon and Theology* (Minneapolis: Fortress, 1998).

24. Sulak Sivaraksa, *Seeds of Peace: A Buddhist Vision for Renewing Society* (Berkeley: Parallax Press, 1992), 57. See also, Michael Phillips, The Social Dimensions of "Rightlivelihood," *Mindfulness and Meaningful Work: Explorations in Right Livelihood,* Claude Whitmeyer, ed., (Berkeley: Parallax Press, 1994), pp. 111–116.

25. For example, the worldview that permeates the cultures of the developed world stresses the value of the individual over the importance of the community. This fundamental imbalance in our worldview has had benefits, such as encouraging individual freedom and initiative. But this imbalance has also had a number of negative consequences, specifically, the lack of attention to the common good.

26. Numerous prophetic voices call us to pay attention to this. The Parliament of the World's Religions says in its Global Ethic that the world is in pervasive and urgent agony. All spiritual reflection must take this into account. (Hans Kung and Karl–Josef Kuschel, eds., *A Global Ethic: The Declaration of the Parliament of the World's Religions* (New York: Continuum, 1993), 13.) The authors of the Earth Charter say we "stand at a critical moment in Earth's history, a time when humanity must choose its future. As the world becomes increasingly interdependent and fragile, the future holds at once great peril and great promise . . . . We must join together to bring forth a sustainable global society founded on respect for nature, universal human rights, economic justice, and a culture of peace." (The Earth Charter Commission, *The Earth Charter* (San Jose, Costa Rica: Earth Council, 2001), preamble. Available at www.earthcharter.org.)

27. Theology should help us see spirituality in our workplace not only from our perspective, but also from the perspective of the transcendent. Sallie McFague (*Life Abundant*, 52) says, "the theology we North Americans need is *one for the world*, one in which God and the world are the focus, not your or my personal problems. *We* fit into this theology as workers called to be God's partners in maximizing delight in the world and minimizing its pain."

28. Thomas Berry, *The Great Work: Our Way into the Future* (New York: Bell Tower, 1999), 10.

29. Wayne Teasdale (*The Mystic Heart*, 141) says daily practice is to the spiritual life what food and drink are to the body. We cannot survive or grow as spiritual persons without them.

30. On the difference between practice and technique, see William Spohn, *Go and Do Likewise: Jesus and Ethics* (New York: Continuum, 1999).

31. Raimon Panikkar, *Cultural Disarmament: The Way to Peace* (Louisville: Westminster John Knox Press, 1995) 63.

32. Joanne Ciulla calls this the search for "the ghost in the machine" and it is one of the themes of her book *The Working Life: The Promise and Betrayal of Modern Work* (New York: Crown Business, 2000).

33. For one account of such assumptions see Lois Sekerak Hogan, "A Framework for the Practical Application of Spirituality at Work," *Work and Spirit: A Reader of New Spiritual Paradigms for Organizations*, Jerry Biberman and Michael D. Whitty, eds., (Scranton: The University of Scranton Press, 2000), pp. 55–76.

34. Peter Senge, *The Fifth Discipline: The Art and Practice of Learning Organizations* (New York: Doubleday, 1990); and, Chris Argyris and Donald A. Schön, *Organizational Learning II: Theory, Method, and Practice* (Reading: Addison–Wesley Publishing, 1996).

35. Just one example of these traditions is Jean Leclercq, *The Love of Learning and the Desire for God: A Study of Monastic Culture* (New York: Fordham U. Press, 1961).

36. See Peter Hawkins, "The Spiritual Dimension of the Learning Organization," *Management Education and Development* 22 (1991) 172–187.

37. One particularly provocative account of this comes from Argyris and Schön. They demonstrate how the organizational learning disfunctions that they express in their Model 1 are rooted in notions of social virtues that have everything to do with spirituality.

38. David R. Loy, "The Religion of the Market" *Journal of the American Academy of Religion* 65/2 (1997) 275–290.

39. Raimon Pannikar (*Invisible Harmony: Essays on Contemplation and Responsibility* (Minneapolis: Fortress Press, 1995), pp. 10–11) indicates how dehumanizing these surrogate spiritualities can be when he says that they tell us, "You are real in as much as you are a worker and a producer. There are no other criteria for the authenticity of your work than its results. You will be judged by the results of your work . . . . Your discipline and asceticism must be channeled into better production and more work. You may relax and even entertain yourself but only in order that you may be able to work better and produce more. It is this very work that will entitle you to the reward, the relaxation, and peace which you may, in rare moments of reflection, sometimes

long for. You may be able to choose your type of work, because if you work with pleasure you will produce more and with less attrition. Even cows are given music."

40. See note #7 above for some of the better Christian versions of this. A Buddhist example is Shinichi Inoue, *Putting Buddhism to Work: A New Approach to Management and Business* (Tokyo: Kodansha International, 1997).

41. Many of these faith-based spiritualities of work are derived from particular theologies of work. Important parts of the history of these theologies can be found in: William E. May, "Work, Theology of," *The New Dictionary of Catholic Social Thought*, ed. Judith A. Dwyer (Collegeville: Liturgical Press, 1994), 991–1002; Karen Ready, "Work," *The Encyclopedia of Religion*, vol. 15, ed. Mircea Eliade (New York: Macmillan Pub. Co., 1987), 441–444; Sellner, Edward C., "Work" *The New Dictionary of Catholic Spirituality*, ed. Michael Downey (Collegeville: Liturgical Press, 1993) 1044–1051; Francis Schussler Fiorenza, "Religious Beliefs and Praxis: Reflections on Catholic Theological Views of Work" in *Work and Religion*, ed. Gregory Baum (New York: The Seabury Press, 1980), 92–102.

42. Religious institutions provide a wealth of insight into our potential for both delusion and enlightenment. They offer communities of experienced practitioners to guide the spiritual growth of those with less experience. And they provide practices and rituals to foster the implicit spiritual dimensions of everyday life.

43. See Wayne Teasdale's notion of interspirituality in his book, *The Mystic Heart: Discovering a Universal Spirituality in the World's Religions* (Novato: New World Library, 1999),

44. This view is powerfully expressed in Gerard Manley Hopkins' poem "In Honour of St. Alphonsus Rodriquez, Laybrother of the Society of Jesus."

45. Karl Rahner, "Concerning the Relationship Between Nature and Grace," *Theological Investigations*, vol. 1 (Baltimore: Helicon, 1961), 297–317; "Nature and Grace," *Theological Investigations*, vol. 4 (New York: Crossroad, 1982), 165–88; *Foundations of Christian Faith: An Introduction to the Idea of Christianity*, (New York: Crossroad, 1978).

46. This is true even in many religiously affiliated organizations, e.g., catholic universities.

47. Soelle, *The Silent Cry*, 57, 88–93.

48. He continues, "Like any other public institution so organized, the organized church is dependent on "the economy": it cannot survive apart from those economic practices that its truth forbids and that its vocation is to correct. If it comes to a choice between the extermination of the fowls of the air and the lilies of the field and the extermination of a building fund, the organized church will elect–indeed, has already elected–to save the building fund." Wendell Berry, What are People For? (New York: North Point Press ) 97.

Spiritualities are also susceptible to embracing the status quo and choking off the prophetic voice. Religions typically do this by becoming fundamentalistic or doctrinaire. Spiritualities today are more often tempted to do this by minimizing the social and ethical challenges involved in spirituality.

49. That is why Marie–Dominique Chenu, a pioneer in the modern effort to develop theologies of work, said that the question of the relationship be-

tween nature and grace is fundamental to the spirituality of work. Chenu, Marie–Dominique, "Work," *Sacramentum Mundi: An Encycolpedia of Theology,* vol. 6, ed. Karl Rahner (New York: Herder and Herder, 1970).

50. Including much of the "new–age" approaches.

51. Peter B. Vaill, *Spirited Leading and Learning: Process Wisdom for a New Age,* (San Francisco: Jossey–Bass), 1998.

52. Michael Skelley, "Learning Communities: A Spirituality of Work for the Information Age," *Review for Religious* 57 (1998) 454–471.

53. See Claude Whitmyer, ed., *Mindfulness and Meaningful Work: Explorations in Right Livelihood* (Berkeley: Parallax Press, 1994).

54. Thich Naht Hanh, *Peace is Every Step: The Path of Mindfulness in Everyday Life,* (New York: Bantam Books, 1992).

55. Ernest E. Larkin, "Contemplative Prayer Forms Today: Are They Contemplation?" *The Diversity of Centering Prayer,* Gustave Reininger, e.d, (New York: Continuum, 1999), p 30.

56. This is one of the areas of research connected with their "good work" project. See Howard Gardner, Mihaly Csikszentmihalyi, and William Damon, *Good Work: When Excellence and Ethics Meet* (New York: Basic Books, 2001).

57 Thomas Keating's attention and intention practice is also appropriate here. See Thomas Keating, "The Practice of Attention/Intention," *Centering Prayer in Daily Life and Ministry,* Gustave Reininger, ed., (New York: Continuum, 1998), pp. 13–19.

58. Wendell Berry, "Healing," *What are People For?* (New York: North Point Press, 1990) p. 11

59. Peter Senge, *The Fifth Discipline· The Art and Practice of Learning Organizations* (New York: Doubleday, 1990); and, Peter Senge et. al., ed., *The Fifth Discipline Fieldbook: Strategies and Tools for Building a Learning Organization* (New York: Doubleday, 1994). Senge's disciplines blend individual and collaborative practices.

60. Edgar H. Schein, *Process Consultation Revisited· Building the Helping Relationship* (Reading, MA: Addison–Wesley, 1999)

61. David Bohm, *On Dialogue,* Lee Nichol, ed., (New York: Routledge, 1996.); and, Linda Ellinor and Glenna Gerard, *Dialogue: Rediscover the Transforming Power of Conversation* (New York: John Wiley and Sons, 1998).

62. The field of interreligious dialogue has done an immense amount of research on this. See for example, Raimon Pannikar, *The Intrareligious Dialogue* (New York: Paulist Press, 1999). Kay Lindahl has a helpful set of guidelines in: Kay Lindahl, "The Art of Dialogue and Centering Prayer," *The Diversity of Centering Prayer,* Gustave Reininger, ed. (New York: Continuum, 1999), pp. 65–76.

63. Panikkar, *The Intrareligious Dialogue,* p. 32:

64. David Chappell, Buddhist Peacework, p. 208: David Chappell ("Buddhist Peace Principles," *Buddhist Peacework: Creating Cultures of Peace* David W. Chappell, ed. (Boston: Wisdom Publications, 1999), p. 208) says, "Mindfulness training was the method developed by the Buddha to develop inner peace, but regular and frequent dialogue leading to consensus was his

method for social well–being." (See his whole discussion of dialogue as social mindfulness and dialogue as soft power.)

# 11

## Why Do Good People Do Bad Things? The Challenge of Business Ethics and Corporate Leadership

### Patricia H. Werhane

Since the time of Aristotle, people have been debating why it is that good people engage in questionable behavior and even repeat their mistakes. Arthur Andersen was commonly cited as the best as well as the largest audit company in America. (e.g., Bollier, 1996, Collins and Porras, 1994) Its founder, Arthur Andersen, wrote the code for the American Institute of Certified Public Accountants, the certifying board for professional public accountants. Andersen was always profitable, it was a company that was constantly evolving to meet changing global demands, and books have been written about the ethical demeanor of its founder as setting the gold standard for behavior in the audit community. Yet just prior to the Enron scandal that brought the company down, Andersen was involved in questionable auditing practices at Waste Management, at Sunbeam, and even at the Baptist Foundation of Arizona! Why did these incidents continue to occur and repeat themselves in a company allegedly as fine as Arthur Andersen run by well–trained professionals?

In their 1994 book, *Built to Last: Successful Habits of Visionary*

*Companies*, James C. Collins and Jerry I. Porras studied the characteristics of the "visionary companies" (as identified by polling CEOs of 700 major corporations), and examined how these companies differed from other "comparison companies." Collins and Porras define a visionary company as the premier organization in their respective industry, as being widely admired by their peers, and as having a long track record of making a significant impact on the world around them. Each of the visionary companies chosen by the CEO poll has faced setbacks, and each has made mistakes. Still, the long–term financial performance of each has been remarkable. A dollar invested in a visionary company stock fund on January 1, 1926, with dividends reinvested, and making appropriate adjustments for when the companies became available on the stock market would have grown by December 31, 1990 to $6,356. That dollar invested in a general market fund would have grown to $415.

What was different about visionary companies as compared to the comparison companies? Each operates in the same market and each has relatively the same opportunities. What is critical for the visionary or successful companies, according to Collins and Porras' findings, is that a visionary company is driven by an ideology that "it lives, breathes, and expresses in all it does . . . . A visionary company almost religiously preserves its core ideology–changing it seldom, if ever."[1] (Collins and Porras, 1994: 8). Moreover,

> [c]ontrary to business school doctrine, 'maximizing shareholder wealth' or 'profit maximization' has not been the dominant driving force or primary objective through the history of the visionary companies. Visionary companies pursue a cluster of objectives, of which making money is only one–and not necessarily the primary one. Yes, they seek profits, but they are equally guided by a core ideology–core values and a sense of purpose beyond just making money. Yet, paradoxically, the visionary companies make more money than the more purely profit–driven comparison companies.[2]

Yet, despite this study and it claims that the most profitable companies are run from a values ideology and by good managers, in the last two years we have seen a plethora of bad corporate behavior. Beginning with Enron, and most recently questionable market timing and late trading by allegedly reputable mutual funds the tales of corporate misdeeds seems endless. In this chapter I shall examine some of the commonly cited reasons for these misdeeds. I shall conclude that the primary causes are not self–interest of greed but rather an inability to take ethics seriously in economic transactions, the separation of ethics from compliance, and a weak definition of corporate social responsibility. I shall end with a case that illustrates how a company might put all of these in place.

Why do misdeeds occur in allegedly legitimate businesses run by well–educated and seemingly good people? A number of reasons are commonly cited.

- First, none of us is perfect, and we all make mistakes. So in large companies with thousands of managers, companies such as WorldCom, there are bound to be errors of judgment.

- Second, it is alleged, human beings are primarily motivated by self–interest, and it is managerial or corporate preoccupation with their own interests, sometimes, even, greed, that accounts for questionable and even egregious behavior in business.

- Third, and following up, from the psychology of moral development one might conclude that at least in some instances some of these people evidence lower stages of moral development, acting primarily without much regard to the social or legal networks of relationships and in disregard to untoward consequences either to themselves or to their company.

- Fourth, each of these recent cases occurs within a complex network of professional, managerial, and legal relationships. It is then sometimes argued that corporate culture and the particular roles and role responsibilities of managers and professionals create a causal nexus that constrains what we might consider, as outsiders, morally appropriate behavior for professionals and managers, and precludes the consequential avoidance of harms.

- Finally, both on the individual and corporate level, it is sometimes argued that many companies and their managers are either unaware of the moral dimensions of their activities or are lacking skills in moral reasoning. Proper moral education could raise the level of individual and institutional moral awareness, enhance moral development, and give managers theoretical tools from moral theory with which to deal with ethical issues. If one could in fact train managers in moral reasoning and moral theory, the conclusion is that they would apply such training to their decision processes with more positive results.

Let us examine each of these in more detail.

## Human Nature and Self–Interest:

All companies are made up of people. It follows that companies, like individuals, will make moral mistakes. This seems obvious, and it is also obvious that some of us repeat our mistakes at least some of the time. What seems less clear is why and how collections of managers or professionals, when faced with issues that are similar to those they have faced in the past, and when those former issues were public incidents that received media, regulatory, and/or public attention, repeat similar mistakes, as Arthur Andersen apparently did at Waste Management, then at Sunbeam, then with the Baptist Foundation, and finally at Enron. The former Federal Reserve Chairperson, Paul Volcker, has contended that the common thread in all these scenarios is "good, old–fashioned greed."[3] In other words, Andrew Fastow, the CFO of Enron, and other managers there, and audit partners at Andersen simply acted in their own self–interest trying to accumulate as much wealth for themselves as is possible by manipulating the system. This is an interesting accusation and surely partly true.

Moreover, acting in one's own self–interests in either sense is not necessarily evil. One must be careful to distinguish not only the quality of the action itself and its object, e.g., oneself or one's company, but also the motivation, e.g., greed, avarice, well being of certain stakeholders, and what in fact that action produces. Many self–interested actions do not harm others, and even greedy ones do not necessarily do so. If, for example, it was true that some of Enron's executives wished to amass a fortune, they would not be alone in that motivation nor would they necessarily be bad people. It is only when that interest overwhelmed any sense of propriety or law that such actions became unconscionable. While we may question Ivan Boesky's alleged famous statement that "greed is good", one must nevertheless be careful when misidentifying self–interest with greed and proclaiming that self–interest is always questionable. So analyzing corporate or managerial wrongdoing or unintentional harms from the perspective of self–interest or greed does not always get us very far.

But let us suppose that personal greed was the only motivation in the cases we have cited. Even if this is so, most of these executives and managers would not get "A" in successful practices of greed. The Andersen partners have lost everything when the company went out of business. Others such as Bernard Evers of WorldCom have virtually worthless stock and he has been convicted of "willful ignorance." Andrew Fastow, the CFO of Enron, indicted on 200 counts of fraud, has been convicted for two.

## The Case for Moral Development:

Still, it is tempting to imagine that the top management at Enron gauged their moral judgments mostly by focusing on their own personal gain as the object of their self–interest, and based their actions on whether or not they would be caught. According to moral psychologists such as Lawrence Kohlberg, if that was true, these executives at Enron were operating at a low level of moral development.

From their studies one can conclude that people deal with moral issues differently, some of us more naively than others, some of us primarily from interests in ourselves, some of us depending on law and convention, and others seeking more ideal or universal principles through which to ground and evaluate moral decisions. Moreover, human relationships play central roles in morality, moral decision–making and moral evaluation. We are born into and affected by human relationships even in acts of solitude and rejection, and these relationships are part of what it is defined as being moral or immoral.

Moral development theories are descriptive of human cognitive and moral development. At least in part, they account for human moral error, and repeatability of mistakes. What theories of moral development have more difficulty explaining is why an intelligent, well–educated person such as Andrew Fastow, the CFO of Enron, even if he is at a low stage of moral development, would get so involved in his job, his company, or himself that he did not perceive that he was very likely to get caught. Alternately, Fastow may have been acting on a conventional level, responding to pressure from his past experiences and role expectations for executives at Enron. But such an explanation places Fastow in disregard to social convention and the law, again belying the expectations of that level of moral development. Fastow cleverly created perfectly legal off–book partnerships (SPEs) at Enron. But these partnerships became vehicles for unprofitable Enron ventures, and they did not meet the legal requirement of "arms length" distance from the parent company, Enron. Fastow himself convinced the Board at Enron to suspend its conflict of interest rules so that he and some of his friends could direct these partnerships, for additional compensation.[4] On any level of moral development Fastow has everything to lose by instigating and participating in the off book partnerships. Fastow himself is a religious, practicing Jew, he created a charitable foundation, and he coaches his son's little league team. The moral development literature, then, does not go far enough in accounting in each case why it is that good people and good companies repeatedly get into trouble. Similarly, in all the cases we have cited, the companies had only to lose when these situations went awry, and many executives will find themselves in jail. There is no self–interested "pay off" either in the short run or long run, nor little in the way of conventional explanation to account for these sets of behaviors.

## Role Definitions of Job Responsibilities

There are, in every incident or set of events, a number of related common causes of the incident, factors that influence managerial and corporate behavior. We shall discuss two: (1) an identification of professional responsibility with institutional or client responsibility, and (2) the identification of moral responsibility with role responsibility, any or all of which can result in the abdication of individual moral responsibility in institutional settings. While each of these factors (and there are others) are important and necessary, indeed, crucial, to explaining the occurrence of events, none is sufficient to account for moral responsibility nor is any sufficient to absolve managers and companies of moral culpability.

An important factor affecting managerial moral judgment is how managers and professionals prioritize client, corporate, and professional responsibility. The dilemma of which constituency should take precedence is well illustrated in the WorldCom case. At WorldCom, whose outside auditors were Arthur Andersen, the vice–president of internal audit, Cynthia Cooper began to question Andersen's method of financial audits. Following the mandate of WorldCom's CFO, Scott Sullivan, billions of dollars in operating expenses were being booked as capital expenses, thus allowing WorldCom to show a profit instead of a loss for 2001.[5] At least two sets of accounting professionals played key roles in this case: its outside financial auditor, Arthur Andersen, and its internal auditors, led by Cynthia Cooper. Both sets of professionals are CPAs, members of the American Institute of Certified Public Accountants (AICPA). Their code proscribes certain actions of these professionals just because they are members, and at least some of these code–proscriptions are meant to override personal inclinations and institutional or corporate demands, even for inside employee–auditors. Specifically, the AICPA code states,

> A member who knowingly makes, or permits or directs another to make, false and misleading entries in an entity's financial statements or records shall be considered to have knowingly misrepresented facts in violation of rule 102.[6]

Both Sullivan and the Andersen auditors violated their professional code in countenancing booking ordinary expenses as capital expenses. Andersen seemed to have placed the demands of its client, WorldCom as more important than its independent professional obligations.

Given these professional guidelines, it is not clear that in defending these companies, to the letter of the law, its lawyers acted within the guidelines of their profession, since it was scarcely in the best interest of shareholders. What is most troubling is that there is little evidence to suggest that either set of professionals: lawyers or auditors, considered a *possible* conflict of interest between their professional codes and what they were engaged in at any of these companies. They allowed client demands to override professional ones despite the priority of the latter.

As Barbara Toffler has argued, Arthur Andersen's corporate culture decision dynamic may have obscured clarity of individual independent judgment so that such judgments do not take place or are ineffective.[7] That the fact of the Waste Management, Sunbeam and Baptist Foundation incidents for which Andersen was reprimanded and fined by the Securities and Exchange Commission, did not seem to play a role in their Enron activities supports that contention. Andersen's auditors may have misidentified their role responsibilities, confusing the legal with the moral, conflated professional with bottom–line obligations to clients, or identified role responsibilities as purely client–related. Let us qualify what we just stated. It would be a gross exaggeration, at best, and indeed false, to say that a number of auditors at Andersen did not think for themselves as independent morally responsible individuals and merely do as they are told. Yet in every institutional setting there are some practices that do not encourage independent decision–making nor provide avenues for questioning what might be, by standards outside the institution, unacceptable activities. Sometimes, too, professionals as well as managers become so involved in their roles and what is expected of them in those roles, that their judgments become identified with what they perceive to be their role responsibilities.

We have used Andersen to dramatize two simple and common phenomena, the confusion of role responsibilities to do one's job well with the role responsibility to follow management or client orders, and second the abdication of concern with independent professional and more general moral responsibilities to those of one's role. By definition, people in every society have a number of roles that define various relationships between individuals, between individuals and institutions, and between institutions themselves. Each of us as individuals has a large number of interacting and overlapping cultural, professional, religious, and social roles, and these change. For example, one of the authors of this text is of Irish background, a mother, a child, a professor, a writer, a student, a

consultant, an employee, an employer, a Protestant, an American, a
member of the world community, an environmentalist, a liberal, a
humanist, etc. All of these adjectives describe intricate social
relationships, and some of them refer to my social roles.

We are enmeshed in a collection of overlapping social, professional,
cultural, and religious roles each of which makes moral demands. This
becomes problematic when the demands of a particular role become
confused, when these demands come into conflict with another role or
when role demands clash what we might call common morality or
society's moral rules. For example, the lawyer who protects a known
repeated murderer, the psychologist or priest who honors the
confidentiality of a criminal's confession, or the reporter who witnesses a
spouse committing a crime face role conflicts because of contradictory
demands of the profession, personal ties, and commonly held societal
moral norms. In business, the managerial pressure to be competitive,
efficient, and profitable can often conflict with demands of common
morality to go out of one's way to prevent harm or further harm as both
the Enron and Johnson & Johnson cases illustrate, albeit with different
consequences.

There is another kind of problem with role morality. Sherron
Watkins, a former manager at Enron became an inside whistle blower.
Observing what she believed to be unethical and illegal activities when
Enron booked losses to off–book partnerships, she wrote an anonymous
letter to Kenneth Lay, then CEO of Enron stating her doubts about these
activities. She saw herself as a manager with the important role of
flagging improprieties. In contradistinction, Kenneth Lay probably saw
himself as Chairman of the Board, whose first responsibility is to preserve
the reputation of Enron and its stock price, and he did not investigate
Watkins' allegations. Interestingly, too, Watkins did not blow the whistle
outside Enron, despite her accumulation of good data to support her
suspicions. She was herself first in the role as Enron manager, perhaps
placing company loyalty rather than public and shareholder interests first.[8]

There are two other interesting role phenomena. At times some of us
adapt contradictory roles simultaneously without perceiving possible
conflicts of interest. The most obvious examples are members of the US
crime syndicate who are known to be exemplary church members, good
family persons, and yet use a decision–model in business dealings that
contradicts the values of church and family. "Mafia mentality" as we
crudely label this phenomenon, is the ability to function in such
contradictory roles simultaneously. That this phenomenon is limited to
criminal activities is belied in cases such as Adelphia Cable. Adelphia
Cable was founded by John Rigas and grew from a small family company
to the sixth largest publicly traded large cable television provider. The

Rigas family was always extremely generous to their community, and even today the family is revered in the town of Coudersport Pennsylvania where the company was located. According to one newspaper columnist in Coudersport, John Rigas "is our Greek god."[9] Despite these good works, in recent years the family has borrowed and not repaid hundreds of millions of dollars from the company. The company itself has engaged in a series of accounting improprieties, and has grossly inflated the number of subscribers it has. What accounts for the disparity between the Rigas family's "good works" in the community and fraud at the corporate level? Somehow John Rigas and his sons are able to compartmentalize their ethics, dividing community social responsibilities from their commitment to shareholder interests.

Returning to the question of role morality and moral responsibility, what we may conclude from this discussion is that the identification of legal and moral responsibility, the priority of institutional or managerial demands over professional codes or just good sense, and role morality explain, at least in part, why good managers engage in questionable behavior. These explanations serve as pathological descriptions. But role morality does not explain all moral or immoral behavior nor does it offer avenues for resolving conflicts of interest or professional or legal dilemmas.

During the Enron scandal, when it appeared that things were and would go badly for the company and for Arthur Andersen, David Duncan, the Arthur Andersen Houston partner in charge of the Enron account, directed Andersen's audit managers to shred documents, an activity that is forbidden by the AICPA code of ethics if the documents in question are known to be material for further audit or investigation. Assuming one's assignment was to shred, one needed to examine one's roles and role obligations first in terms of professional standards, then in terms of the institution in question, Enron, and then in terms of the system, in this case the institution of free enterprise, AICPA code, SEC rules, etc.. At this point one might argue that business corporations are justified as socio–economic institutions if they in fact improve well–being (e.g., by providing jobs, goods, and services), or at least if they do not create additional harms, if they are good corporate citizens or at least, not bad citizens, and if they do not create a net balance of harms in their activities. Then, one would ask, does the well being of Enron and/or Arthur Andersen justify shredding material documents, documents that could prove invaluable in any investigation? Does my role as an employee of Andersen override my role as an auditor, and/or is my role as Shredder so important that it overrides the value of what it is shredding and my professional and legal obligations? Obviously, it is difficult to evaluate every action one takes in every role without becoming consumed with evaluation as a full–time activity, and there are limits to one's impartiality and disengagement. But the act of stepping back, creating a distance from institutions in which one is deeply involved is an activity that can put into perspective the relative importance of the institution and its role demands. Such steps of evaluation are crucial, I would conclude to avoid problems such as Andersen found itself embroiled in, and on the corporate level to avoid the demise of the firm.

## Training in Moral Reasoning

There is another temptation in trying to answer the questions, "Why do good people or fine institutions engage in questionable behavior," or "Why do we repeat our mistakes?" This temptation is to argue that what is missing in the cases we cite in this chapter are managerial skills in moral reasoning. Given limits of role morality and complications in arguing that managers are primarily motivated by personal gain or even greed, one is challenged with the contention that what is missing in these companies is traditional moral education. Managers at Enron, WorldCom, Adelphia Cable, and elsewhere are responsible, morally responsible for what happened at these companies. So, this argument continues, let us talk to the managers of these companies about professional and moral responsibilities through the introduction of moral theory, locate the moral culprits, and begin moral education. We might then test their stage of moral development. e.g., are they egoists, conformists, rule–followers, law–abiders, precedent setters, or philosophers, and give them workshops on moral reasoning. We should then discuss professional and institutional codes of ethics, demonstrate the limits of role responsibilities and role morality, present some ethical theories, e.g., utilitarianism, deontology, virtue theory, and some theories of justice, and engage these managers in a series of practice sessions that apply moral theories to cases studies.

The Enron and Andersen scenarios suggest, in particular, that one needs to get at a distance from the institution and its decision–making habits. A less biased perspective is crucial, because unless a manager can disengage herself from the context of a specific problem, and unless an institution can do so also, decisions are parochially imbedded such as to result in an iteration of the very kinds of activities that invite repeated moral failure. Scenarios such as accounting fraud tend to repeat themselves when one lacks a perspective on one's role, one's institutions, and its demands from the view of more general principles of morality.

Therein lies the problem. Just as auditors are bound by professional codes of ethics while questionable activities persist in these professions, so too, most of the *Fortune* 1000 companies in the United States have codes of ethics, credos, or mission statements. At least one–third of them have ethics officers and ethics programs in place.[10] Yet improprieties continue to occur in companies with a strong code of ethics and a well–developed ethics program for its managers. Enron, for example had a clear mission of Respect, Integrity, Community, and Excellence, even though, according to Enron employees the practice was "Rank and Yank,"[11] that is, make your numbers or be fired.

The difficulty is not that moral principles are wrong–headed; nor is it always the case that morality reduces to role morality. It is that sometimes there is a disconnect between theory and practice when one begins from the general, starting with moral theory or theories and then applies these theories or generalities to particular cases. In these instances one tends to divide theory from practice, or the general from the particular. The subject matter of morality is the real—particular actual cases, characters, events, situations, and dilemmas. To begin with abstract moral theory distances it from the particular in such a way as to create two realms of discourse as if they were separate. The disconnect between theory and practice is created in part because moral theory is formal or general, not contextual.

There is an attendant problem, a problem with what many call "limited rationality." It is possible within a particular institutional or theoretical context to develop limited objectivity so as to create a closed loop of decision–making. At WorldCom Scott Sullivan defended his accounting practices as in the best interest of preserving shareholder value, and he claimed that he was going to correct the expense booking errors during the next fiscal year. He was able to justify these improprieties because of his preoccupation with preserving WorldCom's reputation with profitable returns. His goals, then, appeared to be those that every manager aspires to; but the means to attain them was fraudulent. What this suggests is that what appears to be a rational perspective, while crucial to moral decision–making, may create a disconnect between what appears, *in theory* to be correct, and what, in particular fact, is so. What we are suggesting is that what seems to be a rational perspective may be mere rationalization and thus not be enough, by itself, to avoid moral disasters. The separation of ethics from commerce only exacerbates the possibility of misbehavior and perhaps even encourages it. No codes of ethics, credos, ethics officers, or ethics programs will work unless a company is committed to consistently behaving morally. And that behavior has to be exemplified in business practices, not merely in the mission statement or in the annual report.

This conclusion, while morally satisfying, leaves open the question, "Can a company engage in morally and socially responsible behavior and still be profitable?" as the Collins and Porras' study suggests. Companies have been doing so for at least a century. But that is the problem. We never hear about good companies engaged in best practices. We only hear the 'bad news' in the press. No wonder the public is concerned about the state of free enterprise! In the next section a contemporary example of one company attempting to engage in morally and socially responsible behavior will be considered. It will be argued that what is needed for such an achievement is not merely good will and a strong corporate values statement but also a great deal in the way of moral imagination and a systems approach to corporate thinking.

## Moral Imagination, Systems Thinking and Moral Change: ExxonMobil in Chad and Cameroon

ExxonMobil, in partnership with ChevronTexaco and Petronas (a Malaysian company), considered investing $3.5 billion in oil drilling in Chad and in building a 600–mile pipeline through Cameroon. The project would generate over a billion barrels of oil, $5.7 billion in revenues for ExxonMobil, $2 billion in revenues for Chad and $500 million for Cameroon over the 25 year projected drilling period. The project would be a challenging one and has attracted a great deal of world attention.

Chad and Cameroon are two of the poorest countries in the world. Per capita income in each country is less than $1./day. As a comparison, ExxonMobil's 2001 revenues were $190 Billion; Chad's GDP was 1.4 billion According to Transparency International, Chad and Cameroon are also two countries with very poor records for corruption in the world, and they repeatedly come out near the bottom of TI's corruption list it publishes every year.[12] The pipeline would go through Cameroon's rain forest, an ecologically fragile but important environmental outpost in Africa. Several tribes of Pygmies and Bantu, whose lifestyle depends on forest products, inhabit that forest.

Originally the Chad–Cameroon project was to be a joint venture between Shell, TotalFinaElf and ExxonMobil. However Shell and FinaElf pulled out. According to sources close to these companies, Shell feared another Ogoniland, its often–sabotaged oil fields in southeast Nigeria. Ogoniland proved to be Shell's nemesis for environmental, social, cultural and political reasons. This project had generated years of allegedly environmental and social degradation and very bad press for Shell.[13]

Shell, like many oil companies drilling in remote areas or in less developed countries, had approached the Ogoniland project using their standard operating procedures for oil drilling, an approach, as Shell now admits that was a simple one, too simple. This is an over exaggeration, but sometimes in the past the oil drilling philosophy was to apply almost identical drilling processes in every site all around the world. One found prospects for oil, got government permission to drill, brought in drilling equipment and foreign drilling experts, hired a few local people for more menial temporary jobs, drilled, laid pipeline, pumped out oil, and paid royalties to the government in question. More enlightened companies took into account the local communities that were affected by the drilling (building a school or hospital), and of late the pipes themselves have been improved to minimize spills, which, even under the best conditions account for 2–3% loss of oil every year at every site. Still, at least according to protesters living in Ogoniland, local conditions, culture, governmental structures or the lack thereof, (except when sensitive payments were required) environmental issues, and the long–term effects of these projects on the people, the area, and the country were not always taken into account in a serious way from the perspective of those living in oil drilling areas.

ExxonMobil is a new company formed by the merger of Exxon and Merger, each of which having been in the oil business for a very long time. Each had been economically successful in drilling in less developed countries in the past, and each had developed well–proven formulae for drilling and extracting oil. Why should the company change its modus operandi? However, the history of Shell in Ogoniland, Mobil's alleged payoffs to government officials in Kazakhstan, and Exxon's Valdez disaster were reason enough for a company to re-think its approach to new drilling in less developed countries with reputations and environmental challenges of the ilk of Chad and Cameroon.

The Chad/Cameroon project presented a challenge, not to their expertise at drilling, but to thinking about how to expedite this venture while avoiding problems of previous explorations. To do this would require that ExxonMobil rethink their traditional exploration models and that they revise their "standard operating procedures" or traditional mental models for oil exploration that have worked well in developed countries to be applicable in places such as Chad and Cameroon.

Werhane defines moral imagination as

> the ability in particular circumstances to discover and evaluate possibilities not merely determined by that circumstance, or limited by its operative mental models, or merely framed by a set of rules or rule–governed concerns.[14]

The notion of moral imagination is by and large a facilitating reasoning process that helps us out of a particular framing box, leading us to refocus our attention, critique, revise, and reconstruct other operative mental models, and to develop more creative normative perspectives. Moral imagination begins with the particular–a particular person, an event, a situation, a dilemma, or a conflict. It requires the ability to disengage–to step back from the situation and take another perspective, or at least, be able to begin a critical evaluation of the situation and its operative mental models. Thus part of being morally imaginative is to perceive the ethical dimensions of a managerial or corporate situation and its operative mindsets, activities that are only possible when one disengages or steps back from the situation. Of course, if it is true that we deal with the world only through socially constructed mind sets, no one can ever disengage themselves completely or take a "view from nowhere." Our revisions, critiques, and evaluations are still context driven by history, circumstances, culture, education, and personal framing choices. However, just as children we can play act, so too we can devise ways to disengage and step back to examine ourselves and our projects, from a somewhat disinterested or distanced perspective.

Unlike other forms of imagination, moral imagination deals not with fantasies, but with possibilities that if not practical, are at least theoretically viable and actualizable. Further, because we are talking here of *moral* imagination, these possibilities have a normative or prescriptive character; they concern what one ought to do, with right and wrong, with virtue, with positive or negative outcomes, or with what common morality calls "good" or "evil." That is, these judgments involve principle based reasoning.

Moral imagination involves not only perceiving ethical nuances, disengagement from the situation at hand, and fantasizing creatively about fresh opportunities or new possibilities from a normative perspective. It is not mere "second guessing." It also should entail work at developing fresh solutions based on revised or even different mental models. Finally being morally imaginative requires that one evaluates new possibilities or solutions form a normative perspective, judging not only the possibilities but also the mindsets in which such possibilities are operative.

In summary, being morally imaginative includes:

- Self–reflection about oneself and one's situation, perhaps taking the point of view of another.
- Disengaging from and becoming aware of one's situation, understanding the mental model or script dominating that situation, and envisioning possible moral conflicts or dilemmas

that might arise in that context or as outcomes of the dominating scheme.

- Moral imagination entails the ability to imagine reformulated or even new possibilities. These possibilities include those that are not merely context–dependent and that might involve another set of mental models, within the range possible given one's situation.

Moral imagination requires that one evaluate from a moral point of view both the original context and its dominating mental models, and the alternatives one has envisioned. [15]

ExxonMobil's projected oil exploration in Chad and Cameroon involved a complex network of relationships imbedded in a complex set of systems and subsystems, including the cultures of two countries and their diverse indigenous populations, environmental issues, financing, pressures from nongovernment organizations (NGOs), and it will turn out, the World Bank. To deal with ethical issues in these and other cases either from an individual or even from an organizational perspective, may oversimplify what is really at issue and thus ignore a number of important elements. To evaluate these cases and to develop rich decision making skills may require what the organizational and scientific literature call "systems thinking" or a systems approach.

What do we mean by "systems thinking" or a "systems approach?" For our purposes systems thinking presupposes that most of our thinking, experiencing, practices and institutions are interrelated and interconnected. Almost everything we can experience or think about is in a network of interrelationships such that each element of a particular set of interrelationships affects the other components of that set and the system itself. Almost no phenomenon can be studied in isolation from all relationships with at least some other phenomenon.

A systems approach that engaged moral imagination should include the following: Concentration on the network of relationships and patterns of interaction, rather than on individual components of particular relationships, Spelling out the networks of relationships from different perspectives

- A multi–perspective analysis
- Understanding the various perspectives of the manager, the citizen, the firm, community, state, law, tradition, background institutions, history, and other networks of relationships.
- Taking an evaluative perspective, asking, What values are at stake? Which take priority, or should take priority?

- Becoming pro–active both within the system and in initiating structural change.

In this process one should describe the system and its networks of interrelationships to grasp the interconnected of the system. One should investigate what is not included in the system (its boundaries and boundary–creating activities) and what mindsets are predominant, asking, who are the stakeholders (individuals, associations, organizations, networks, agencies) and what are the core values of each set of stakeholders. Additionally one needs to outline the core values of the system and speculate as to what these *should* be. Finally one should think about whether and which organizations or individuals within the system might be capable and willing to risk challenging bits of the system and carry out change. Thus moral imagination and systems thinking encourage networked systems analyses that are engaged and critical, creative and evaluative, and values grounded and encourage constructive change within a network of relationships.

Given the character of Chad and Cameroon overridden with poverty, corruption, environmental challenges, fragile indigenous cultures and the past checkered history of oil exploration in less developed regions, ExxonMobil made the decision to experiment with a new, more systemic approach to this oil exploration project What that company has done is to create a new model for oil exploration based on an alliance model.

ExxonMobil has formed a partnership with the Chad and Cameroon governments, the World Bank and a number of NGOs. The World Bank's interest is in improving the well–being of the people in Chad and Cameroon. The rationale for considering and then approving the project was that, according to the World Bank,

> [t]his project could transform the economy of Chad . . . . By 2004, the pipeline would increase Government revenues by 45–50% per year and allow it to use those resources for important investments ink health, education, environment, infrastructure, and rural development, necessary to reduce poverty.[16]

The World Bank has set up a series of provisos to ensure that there is sound fiscal management of the revenues received by Chad and Cameroon, it has set up strict environmental and social policies, and has consulted with a number of NGOs involved in the project.

According to a World Bank report, by the middle of 2002 the project employed over 11,000 workers, of whom at least 85% are from Chad or Cameroon. Of these local workers, over 3700 have received high–skills training in construction, electrical and mechanical trades, and 5% of the local workers have supervisory positions. In addition, local businesses have also benefited from the project to a total of almost $100 million. Through the Bank micro lending projects have been developed accompanied with fiscal and technical training. The aim is to establish permanent micro lending banks.[17]

The World Bank in partnership with ExxonMobil have created new schools, and health clinics, provided vaccines against tuberculosis and medical staff to monitor the applications, distributed thousands of mosquito nets for protection against malaria, and provided farm implements and seeds to develop indigenous agriculture,

The NGOs involved have goals to improve the economy of Chad and Cameroon, as well as the aim to protect indigenous traditions and the environment. Before approving this venture the World Bank conducted an extensive series of environmental studies to determine if this project could be done without drastic environmental degradation. It was concluded that with careful drilling and care to the surrounding landscape, and with safety measures that would prevent illicit tapping into the pipeline, the project was environmentally safe. The Chad and Cameroon governments, in turn, pledged to use the profits they received from the venture to improve the standard of living of their citizens.

ExxonMobil has hired a former Prime Minister of Chad to coordinate the project and an anthropologist, Ellen Brown, who was in Chad in the Peace Corps some years ago. Under her and other NGO supervision ExxonMobil is building schools, funding clinics, digging wells, fielding AIDs education units and providing anti–malarial mosquito nets. In some areas where sacred trees are in the way, villagers must give permission to remove the trees and Brown orchestrates chicken sacrifices to preserve the spirit of the trees. [Brown is referred to as Madam Sacrifice by the Chadians.][18]

**The Perspective of the Critics:** The project is not without its problems and critics. Despite good intentions, environmental hazards are inescapable. In any oil drilling project, even with the strictest safety measures, there will be oil spills. According to World Bank estimates, annual spill rates will be between 1 and 4%. There will be increased greenhouse gas emissions, although the level of these has not been accurately calculated. There will also be forestry and bush product losses (e.g., nuts, herbs, and fruit) all of which are to be compensated.

In addition, large projects such as these usually spawn an increase in HIV infections and other health risks. Agricultural and livestock losses for displaced farms will occur, although ExxonMobil has guaranteed compensation and/or relocation.

According to the Cameroon Environmental Defense (CED) report, there are a number of almost insurmountable negative aspects of this project. First, as ExxonMobil, the World Bank, and NGOs working in the region are well aware, there exists no sound rule of law in either country so that any contracts or promises are not backed with a well-developed legal system to enforce those agreements. This is not only problematic in terms of agreements between the drillers and the government, but there is no legal guarantee that monies given to these governments will actually be spent on citizen welfare. Indeed, despite World Bank protests, the President of Chad bought arms with his first payment of oil revenue. (He has promised not to do this in the future, but there is no legal framework by which to hold him accountable.[19]

The CED also questions whether adequate compensation is being provided for land use and displacement of people. There have been some intertribal wars between Pygmies and Bantus concerning whose land is actually being compensated. This sort of quarrel upsets the delicate balance between these tribes, and again, there are no enforcement mechanisms to remedy any injustices of thefts. So there are questions concerning the protection of rights and cultural values of indigenous peoples in this region. Even *Fortune* reports that not every citizen will be satisfied with the company's efforts. Even as they begin drilling, local people are complaining that they are not getting jobs, and worries about Pygmy peoples (the Baka and Bakola tribes) rights abound.[20]

The CED and the Rainforest Action Network question the environmental viability of the project, arguing that issues of water pollution and rain forest protections have not been adequately addressed so that part of the ecosystem may be negatively impacted. Many of the local tribes depend on the forest for food, and changing this ecostructure may not be prodigious to preserving these traditional food supplies.

> The Chad/Cameroon project is not the help we asked for or needed. In the absence of the rule of law and respect for human rights [in both countries] and the environment, financing of large–scale development is destroying the environment and us." —Archbishop Desmond Tutu[21]

**The Required Last Step:** The moral risk involved in this project cannot be eliminated. But it can be reduced. When a company does an analysis of its responsibilities in a particular project, it tends to put itself at the center and look at the situation from its corporate point of view, from its mental model as to how the various stakeholders will be affected and how their interests should be balanced. To mitigate the dangers of a biased point of view, one might try to see the world from the perspective of one of the affected stakeholders as if they were conducting the stakeholder analysis. For example, what decisions would be made if the Bakola Pygmy Tribe was doing the stakeholder analysis and that tribe was asking how to balance the interests of its other stakeholders with the interests of ExxonMobil. Quite possibly a different set of decisions would result. Of course even this reordering of priorities will not eliminate the moral risk of drilling in Chad and piping oil through Cameroon. Exxon Mobil still faces the risk of creating more harm than good in these two countries. Because it is dealing with multiple stakeholders in a situation where there are no enforceable legal mechanisms, the company and the World Bank cannot control or mitigate all these risks, although of course ExxonMobil will profit extensively from this very rich oil source, and expand the oil supply for its consumers. We would classify this as moral risk since it is hard to calculate, in advance, whether the good of producing oil will balance the harms, and indeed, that may never be determined with certainty. However, not developing this oil will exclude the chances for prosperity in Chad or in Cameroon. If ExxonMobil continues with its alliance model it will have attempted to apply a morally imaginative systems approach that is novel in the oil business.

Finally, the project is expected to deliver to markets for consumption 800–1,000 million barrels [of oil] over the 28–year production life of the fields.
However, given existing consumption levels, this supply of oil is expected to have a minimal impact, if any, on the global level of oil consumption.[22] So we still need to ask,

- Would $3.7 billion (the investment in Chad/Cameroon) be better spent on new energy exploration?
- Are the trade–off losses to Chad and Cameroon balanced by this long–term investment?
- What IS Exxon/Mobil's corporate moral responsibility in this case?In the end ExxonMobil might have even concluded that $3.7 billion in solar energy exploration would be a better long–term bet, all things considered.

## Conclusion

We have before us, then, a number of factors that contribute to moral mistakes: self–interested greed and retarded moral development may be contributing phenomena. A confusion of legal and moral demands, possible conflicts of interest between professional and institutional commitments, conflicts of role responsibilities, and/or the identification of moral responsibility with role responsibility may lead to the subsequent abdication of individual moral responsibility to institutional or client demands. Analyses such as these are helpful in pinpointing weaknesses in individual, managerial, and corporate decision–making. But such analyses do not successfully attack the problem of repeated moral errors.

Moral imagination coupled with systems thinking is essential if we are to understand, evaluate, and institute structural, organization, and individual change. The importance of systems thinking and systems analysis, and this is the final point, reminds us no organization, system or subsystem is or need be thought of, as a closed static system. Systems thinking is necessary when one tries to apply the stakeholder approach to management ethics and seeks to avoid moral mistakes. Until we comprehend the complexity of systemic interrelationships we cannot successfully evaluate the issues in question and begin to make changes that are critical if we are to make moral progress.

## Notes

1 Collins, James and Porras, Jerry. *Built to Last.* New York: Harper-Collins, 1994. p. 8.

2. *Ibid.* p. 8.

3 Bacon, Kenneth H. and Salwen, Kevin G., "Summer of Financial Scandals Raises Questions about the Ability of Regulators to Police Markets." *Wall Street Journal,* August 28, 1991, p. A 10.

4 Fastow admitted that he made over $45 million on the partnerships between 1999 and 2001. "Special Report: Corporate America's Woes, Continued–Enron One Year On." *The Economist.* November 30, 2002, pp. 59–61.

5 www.money.cnn.com/2002/07/19/news/worldcom_bankruptcy/

6 American Institute of Certified Public Accountants, Code of Ethics, section 102.01.

7 Toffler, Barbara and Reingold, Jennifer, *Final Accounting.* New York: Broadway Books, 2003.

8 Swartz, Mimi and Watkins, Sherron. *Power Failure.* New York: Doubleday, 2003.

9 Leonard, Devin, Harrington, Ann, Burke, Doris, Rigas, Michael, Rigas, Tim, and Cohen, Oren. "The Adelphia Story." *Fortune* August 12, 2002, pp. 136–143.

10 www.eoa.org [Ethics Officers Association]

11 From McLean, Bethany and Elkind, Peter, *The Smartest Guys in the Room.* New York: Penguin and Fortune [Time}, 2003.

12 www.transparency.org/pressreleases 2005

13.Shell has drilled for oil in Nigeria since 1937, and until recently was the largest oil operation in that country. In the early 1990's its joint venture with Elf and Agip produced over 900,000 barrels of oil a day, most from a region inhabited primarily by the ethnic group, the Ogoni. At the same time, between 1982 and 1992 approximately 1.6 million gallons of oil were spilled in the Nigerian oil fields, some precipitated by dissident Ogoni unhappy with the oil ventures, the environmental degradation, and the lack of improved social impact the drilling had on the local villages and communities. Although Shell claimed to have invested over $100 million on environmental projects in Nigeria, there is little to show for this investment. Finally, when Shell did not try to intervene or protest the government's assassination of a number of prominent dissidents including Ken Sari–Wiwa, worldwide media attacked Shell for what was perceived to be complicity in these deaths. Newberry, William E. and Gladwin, Thomas L. "Shell and Nigerian Oil." In *Ethical Issues in Business.* 7th edition. Upper Saddle River NJ: Prentice–Hall, 2002. pp 522–40) Despite $300 billion earned from oil since 1975, Nigeria's per capital income has dropped 23% in that time period. In 1993, Shell shut down its operations in Ogoniland, but it still drills for oil and gas in other parts of Nigeria. Shell it has dramatically revised its Code of Ethics, it has invested at least $100 million in cleaning up Ogoniland, and has pledged over a ½ billion dollars in exploring alternate energy sources. (www.shell.com. 2003)

14 Werhane, Patricia. *Moral Imagination and Management Decision–Making.* New York, Oxford University Press, 1999. p. 93.

15 Werhane, 1999.

16 www.worldbank.org/afr/ccproj/project/pro_overview.htm

17 www.worldbank.org/afr/ccproj/project/pro_overview.htm

18 Useem, Jerry. "Exxon's African Adventure. *Fortune.* April 15, 2002. pp. 102–113.

19 Useem, 2002 and Cameroon Environmental Defense, *The Chad–Cameroon Oil and Pipeline Project: A Call for Accountability.* New York: Association Tchadienen pour la Promotion et la Défense des Droits de l'Homme, Chad: Centre Pour l'Environnement et le Développement.

20 Useem, 2002, p. 114.

21 www.environmentaldefense.org/documents/728 Chad Cameroon pipeline

22 www.worldbank.org/afr/ccproj/project/pro_overview.htm

## 12

# "It's Business; We're Soldiers" *The Sopranos*, Liberal Business Ethics, and this American Thing of Ours

## H. Peter Steeves

The twisted and demented psychos who kill people for pleasure. The cannibals, the degenerate bastards that molest and torture little kids. They kill babies. The Hitlers, the Pol Pots. Those are the evil fucks that deserve to die . . . . We're soldiers. Soldiers don't go to hell. It's war. Soldiers, they kill other soldiers. We're in a situation where everybody involved knows the stakes. And if you're gonna accept those stakes . . . . You gotta do certain things. It's business; we're soldiers. We follow codes . . . . [L]et me tell you something. When America opened the floodgates and let all us Italians in, what do you think they were doing it for? Because they were trying to save us from poverty? No, they did it because they needed us. They needed us to build their cities and dig their subways and to make them richer. The Carnegies and the Rockefellers, they needed worker bees and there we were. But some of us didn't want to swarm around their hive and lose who we were. We wanted to stay Italian and preserve the things that meant something to us: honor and family and loyalty.

And some of us wanted a piece of the action. We weren't educated like the Americans, but we had the balls to take what we wanted. Those other fucks, those other . . . . The J. P. Morgans? They were crooks and killers too, but that was a business, right? The American way.

                              –Tony Soprano, "From Where to Eternity"

## Envelopes of Cash

I'm not sure how many connected men I've met in my life. At least three. Likely more. The number seems high to me as I've lived most of my life in the quiet American Midwest–not a hot–bed of *Cosa Nostra* activity by most regards. And yet, I have . . . stories.

When I was just out of my first year of college I was in search of a summer job and thus came to tutor the only son of a rich Italian businessman in a town in Illinois. The boy was attending summer High School and it was my job to see he passed every class, especially the math and science courses, his greatest challenges. We worked for hours each day (it was a struggle; he bore more than a passing resemblance to A. J. Soprano in body as well as mind); and I would reward myself most nights by accepting the hospitality of the family, especially happy to take home a Tupperware container of the mother's manicotti or the grandmother's freshly made and frozen *cassatta siciliana*–exotic foods to my Ohio–born, Hamburger Helper–acquainted, Velveeta–accustomed palate.

In my memories, twisted and interpreted as memories necessarily are, the grandmother was a lovely stereotype. Not a scheming Livia Soprano, but a Hollywood creation nonetheless: the happy Italian *nonna* committed to her family, talking about "the Old Country" with a tear in her eye, offering food as the solution to all of life's problems. She had been born in Italy and moved to the U.S. as a young girl; and after more than seventy years in this county she still seemed "Italian" to me in a way that was somehow deeper than her son.

Is thinking in such a stereotype itself somehow immoral? Was I wrong to think this way, am I wrong to remember this way? Was I wrong to care so much for this woman and her family, knowing–no, not quite *knowing*–but "knowing" how it was that the bills were paid? Where is the beginning and the end of my own complicity?

Have another plate of *mani–got* for now, my "adopted" grandmother would say. Don't worry. You'll figure it all out tomorrow.

The father's business had something to do with construction, though it was impossible for me to imagine him ever having a speck of dirt on his clothes. The materials from which his suits were made seemed flowing and smooth, like running wine. No jogging suits and see–through socks in his closets. He seemed to me such a good and kind man as well. He clearly loved his family. He slapped me on the back each day with a smile, thanked me for doing a commendable job with his son, treated me with respect and good humor, and paid me every Friday. In the middle of trying to get out of a geometry lesson one particularly sunny morning, his son once spoke of the family's boat out on the lake, eventually making a passing reference to his father's work and letting the word "construction" hang in the air with an ironic tone. But it's not as if I accidentally came across $50,000 in Kruger-rands and a .45 automatic while hunting for a pencil sharpener in the house. And yet . . . .

At the end of the summer, "A.J." passed all of his classes to the delight and surprise of his parents (and his tutor), and everyone insisted that I come to the house one last time that final Labor Day weekend as part of the family, part of the party, part of the collective celebration of the ending season and the accomplishments of the previous months.

It was an unseasonably cool September. We ate sausage cooked outside with peppers and onions grown in the family garden. We played horseshoes and bocci in the finely kept lawn beside the tennis court which I had never seen being used, and came back to sit close to the grill in the early evening, the imported handmade tiles beneath us cool and red, shadows of their surface imperfections appearing and disappearing in the blue flame light. I was in a different world, a world I was soon leaving, and I took time to take it all in as such. At the end of the day the father called me into the house, into the kitchen, and thanked me for the miracle I had worked with his son. I assured him that the boy had truly worked hard, but he wouldn't hear it. He said that he wanted to give me a bonus for having done such a fine job. I refused, sincerely needing the money but just as sincerely not wanting to take anything away from his son's accomplishment or to take a greater payment than that on which we had agreed. I had my honor as well. He definitely wouldn't hear it. With a warm smile that should have–but somehow did not–clash with his serious eyes and the deter-mined force with which he took my hand and made the decision for me, he placed an envelope of cash against my open palm then pushed my hand up to my body toward my heart before letting go and walking away. I didn't look in the envelope but folded it and stuffed it into my pocket, playing my part. I would not see him again.

Later that evening the grandmother kissed me on the cheek and wrapped up three sausages in aluminum foil for me. The cream flood-lights that shone up the sides of the house were turned on, the lightning bugs scattered out of the garden, and I left for home.

# Tony and the B of A

Tony Soprano feels disappointed that he came in at the end of *this thing of ours*. "The best," he says with great remorse and in the grips of depression, "is over" ["The Sopranos" (Pilot)]. Yet regardless of the fact that the Mafia seems to have lost the code of honor that once–at least so goes the collective myth–held it together, Tony's identity, his sense of self, his set of values, are direct creations of the community in which he finds himself today. Against the tide of modern life with its constant undertow of Liberal metaphysics and relativistic ethics, Tony treads purely communitarian waters: he *is* his roles and relationships– father, husband, lover, Don, friend, and executioner; the point of over- lap of the many narrative threads that converge in modern Jersey to constitute this man. And yet he is in a state of crisis. It is a crisis that can, in part, be traced to the tension between Liberalism and communi- tarianism in the Western world. Liberalism, finding its roots in the seventeenth century thought of Descartes and Hobbes maintains the radical isolation of the individual: we are each radically distinct mo- nads, separate, equal, and armed with rights to keep each other at bay. Versions of this sort of thinking essentially found our society: capital- ism, contemporary democracy, the U.S. Bill of Rights, our justice sys- tem, our educational institutions, our cultural myths all take this indi- vidualism–this view of what it is to be a self–as fundamental. To Liberal eyes, even, the Mob boss comes close to a Hobbesian Sover- eign, with the *Omertá* oath which one swears upon entering the Mob akin to signing a social contract. The Mafia requires a Sovereign not a community in charge, goes the thinking–or as Sylvio Dante remarks: "We need a supreme commander at the top, not the fucking Dave Clark Five" ["Meadowlands"].

And yet, the Mafia is all about community, being–together, defin- ing one's self in terms of one's relationship to the group. It is, at its very core, more communitarian than Liberal. Communitarianism re- jects the assumption that all we can know, count on, or take to be fun- damental in our politics, metaphysics, and ethics is the isolated individ- ual. Instead, to be is to be a member of a group. We are born into–and throughout our life find ourselves caught up in–roles and relationships that, at a fundamental level, define who we are. The self is thus defined in terms of its relation to Others. First and foremost, one is someone's son or daughter, brother or sister, a member of this culture or that. We might then make decisions to go one direction or another, but it is al- ways from a starting point over which we have no choice and by means of which we found our core identity. And even after we leave this ini- tial position, we continue to be communally defined. The rejection of

Liberalism is not the rejection of free will, but it is the acknowledgment that one's will is always tied to others' and thus is not radically individual. When his psychiatrist, Dr. Melfi, for instance, ushers in a discussion of free will with Tony, he rejects any radically individual formulation of it as a cause for his "chosen" line of work. "How come I'm not making pots in Peru?" he responds. "You're born to this shit" ["Down Neck"].

Saying one is born to a line of work and a way of life seems to be a way of sidestepping ethics–not just business ethics, but ethics in general. It seems to be saying that one has no choice. But *choice* is a Liberal value–the ultimate individual noninterference right for the ultimate radically self–creating individual. Choice is thus at the forefront of Liberal business ethics: did you choose the correct thing in releasing that product, blowing that whistle, hiring that person, cooking those books? Business ethics in America faces crises, though, under this Liberal model. Are corporations, for instance, individuals? Can they choose? Can they be held accountable? As a culture, we have yet to come to terms with such questions, extending first amendment rights but not fifth amendment rights to corporations.

It is easy to offer a Liberal critique of the Mob's way of doing business: individual rights of noninterference are being violated; universal human rights (based on a belief in a universal human nature) are being rejected; Tony and his crew don't play by the appropriate Liberal rules. But if we accept a communitarian metaphysic of the self and thus an ethic as well, mustn't we admit that this is the life those in this community know, this is the set of traditions they hold in esteem? If one's identity is constructed within the Mafia business community, what right does a non–made man have to come in and say it is a bad identity, a pathological community, an immoral moral code?

In "From Where to Eternity," Tony gives a defense similar to this when Dr. Melfi asks a rare judgmental leading question about whether Tony thinks his violent ways will send him to hell. Tony is clear: hell is not for him; hell is reserved for

> the twisted and demented psychos who kill people for pleasure. The cannibals, the degenerate bastards that molest and torture little kids. They kill babies. The Hitlers, the Pol Pots. Those are the evil fucks that deserve to die . . . . We're soldiers. Soldiers don't go to hell. It's war. Soldiers, they kill other soldiers. We're in a situation where everybody involved knows the stakes. And if you're gonna accept those stakes . . . . You gotta do certain things. It's business; we're soldiers. We follow codes . . . . [L]et me tell you something. When America opened the floodgates and let all us Italians in, what do you think they were doing it for? Because they were trying to save us

from poverty? No, they did it because they needed us. They needed us to build their cities and dig their subways and to make them richer. The Carnegies and the Rockefellers, they needed worker bees and there we were. But some of us didn't want to swarm around their hive and lose who we were. We wanted to stay Italian and preserve the things that meant something to us: honor and family and loyalty. And some of us wanted a piece of the action. We weren't educated like the Americans, but we had the balls to take what we wanted. Those other fucks, those other . . . . The J. P. Morgans? They were crooks and killers too, but that was a business, right? The American way.

Let's first admit that this "apology" makes some sense–as hard as that is to face. Tony is actually making a nuanced, thoughtful, philosophic response to Dr. Melfi's simple black–and–white take on the Mafia. The argument is that only those who enjoy violence (as an end in itself?) are evil, and that in a community where everyone knows the standards and codes, acts of violence are not necessarily immoral–the implication being that Tony does not take pleasure in violence but merely accepts it as part of his communal code, knowing he must dish it out and may someday have to take it. Furthermore, if outsiders critique the Mob's code, they should first look to their own history and their own traditions–the implication being even clearer that the American Mafia was a response to the subjugation of Italian immigrants, and that the "American Way" has its own violence hidden just beneath the surface. Indeed, in some ways one could extend Tony's line of thinking and suggest that there is something inherently morally superior to the Mafia as opposed to the standard "American Way" of business in that Mafia violence is not hidden, its codes are out in the open to all who are involved, there is no attempt to "pretty it up."

Let us be clear. Tony lends money to people. If they don't pay, he hurts them. He beats them, runs them over with a car, takes over their business and runs it into the ground, sends Furio to shoot them in the leg, etc. How is this unlike the Bank of America?[1] The B of A loans money to people. If they don't pay, the bank hurts them. In the meantime, Bank of America uses that money to invest in all sorts of nastiness that causes bodily harm to real people (e.g., Vietnam received that much more napalming thanks to the Bank of America). If someone doesn't repay the B of A after a couple of "friendly" warnings, the bank might take over that person's business, or take the person to court and force him into bankruptcy. When the bank comes to foreclose on the house, we do not call this violence. It is part of the system, a faceless corporation merely doing what it is legally entitled to do to someone who has not paid on his or her loan as promised. That this person might be put out on the street, that his or her family might then be hungry and homeless or even dying, none of this matters or counts as violence. In America, if your business fails or your pony doesn't place or whatever your story for running out of money to make good on your debts happens to be, that's simply an instance of The Invisible Hand: you can't compete, you lose. Yet surely as much as the hand is invisible, it is bloody as well–and all the perfumes in Arabia, all the scrubbing with Lava and Clorox over a bathtub, will not render it clean.

The Liberal sees the body as the vessel for the individual and thus associates bodily violence with the most threatening type of violence. Thinking that the self is solitary and unitary, the skin barrier fools the Liberal into thinking that the body is sacred, the boundary of the individual, that which marks the difference between me and you. To do bodily violence, then, is to threaten the sanctity of the individual. One can scream at a protester all one wants (that's a right to free speech), but don't lay a hand on him. The communitarian realizes that there is nothing special about personal body violence. There are other forms of violence as well: to communities, to families, to a way of life. The communitarian realizes that there is nothing "real" about the skin barrier. Flesh is communal, bodies are socially constructed, we are all in this together. To call beating a man for not repaying a loan a form of violence, but to refuse to call foreclosing on a man for not repaying a loan the same is merely a Liberal prejudice. Both are violations, painful disruptions, castigations by those with power for failure to make good on a promise. How can we condemn one and celebrate the other? Furthermore, Tony may have whacked Matt Bevilaqua for having tried to kill Christopher, but if the State had caught up to Matt first, they would have done the same–only after a supposedly straightforward and fair trial, in a nice clean sterile environment, with public approved gas or electricity or chemical injections, all so that the death could be orderly and peaceful and just and acceptable and nice. Who's scamming who?

The Mafia code suggests there be no "collateral damage," that only those within the community who know the stakes can be harmed. The violence is thus supposedly, though not always, *controlled*–not all violence is accepted–and this seems to be based on a social construction of different categories of players: some within the business and others outside. Even within the ranks, everyone knows you cannot lay a hand on a made man without permission from the top Boss–a rule Tony forgets when he roughs up Ralphie after Tracee is murdered and later kills Ralphie after Pie–O–My is murdered. Still, such moments aside, there is indeed allowable, sanctioned violence within the Mob community, violence as a legitimate way to operate a business. Must we be silent when we are asked if whacking a guy is *generally* wrong as a community business tradition?

It's not that each community has standards and that there is no way to critique one in favor of another. It's not that communitarianism must be a form of relativism. Hopefully this much is clear. There are universal truths according to the communitarian—universal truths about how identity is constructed, how we are always intertwined with Others and our Goods are intertwined as well, how we should not treat Others as if they were something they are not, etc. None of this is relative. But the problem with thinking that life is sacred and murder is wrong or—following Levinas—the face universally commands us not to kill, is that "life" and "murder" and even "the face" can be understood and constituted quite differently in different communities. Some constructions can be critiqued if they go phenomenologically wrong, but as general place—holders for the ultimate moral commands, they don't do much work. Something more fundamental must be decided, something that tells us how these terms came to be used the way they are being used and if those uses are *right*. In our own society—the "American Way"—we use set definitions that could have been otherwise.

To put the problem another way, perhaps we could argue that the immorality of Ralphie killing Tracee (the stripper carrying his baby) centered on phenomenologically taking her to be less than a real person, less than an Other in the community. But when Tony is faced with killing Febby Petrulio, the government witness rat he encounters while visiting colleges with Meadow, would he not be taking Petrulio as somehow less than a real person, less than a true Other in the community, if he decided that Petrulio should *not* be killed? The guy took an oath. He confirmed his membership in a community in which he agreed to be killed should he ever betray his friends and business partners. If Tony did not follow through, would he not then be constituting Petrulio as less—than—an—Other, as less than a thoughtful and willing person? Petrulio must die—given the moral code to which he agreed long ago. And Tony must play his role—in order to keep up his end of the code as well. It is a strange problem for Mafia—business—ethics: at first glance it might seem a sort of anti—whistleblowing; but this would be applying Liberal categories to an illiberal tradition. The categories are all different here, the rules never the same.

But let's put aside for the moment the larger question of generally critiquing Mafia business and instead admit that many of the apparently terrible things Tony does in the course of running his business are things in which we, as an audience, take pleasure. This is not only an aesthetics question, then, but a moral one. Is it merely that we wish we could run our business this way, living above the law and only by our own codes as Tony does? I don't think so. Al Swearenger, from HBO's "Deadwood," is an interesting character who runs his Old West town making the rules as he goes; but he is much harder to identify with, much less sympathetic, than Tony Soprano. Rather, we revel in Tony's violence, I think, because it is so often a symbolic attack on the institutions of Liberalism–institutions we know, we feel, are killing us, our inherently violent to our true selves. Let me, in conclusion, try to make this claim clear.

### To Kill a Rat

Friendship is most likely the glue that keeps all communities functioning. This is a truth that goes all the way back to Aristotle, a man who knew that one can only have a limited number of friends and that a community has an upper size limit beyond which it will not function justly (for lack of real face–to–face relations and thus true community). Friendship appears in many different forms and has multiple cultural incarnations, but one way or another, without this close bonding, face–to–face connection, and the true sharing of a life in common, we could not be human. Liberalism, however, inevitably destroys friendship as a means for social organization and thus for doing business. Personal relationships are not supposed to make a difference in Liberal interactions: judges and jury members must leave a case if they know the litigants; bank loans are decided by mathematical formulae rather than acquaintance or trust; doctors see multiple strangers as patients each day; friends and strangers all pay the same price for bread at ones bakery; and Franco–American (come on, the *French*–Americans producing your macaroni?!) makes sure their SpaghettiOs are not poisonous only because the huge corporation is afraid of lawsuits, not because it cares one bit about you and me having a healthy dinner, feeling well, living or dying in horrible gastric pain. How can it care: it has no feelings. And worse yet, the people that run it do not know you and me, they have no stake in how we feel as real people, only as potential customers, because we do not share a common life, we have no face–to–face interaction, we meet only as strangers on a huge playing field designed to make living morally all but impossible.

When Tony resorts to violence it is typically of a personal kind. He does not run shareholders and stakeholders into bankruptcy from high above, as the leaders of Enron did. He does not allow others to take his fall while still making money and supporting wide–spread violence as Dick Chaney did with his Haliburton cohorts. No. Tony shows up at your house if you do him wrong. At times he sends his most trusted friends to take care of business: Furio beats the Frenchman who swindled Artie in a bad business move; Sylvio takes Adriana for her last ride upstate. But typically, at the crisis moments, Tony himself takes care of business. He waits at the country home with a shotgun to blow away his cousin without a word; he cuts off Ralphie's head and puts it in a bowling bag; he garrotes the rat and puts Pussy to bed with the fishes.

Part of the reason we take a certain pleasure in some of Tony's violence, then, is that we see him using it out of frustration in a Liberal world where friendship, acquaintance, and close personal relationships are being ignored. When Uncle Junior's doctor starts ignoring him and his worries about his cancer, for instance, we all know the feeling. Uncle Junior does not want to put faith in a system, in an HMO, or in a scientific treatment plan. He wants to put faith in another person. But Dr. Kennedy is part of the Liberal world. He doesn't care about Junior. How could he? He doesn't really know him at all. The doctor is trained to do a job like any other, and he does his best because he does not want to be sued and have his malpractice insurance go up, not because he takes Junior's Good as such as his own, a Good that is necessarily unknown to him. What Junior wants–what we all want–is for someone to be working to cure our illnesses because he or she cares, because he or she takes our best interest to heart and truly sees how our Goods are intertwined. When Dr. Kennedy continues to snub Junior, then, Tony and Furio pay him a visit on the golf course and convince him at least to play the part of a caring physician so that Uncle Junior does not give up hope in curing his cancer. As Tony threatens Dr. Kennedy in a "friendly" yet deadly–serious way, he slowly backs him into a water–trap on the golf course. Furio "playfully" smacks the doctor's hat off because it had a fictional bee on it, and they let the man know "[t]here are worse things that can happen to people than cancer" ["Second Opinion"]. Tony knows that he needn't harm this man, that the threat will work just fine, and we are happy with this as well.[2] We are happy to see someone chip away at Liberalism.

Something similar is working in the case of Dr. Melfi's rapist ["Employee of the Month"]. When the attacker goes free on a technicality, we are outraged; but having such a rule is important in a faceless, bureaucratic, Liberal justice system. Without guaranteeing the accused his or her rights, there can be no justice on a large scale. Without guaranteeing a secure chain of custody in handling evidence, how can we go about prosecuting the millions of people we end up prosecuting each year? No matter that it is personally clear to all involved that this particular man is guilty of this particular rape. The procedure outweighs personal experience in importance in the Liberal system. And so, the attacker walks away a free man. We would understand if Dr. Melfi acted on her impulse to mention what has happened to Tony. Tony–the protective bulldog–would surely set wheels in motion that would punish this man and "squash him like a bug." And yet Dr. Melfi chooses to remain silent.

Her silence is not for fear of having Tony do something unjust. Tony's is a less Liberal, and surely more outwardly violent, system of justice, but he does not dispense punishment thoughtlessly. He will, that is, do everything he can to find out if the fellow he saw in Maine really was Febby Petrulio, the rat who sold out his friends. When Tony threatens a doctor, he does so in the name of what could have been, what should be, of someone truly caring for another. Is it ironic that Tony's threat of violence is actually an echo of a call for trust, caring, and friendship? When Tony murders Petrulio, he does so in the name of trust, loyalty, and honor. Petrulio, too, has rejected friendship. Is it ironic that Tony then murders in the name of friendship? Is it absurd to say that the only way left to be a true friend to Petrulio is to murder him?

We are big–pussy footing around a dangerous point: to take this person as a true Other, one must respect him enough to kill him? There are Kantian echoes here, I know. Kant (in)famously outlawed all murder–for any reason (even self–defense)–but was in favor of capital punishment, arguing that to *not* kill the killer is to treat him with less respect and dignity than he deserves, to treat him as if he did not possess a free will, as if he were not capable of realizing that murder is a false maxim (one that cannot be universalized without logical contradiction). In order to treat the murderer as an end in and of himself, then, Kant would whack him.

A critique of this bad Kantian reasoning would take us too far of course now, but it is important to note the general sense in which Kant goes wrong. His equation of logic and ethics, his Liberal view of the individual in general, and his suspect reasoning that an executioner is not a murdered himself all deserve attention, but more to the point we should look at the sense in which Kant would argue that the murderer freely willed to commit his crime. Free choice, as we have seen, is the ultimate value for a Liberal. Since the Liberal individual is metaphysically disconnected from all Others and from the world, the Liberal definition of freedom is having the individual will disconnected as well. This value of choice, then, becomes a foundation for Liberalism in all of its guises. We think someone is free if he or she can vote for either for Bush or Kerry (choice!), if there are fifty different types of breakfast cereals on the shelf (choice!!), if a man is homeless and sick and destitute yet no one is physically keeping him from getting a job and becoming the next Bill Gates (choice!!!). For a communitarian, choice is a value, but it is one among many–and it is never taken to be radically free. Other wills intersect with my own, and the narratives in which I find myself will always be setting boundaries to my choice. None of us–not Michael Corleone, not Tony Soprano, not John–Paul Sartre, not you, and not me–are doomed to radical freedom.

Still, though, it is unclear if violence is ever truly to be condoned–whether freely chosen or not. Should killing a business associate ever be anything but immoral? Could Tony–however illogically, however impossibly, however absurd it sounds–have let his best friend and greatest betrayer, Big Pussy, live and still have been Pussy's true friend? Could he have found a way to save him *and* remain true to him? Can our violently shattered postmodern identity *not* be a hallmark of our way of interacting as well? Could Tony have chosen something other than what he apparently must have done? Could Pussy have lived and the world stayed in one piece? Could Pussy have lived!?

Have another plate of *mani–got* for now. Don't worry. You'll figure it all out tomorrow.

In the end, perhaps the *agita* of identity is a sign, the trace of violence inherent in all becoming and all being. Perhaps it is an indication that we are never fully realized, never truly made, never free from the responsibility of choosing right over wrong even when the choice is less than free, less than really ours. This, then, is what it means to be in the business of a wise guy: to know just how little we know as we simultaneously refuse to accept our short cut. It is to know that even envelopes of cash stuffed into youthful pockets on quiet Midwestern nights make us who we are, and we will echo these moments the rest of our lives in a world that was never fully innocent.

## Notes

1. Bank of America assets in 1998 were $618 billion; in 2004 they are $930 billion.
2. A nearly identical thing is happening when Carmela takes the pineapple ricotta pie to Jeannie Cusamano's sister and asks for a letter of recommendation to Georgetown for Meadow ["Full Leather Jacket"]. (Note that Tony also starts with a gift–a new golf club–for the doctor.) Georgetown will have tens of thousands of applications, with no way to tell who are the best students apart from mathematical, statistical analysis of GPA's and SAT's, etc. A supporting letter from someone that an admissions officer might know can make all the difference. Carmela calls on a friend's family for the favor, but the sister refuses even to look at Meadow's dossier, arguing that she only writes one letter

a year and already wrote that letter (for a disadvantaged youth she obviously does not even personally know). Carmela's threat does the job and makes the Liberal process a bit more personal, even if that personalism is, in the end, a facade.

# 13

# Tissue Banking: Disclosure, Informed Consent, and the Rule of Law

## Michele Goodwin

*Since 1996, 33 infections associated with CryoLife heart valves have been reported. Four patients died, including 5-year-old Sydney Steinberg. She developed a fatal infection after receiving a CryoLife valve. Officials say many more cases go unreported . . . .*[1]

## Introduction

Accelerated growth in biotechnology and medical science are creating new uses for human tissue that were once presumed to have limited value beyond their original function and hosts. Human tissue and organs that once were suited for burial at death or disposed of after medical procedures have found new life and value in research laboratories and commercial biotechnology supply companies.[2] Although cadavers have traditionally been used for educational purposes, the expanded exploitation of human tissues and organs has forced a fundamental reconsideration of legal and moral issues associated with human experimentation.

Human cells are now invaluable to the creation and production of human biologics.[3] Advocates of human tissue usage anticipate cures for cancer, the development of miracle drugs, and an end to genetic ignorance. However, some critics condemn medical practitioners and scientists for masquerading as gods, evading ethical norms, and commercializing biotechnology. These broadly divergent views reveal inescapable ethical, legal, moral, and political conundrums. On one hand, if scientists are correct, the utilization of the human body for scientific research and reprocessing for transplants is imperative for the advancement of biotechnology and saving lives. Yet, the commercialization and underground selling, buying, and reselling of human biological material compels consideration as to whether interests and rights exist in the human body, and if so, in whom do such rights vest. We must also consider the business ethics of an industry that reveals little to altruistic donors and exploits that ignorance.

Annually, about 650,000 Americans have surgery involving soft–tissues and skin, bones, and tendons taken from cadavers. One company, CryoLife, which has been the subject of investigations by the Centers for Disease Control (CDC), and lawsuits from former patients or their estates, supplies 15–20 percent of the overall market. CryoLife is the nation's largest supplier of heart valves from human cadavers. It controls a monopoly–size market share of 90 percent of vascular tissue and 70 percent of heart valves. How companies obtain their cadavers and cadaver parts might shock most Americans. Tissue processing companies purchase parts from hospitals, universities and other institutions to which bodies are *altruistically* donated. Some companies boast that one cadaver reaps over $200,000.00 in value. They trade on the global stock exchanges and enjoy huge profit margins.

The challenge in parsing out the trade in body parts is that it is wedged between two legal processes, altruistic donation and legalized tissue implantation. In between is the black market industry that practically receives bodies and parts for tiniest fraction of their profit and charge huge mark–ups to doctors and hospitals. Controversy erupted at the University of Los Angeles (UCLA) Medical School in 2004, when reporters discovered that Ernest Nelson, a middle man for Fortune 500 companies, regularly emptied the medical school of body parts. Mr. Nelson, in collaboration with at least one medical school official, Henry Reid, the former chief of cadaver procurement, began the first part of reprocessing himself. Nelson sawed off limbs, torsos, and other body parts, disfiguring the donated cadavers, twice per week. He later sold bodies and parts to high–profile, commercial entities that trade in body parts and make new ones that they process and sell to hospitals and doctors who transplant the parts into patients. Henry Reid, the Director of the Willed Body Program at UCLA, is reported to have profited significantly, making about $700,000 over the course of a few years. The subsequent international uproar revealed how little the donors know about the underground market of selling and reprocessing altruistically donated bodies.

The UCLA cadaver robbing scandal revealed an open secret in a lucrative industry, which is estimated to be worth more than a billion dollars per year. Reid and Nelson are simply middle men who help to fuel larger companies that are proscribed from buying body parts directly. Tissue banks usurp federal regulations by obtaining cadaver parts from government–affiliated organ procurement organizations and university hospitals. The National Organ Transplantation Act (NOTA), passed by Congress in 1984, proscribes the selling of body parts. Violation of the act can result in a five year criminal conviction and a $50,000 fine. Yet the law is flaunted regularly through regulatory gaps that allow for cadavers and parts to ostensibly be traded for "reprocessing fees," "packaging," and "transportation costs."

Lack of federal and state oversight with regard to how companies obtain body parts and NOTA enforcement gaps contribute to the underground, nefarious black market in body part trading. Much is to be learned by the UCLA scandal. First, donor outrage indicated that the consent obtained by UCLA from donors was less informed and more illusory than real. Donors reported feeling humiliated and disgraced that their loved ones were desecrated for a pecuniary interest. The nonconsensual harvesting of bodies donated to the UCLA medical school violated donor trust and exposed the weaknesses inherent in informed consent agreements. Informed consent dictates that individuals actually be informed of the risks and benefits associated with their decision–making. In this case, UCLA was obligated to disclose to the donors how the body parts were to be used and that the medical school might generate income from the disposition of body parts. Without valid informed consent injured individuals (even third parties) may have actionable claims against the parties that caused the harm. Yet, informed consent agreements are difficult to enforce, particularly with cadavers; body parts are difficult to trace and unlike an injured patient, cadavers do not communicate.

Second, the scandal also illuminated our limited social understanding or categorical ignorance of the body trading world, collateral health risks and the economics of that industry. Two years ago on May 14, 2003, the Senate Governmental Affairs Committee, chaired by Susan Collins, held a hearing to investigate the risks, and deaths, associated with routine knee transplants in the United States. The focus of that hearing was to learn more about the death of Brian Lykins, a 23 year old college student from Minnesota, and to determine why the Food and Drug Administration (FDA) had failed to implement regulations to protect a largely naïve and unsuspecting public.  This was the first time that Leslie and Steven Lykins, Brian's parents, spoke to government officials about their son's death following a simple knee implant that resulted in his death.

Several years before the hearings, in 1997, government officials at the FDA acknowledged the many health complications and risks associated with tissue transplants as well as the need for greater oversight in light of the rapidly expanding commercial market in human tissues.  However, this acknowledgement seemed largely confined to congress; the public remains in the dark.  Tissue, similar to blood transfusions, can transmit hepatitis, HIV, mad cow disease, bacteria, and various other communicable diseases to the unsuspecting transplant host.  Indeed, most individuals are unaware that human bones, from cadavers (some that were donated never with the intent of being part of a "commercial industry"), are the preferred source for enhancing or replacing knees, heart valves, and other body parts.

Yet, despite the FDA's knowledge of the many health risks associated with cadaver reprocessing and transplantation, including death, paralysis, comas, and other health traumas, the agency did little to respond.  Lack of federal laws, little if any regular monitoring of private, for–profit tissue firms, and often substandard processing facilities where the new body parts are made or the old ones sterilized and reprocessed, are the less desirable aspects of the tissue transplantation industry.

This chapter analyzes the law and ethics of body part trading.  It scrutinizes the clandestine nature of the commercial body part trading industry, including the surreptitious nature of body part procurement and the risks associated with their products.  It focuses in part on one company, CryoLife, which has been the subject of active litigation for placing defective body parts on the market.  CryoLife litigation is an appropriate starting point for this study; as its case against the Superior Court of California was a case of first impression involving the sale and purchase of contaminated human tissue.  This chapter by no means intends to single out this particular company.  However, both the human tragedy and curious legal outcomes of CryoLife litigation deserve serious scrutiny by practitioners, business leaders, and scholars.

This chapter also studies the applicability of strict liability to claims against human tissue manufacturers for breach of duty.  Part II provides an overview of whom the market in tissues is intended to help.  It highlights the narratives of three tissue transplant recipients who became ill or died as a result of receiving contaminated tissue and later sued the company that supplied the tissue. Part III analyzes the strict liability causes of action brought by injured plaintiffs. It examines whether product liability applies to companies that manufacture and sell tissue based products. It considers whether cadaveric tissue is a product or a service. Part III considers whether organs are comparable to tissues for purposes of affirmative defense under the rubric of blood shield laws. Part IV concludes by arguing that strict liability is an appropriate remedy for patients injured by tissue banks placing contaminated products in the stream of commerce. This section supports the strict liability application to tissue bank manufacturers based on their strictly pecuniary organized interests, the public's inability to test their products prior to purchase and implantation, and because such companies are in the best position to avoid accidents.

## Part II:  Buyer Beware

Most surgeries involving the use of cadaveric tissue are elective; the surgeries enhance the quality of life after strain or tensions in the knees or other body parts. Soft tissues used for heart valves, on the other hand, are life saving products, transplanted into patients with life–threatening conditions. Most patients who elect to use life enhancing or life saving therapies may be unaware of the "brands" or manufacturers of the tissues used in these routine operations. Part II visits the stories of several individuals who suffered from fatal or near fatal diseases after transplantation with human tissue. As a market share, they are a very small group. On the other hand, some illnesses will not be detected as quickly as in the stories described in Part II. Weeks, sometimes months later the bacteria may be discovered and its link to the implantation may be overlooked. In addition, patients and their physicians may not attribute the diseases to the cadaveric implanted parts; most might assume that only tested tissues would end up in the stream of commerce and they would be wrong.

## Three Narratives

### Brian

Brian Lykin's life was cut short after a routine knee operation. According to one of his family's lawyers, whom I interviewed for this chapter, he needed only the equivalent of a pin to be placed into his knee. Brian was a healthy, outgoing 23 year old engineering student. He was a self–taught musician and very close to his family. The surgery he required was a routine out–patient surgery. What Brian received was more than he bargained for; CryoLife, the company that sold the tendon to transplant into Brian's knee, processed it from a cadaver, which remained unrefrigerated for nineteen hours. The cadaver from which the allograft was acquired had been rejected by other tissue processing companies.

Despite Cryolife's tests on the cadaver, which revealed infection, the company sold the tendon at a tremendous mark–up to the hospital where the operation took place. On November 7, 2001, Brian's new tendon was implanted. Within hours, his condition rapidly deteriorated. By the evening he was extremely ill. In less than one week's time he was dead. He died on November 11, 2001 as a result of an allograft which had been contaminated with bacteria from the bowel of a cadaver donor which was manufactured and sold by Cryolife, Inc.

### Bonny

Bonny Gonyer lives in Wisconsin. During most of her life, she was an active woman–she was crew chief with the United States Air Force and served during Desert Storm–she now has limited rotation and flexibility in her right leg. Married, with three kids, activities were a important part of her family's life. From horseback riding, running, swimming and even boogie boarding, Bonny was actively involved with her husband and children. On February 4, 2001, Bonny tore her right anterior cruciate ligament while skiing. Her condition was not an unusual sporting accident. Nor was it the type of injury that would result in a Clostridium infection. Two months after the tear, in April 2001, Bonny received a hemi–patellar tendon from CryoLife. Unfortunately, the allograft she received was contaminated with Clostridium, a potentially deadly disease. Bonnie's condition dramatically deteriorated. Several surgeries were required after the initial diseased implant. Unlike Brian, Bonnie did not die, but her knee will only bend to a 90 degree angle.

### Ken

Ken is perhaps the lucky one. He was the only one of a group of patients who did not die from a heart valve implant processed by Cryo-Life technicians in 2001. Like Bonny Gonyers, Ken Alescu was an avid sporting fan and a parent. He skied, hiked, and was scuba diver. Now, after receiving an infected cadaveric heart valve processed by CryoLife, even walking is a challenge for him. Weeks after his surgery, doctors "opened up" his chest and according to Mr. Alescu, "found the heart was covered with growth, fungal growth."[4] Despite health inspectors from the CDC finding unsanitary conditions at the

CryoLife laboratories, federal officials recalled only the CryoLife orthopedic tissues in 2002 and not the heart valves. The FDA noted a lack of confidence in the company's ability to keep cadaver tissue "free from fungal and bacterial infection."[5] According to Dan Jernigan who worked for the CDC, "these tissue heart valves are something that are needed by patients, and CryoLife has a very large part of the market and it is important to make sure we can treat patients appropriately."[6]

## The Problem

Several problems attend human tissue transplantation and the reconstitution of body parts. Some of these problems are illuminated in the earlier narratives of Brian, Bonny, and Ken. There are other incredibly sympathetic stories, including that of Sydney Steinberg, a five year old who died from a heart valve infection possibly linked to CryoLife, the supplier of the valve that she received. The tensions in this area have much to do with the significant demand for body parts and the growth of biotechnology. To the extent that treatments are now available for worn out knees and joints and defective or blocked heart valves, doctors will continue to recommend treatments for their patients. Their failure to do so might be actionable itself; failure to enhance, even by chance, a patient's health outcome. Thus, it appears, orthopedic knee surgeries and heart valve operations involving cadaveric parts are here to stay.

Yet, problems are unresolved, even with the CDC's investigations revealing the numerous problems at the CryoLife laboratories, and as will be discussed, the very direct links between the deaths and illness of Brian, Bonny, and Ken and cadaveric sources used by the company that processed and sold the body parts. Among the problems are that we lack public understanding and awareness about the global industry of body part buying, selling, re–trading, and transplanting. Recent court decisions place the burden on patients to be aware of the industry in order to proactively guard against possible contamination from diseased implants. Yet, how are patients to know where the purchased part comes from–not simply the processor–but the cadaver? Patients and their doctors are at a disadvantage; they are uninformed about the cadaver's (if they know that much), lifestyle, sexual habits, prior illnesses, whether s/he was a smoker, drinker, or drug user. The Food and Drug Administration (FDA) does not require companies to be a registered member of a certified tissue bank association, such as the Tissue Bank Association of America, TBAA. Rather, each company selects its own method for testing tissues, determining whether it will test and treat tissues at all, and whether it will inform patients and physicians about the results of those tests.

It is here that the story of tissue giant, CryoLife, its processes, and its setbacks are instructive for legal, ethical, and business analysis. Although lawsuits have been settled against CryoLife, the Court of Appeal of California determined in 2003 that CryoLife is immune from liability for the body parts it places into the stream of commerce.[7] According to the court, CryoLife's immunity arises from their interpretation that buying collecting, processing, storing, and selling body parts is a "service" and that the parts sold are not "goods," but rather services.[8]

The Appellate court decision forces a fundamental consideration of what exactly cadaveric body parts are. Hardly anyone would think of his or her knee, heart, hip, or spine as a service. Likewise, of course, tissue banks leery of litigation, are equally reluctant to treat knees as goods, exposing the need for a common lexicon and understanding as the legal and social status of cadaveric body parts. Yet, in the changing lexicon and use of body parts, our common understanding of items obtained at hospitals is that they are goods, and the service is that which the surgeon and hospital facilitates. In other words, *what* CryoLife *processes* describes its service, *what* it *produces* through that processing is a good or *product* for which it receives value.

Yet, the California Court of Appeal was not persuaded.[9] It construed CryoLife's claim that its products are similar to that of not–for–profit organizations like the Red Cross and blood banks to be valid.[10] The court determined that despite the language differences between California's Health & Safety Code and the state's blood shield immunity law, that the same laws that protected blood banks from litigation should also protect for–profit tissue banks.[11] The court reasoned that the California Health and Safety Code treated providing blood as a "service" rather than a good.[12] Moreover, the Health & Safety Code provided immunity from strict liability claims for blood related services. The court held that CryoLife was a "health dispensary" and immune from strict products liability, because it dispensed cadaveric tissue for transplantation.[13]

Herein are the praxis and pitfalls that relate to tissue industry accountability, scientific knowledge and practical application of tissue transplantation. First, at the time that blood shield laws were passed, tissue banking was virtually a non–reality. The tissue banking industry did not exist, nor was there gross industry profit from procuring, harvesting, evaluating, selling, preserving, promoting, selling, trading, or distributing tissue as is currently the case. Blood shield laws promulgated in the 1950s and 60s, are now enacted in 47 states. The regulations protect blood banks from future strict liability claims for distributing contaminated blood products, including clotting factor concentrate.

Second, tissue banks do not fit within the legislative exception and could not have been predicted by legislators of the 1950s. To suggest that legislators had a vision of twenty–first century biotechnology in 1955 is illogical and unreasonable. So why should such laws apply to industries that have developed since then? Arguably, tissue banks were not the class of entities legislators sought to protect from litigation. Third, that the tissue industry is a profit–motivated industry, which responds to market demand, share holders, and trades on the global stock exchanges, places its services and the products that result from those services in an entirely different category than blood suppliers. In addition, most of the services for which it provides products are elective. Fourth, it is unreasonable to expect that buyers of tissue products will actually inspect them or have the immediate financial and technical resources to do so. Placing the responsibility on unsophisticated patients, who are already vulnerable, uneducated in the language and reality of tissue processing, is unduly burdensome. Patients are in the least opportune position to serve as a "check" in the tissue processing industry. Finally, biotechnology outpaces regulation and judicial awareness. Part III analyzes these issues, beginning with a negligence framework to test whether tissue banks fall within traditional notions of companies that owe duties to the public.

## Part III:  Strict Liability and Tissue Selling

In *CryoLife v. Superior Court*[14] the Appellate Court of California addressed a case of first impression. Never before, in that state's judicial history, had a claim for strict liability against a tissue processor and distributor been litigated in a California court. Thus, the court's guidance was limited by the very fact that the legislature had not anticipated tissue bank products liability claims and that the court had no prior precedents on which to rely. By contrast, it was well established that "strict products liability does not apply to blood banks or other institutions that provide blood transfusions and blood products."[15] The court wrestled with the question of whether the blood shield law applied, but seemed to skip over the actual elements for the common law tort. Immunity is simply an affirmative defense to the actual negligence claim. Thus, immunity provides a shield for liability, but does not negate the actual wrong; it only signifies that the tort doer will not be responsible for paying for his negligence. Let us compare the facts from one of our narratives, those from the Lykins case, to determine the feasibility of future strict liability claims for contaminated tissue based products.

## Strict Liability

According to the *New York Times*, by December 2001, a CDC investigation uncovered that the cadaveric supplier of Brian Lykin's knee had committed suicide a month before Brian's operation.[16] The body was not refrigerated for 19 hours after being picked up by a tissue bank. Other tissue banks rejected the cadaver finding it was potentially unsafe for use. CryoLife, however, purchased the cadaver and began processing. In a similar case, that did not, however, result in death, Alan J. Minvielle, had a routine knee operation using an allograft consisting of a patellar tendon obtained from a human cadaver. The allograft was supplied by CryoLife. Minvielle's knee pain "increased after the surgery, and, two months later, the allograft was removed because it was infected with bacteria."[17]

Minvielle's product liability claim was based on several theories. The plaintiff claimed that CryoLife's allograft products were not fit for their intended use of implantation in humans. The plaintiff alleged that CryoLife failed to warn the plaintiff and or his physicians about the risks involved in using CryoLife's potentially contaminated tissues. Further, according to Minvielle, CryoLife established a chain of command over the tissue from procurement to distribution and labeling, but failed to reveal that its products were defective. The most serious charges were that the company misled patients and health care providers and "maliciously denied that an infection could be caused by its products.[18]

The first question to consider is whether, if allegations can be established as true, product liability can attach for misleading the public and placing faulty products in the marketplace. Three main theories provide for plaintiff relief for product–related injuries: negligence, warranty, and strict liability. Strict liability provides a more substantive remedy for plaintiffs than traditional negligence law. Most states use Restatement § 402A as the source of doctrine governing strict liability claims. Under strict liability claims, the plaintiff must demonstrate proof of an injury, but she is not required to show a lack of due care by the defendant.

*Greenman v. Yuba Power Products*,[19] another California case, is the landmark decision for modern product liability claims. In Greenman, the Supreme Court of California considered whether the retailer and the manufacturer of a Shopsmith, a power tool "that could be used as a saw, drill, and wood lathe" could be held liable for head injuries sustained by the plaintiff when an attachment advertised and sold for the tool unexpectedly flew out of the machine and struck Mr. Greenman on the forehead.

According to Justice Traynor in the Greenman decision, a manufacturer is strictly liable in tort "when an article he places on the market, knowing that it is to be used without inspection for defects, proves" to be defective and causes an injury to "a human being."[20] The purpose of strict liability is to insure that the costs of injuries resulting from defective products are borne on manufacturers that place goods in the marketplace rather than the powerless individuals who purchase the products and are otherwise unable to protect themselves. Traynor suggested that implicit in products being on the market is the representation by its manufacturer that "it would safely do the jobs for which it was built."[21]

The Restatement (Second) of Torts provides the general framework adopted by most states. § 402 A of the Restatement establishes the test for strict liability for the manufacture or distribution of defective products. It provides:

(1)     One who sells any product in a defective condition unreasonably dangerous to the user or consumer or to his property is subject to liability for physical harm thereby caused to the ultimate user or consumer, or to his property, if

(a) the seller is engaged in the business of selling such a product, and

(B) it is expected to and does reach the user or consumer without substantial change in the condition in which it is sold.

(2)     The rule stated in Subsection (1) applies although

(a) the seller has exercised all possible care in the preparation and sale of his product, and

(b) the user or consumer has not bought the product from or entered into any contractual relation with the seller.

Thus, product liability claims require only that the plaintiff, the injured party, demonstrate that the product is defective. The plaintiff is not required to show privity between the plaintiff and manufacturer. Neither is the plaintiff required to demonstrate that the manufacturer acted "unreasonably." Strict liability has been interpreted to be a "pro–plaintiff" theory of law because of its less rigid requirements to establish manufacturer liability. Part of the rationale for this is that manufacturers are in the better position to prevent the accidents that result from their defective products. Plaintiffs assume that advertisements about the safety and utility of the manufacturer's products are true and that the purchased products are free from defects. The defects covered under strict liability law can be a) manufacturing defects (products that fail to meet the manufacturers' specifications; b) design defects (products with unsafe designs); and c) defects in warnings or instructions or products that lack information to make their use less dangerous.

The public policy rationale for product liability was established by Traynor's concurring opinion in the infamous *Escola v. Coca–Cola Bottling Co. of Fresno* case where he suggested that fairness in a modern, industrialized society, requires making manufacturers responsible for the injuries caused by their products.[22] In that case, a waitress was injured by an exploding Coca–Cola bottle. Although the court affirmed the judgment against the manufacturer based on another tort doctrine, Traynor's concurring opinion opened the door for strict liability consideration.

To determine whether strict liability should apply to tissue manufacturers, we must consider whether its activities fall within the general framework established through the Restatement and prior case law, which albeit, involves non–tissue manufacturers. The primary prong for successfully establishing a product liability claim against a manufacturer is to demonstrate that the product was defective. However, the defendant class is not limited to the manufacturer of products. Rather any entity that plays a role in the manufacture, distribution, or sale of a product is a potential defendant and therefore subject to liability. Within this framework, when a product does not function in a way in which its manufacturer's intend, and the defect contributes to an injury suffered by the plaintiff, the product is characterized as having a manufacturing defect. Moreover, if a product has a manufacturing or design defect, plaintiff can recover under strict liability for injuries related to those defects regardless of manufacturer warning labels being present.

## Strict Liability and CryoLife: Product, Service or Both

Liability in the tissue industry for the distribution, processing, handling, and selling of products is largely premised on whether we consider those processes to be the manufacturing and processing of a "product" or providing a service. Such issues may best be resolved by turning to the dictionary for a better grasp of our social understanding of a product versus a service. According to the *American Heritage Dictionary*, a product is "something produced by human or mechanical effort or by a natural process."[23] A service, on the other hand, is described as "employment in duties or work for another."[24] The dictionary compares it with providing consultation or doing a favor.

Thus, when compared between a "service" or "product," human tissues resemble much more closely a product, almost too exacting to be sure. Human tissue is in fact something produced by human effort, which is a natural process. Next, we must consider the question of defect and whether the manufacturer's having control over the tissues meets the requirements established by the Restatement and prior case law. To help us determine whether CryoLife's human tissue product was actually defective, we should turn to the prior health status of the patient and her postoperative condition. Although it is true that patients could acquire diseases in hospitals, it is far more likely that contaminated implants will definitely result in life–threatening illnesses.

In the case of Brian Lykins, for example, the deadly bacteria found in the tendon implanted in his knee, Clostridium sordelli, was not pre–operatively present in his body. Yet, following his death and several illnesses that resulted from similar implants in Minnesota from Cryo-Life products, the CDC visited the manufacturer. The CDC first learned of the unusual length of time the body was kept unrefrigerated, which was well outside the time permitted by industry standards. CryoLife's claims that its products were safe and that the rare bacterium could have been picked up anywhere were less persuasive when CDC investigators "then found two strains of the deadly Clostridium in the donor's other knee, which was still in CryoLife's warehouse."[25] Moreover, of the nearly twenty tissue samples that were not implanted, at least two contained the exact bacteria that killed Lykins.[26] Scientists from the CDC linked all Clostridium infected tissues to the bacteria in the "cadaver's gastrointestinal tract."[27]

If human tissues are more likely products than services, then their contamination would seem to make them "unsafe" products. Moreover, an unsafe product used for medical processes would seem to be inconsistent with manufacturer intent, and certainly inconsistent with patient, physician, and hospital expectation. Unsafe products by their very definition are defective, no? Likewise, infection of deadly viruses in transplantable tissue must within a legal definition render them defective products. According to the common law and Restatement of Torts, a manufacturer need not know nor intend to distribute a defective product in order for strict liability to attach. Rather, it is sufficient that the item appear in the stream of commerce and a human being is injured by the product. Recovery in strict liability is allowed if those elements are met–and they are in these cases.

That courts are slow to recognize strict liability claims against tissue manufacturers reflects an ultra–conservative stance that reflects the

*Moore v. Regents* decision that held a conversion claim by the plaintiff for nonconsensual harvesting of his tissue could not be sustained against his physicians (even though their extraction was for pecuniary gain) because individuals have no property interests in their body parts. That 1990 case, combined with cautious judiciary largely under–informed about clandestine purchasing of body parts, biotechnology, and the explosive market in the manufacturing body parts arguably led to the California Court of Appeals applying blood shield laws as affirmative defenses to products liability claims involving contaminated tissue.

It also appears from the *CryoLife v. Superior Court* that the court misconstrued the Uniform Anatomical Gift Act, UAGA, and its legislative intent. As to the latter point, this chapter shall not belabor the point, but suffice to draw the reader's attention to the fact that the UAGA was originally passed during the course of one summer in 1968, for the purpose of encouraging organ donation, long before CryoLife and other such companies ever existed. At the time with less sophisticated testing technology, the rationale for limiting hospital liability for implanting a contaminated kidney or liver was far less of a stretch and more reasonable; to encourage organ donation from dying patients and save lives. The sick patient was already in a life–threatened condition and without the organ would certainly die . Anti–rejection medications such as cyclosporine were not invented so that life with an implanted organ did not guarantee–even disease free–a patient's survival. Nor is it wise to view organs as services, but were we to do so, it invites an analysis different from the Appellate Court in *CryoLife*.

As much as a kidney is tangible, were hospitals selling products or providing services when transplants were made available? It seems the latter. Hospitals provided a service in transplanting organs with a limited time frame and chain of command to do so. Hospitals and physicians (even if they might desire to do so) can not legally purchase, nor stockpile, organs for transplantation; the supply is far too limited and organs expire far more quickly than human tissue. Thus, the technology is unavailable should there even be interest in such an industry. The storage life of a kidney is hours, but for tissues it can be years after processing.

Judicial comparison of organs and tissues and the entities that "handle" them is misapplied. The two are vastly different and the "controllers" far differently motivated. Physicians and hospitals lack the ownership interests in the organs they transplant as it also seems with regard to the prospective recipient. Yet, tissue banks have proprietary, legally recognized interest in its tissue products. The company's rights to litigate for the misuse, misappropriation, mischaracterization, and theft of the tissue are all legally protected.  Even with an understanding that hospitals provide a service and not a product, consider that the common law has evolved to allow tort claims to proceed against hospitals for negligent actions involving organ transplantation.

Finally, any tissue related services that existed in 1968, the year of the UAGA's enactment, were on the whole far less pecuniary, and focused on research.  The nature of the industry that seeks protective status through the UAGA and shielding through blood shield regulations does not appear to be the "model" intended for protection from public accountability.

# Part IV:   Conclusion

This chapter began by telling the stories of Brian Lykins, Bonny
Gonyers, and Ken Alescu, three patients whose experiences with tissue
obtained through this complex process illuminates the need for better
regulation, public disclosure, and discourse about body trading. It was
during a gap in time, between 1997 and 2003, that Brian, Bonny, and
Ken's stories unfold. Their stories reveal the clandestine and complicated nature of the tissue transplant industry in the U.S.; an insulated
world where demand for body parts from commercial processors contributes to surreptitious and sometimes downright unethical procurement strategies with limited governmental intervention.

For example, donors as well as recipients may be unaware of what
they are giving and receiving. Unsuspecting donors, now litigants in
lawsuits from Maine to California, claim to be entirely dumbfounded
by the commercial enterprise that lay behind their donations and that
relatives are now products in the stream of tissue commerce. Recipients believe that any tissue delivered to them for transplantation is safe
and disease free. Recipients assume, at times to their detriment, that
companies will voluntarily test, and should the need arise, recall products known to be contaminated.

In Bonny Gonyer's case, CryoLife received the donor cadaver
January 28, 2001, tested it and on February 5, 2001 found positive indication of Clostridium Paraputrification. Days later, on February 8,
2001, Clostridium Septicum was found, and yet, on April 23, 2001, the
tendon from the donor was shipped to Gonyer's doctors and less than
one week later, April 29, 2001, Gonyer's tested positive for Clostridium.

Strict liability is an appropriate remedy for patients injured by tissue banks placing contaminated products in the stream of commerce.
Strict liability application to tissue bank manufacturers based on their
strictly pecuniary organized interests, the public's inability to test their
products prior to purchase and implantation is consistent with contemporary social notions of fairness and legal justice. Ultimately, tissue
banks operate in a risk intense industry and are in the best position to
avoid accidents. Thinking otherwise exempts tissue banks from the
type of liability to which sister industries are exposed, such as intra
uterine device, IUD manufacturers, makers and sellers of tools, and car
manufacturers. It is well established through the *Beshada*[28] line of
cases that courts will impose responsibility on a defendant for its failure
to warn about risks that were scientifically unknowable at the time the
defendant marketed its product. The burden rightfully belongs with

tissue manufacturers to place healthy tissues in the market place or suffer the consequences for their failure to do so.

# Notes

1. CryoLife Heart Valve Patients Cry Foul, CBS News, August 27, 2002, http://www.cbsnews.com/stories/2002/08/27/eveningnews/main519937.shtml (last searched October 22, 2005).

2. See Michele Goodwin, *Commerce in Cadavers is An Open Secret*, LA. Times, March 11, 2004 at B15.

3. Aaron Smith, *Tissue From Corpses In Strong Demand: Market for Allografts Keeps Growing, Outpacing Supply*, CNN Money, October 5, 2005.

4. CryoLife Heart Valve Patients Cry Foul, CBS News, August 27, 2002, http://www.cbsnews.com/stories/2002/08/27/eveningnews/main519937.shtml (last searched October 22, 2005)

5. Id.

6. Id.

7. See *CryoLife, Inc v. The Superior Court of Santa Cruz County* 110 Cal. App. 4th 1145 (2003).

8. Id.

9. Id.

10. Id.

11. Id.

12. Id.

13. Id.

14. 110 Cal. App. 4th 1145 (2003).

15. Id. at 1152. See *also Osborn v. Irwin Memorial Blood Bank*, 5 Cal. App. 4th 272 (1992); and *Hyland Therapeutics v. Superior Court*, 175 Cal. App. 3d. 509 (1985).

16. See Sandra Blakeslee, *Recall is Ordered at Large Supplier of Implant Tissue*, N.Y. Times, August 15, 2002 at A1.

17. *CryoLife, Inc v. The Superior Court of Santa Cruz County* 110 Cal. App. 4th 1145, 1147. (2003).

18. Id. at 1149.

19. 59 Cal.2d 57 (1963).

20. Id.

21. Id.

22. 24 Cal. 2d. 453 (1944).

23. See *American Heritage Dictionary*, 1399 (4th ed. 2000).

24. *Id.* at 1591.

25. See Sandra Blakeslee, *Recall is Ordered at Large Supplier of Implant Tissue*, N.Y. Times, August 15, 2002 at A1.

26. *Id.*

27. *Id.*

28. Beshada v. Johns–Manville Products Corp, 90 N.J. 191(1982).

# About the Contributors

**Kenneth D. Alpern** is George and Arlene Foote Chair in Ethics and Professor of Philosophy at Hiram College. He also directs the College's Center for the Study of Ethical Issues. Professor Alpern received his B.A., magna cum laude, with distinction from Kenyon College, having spent his junior year at Waseda University in Tokyo, Japan. He received both M.A. and Ph.D. degrees from the University of Pittsburgh. His professional interests include ethical theory, the history of ethics, and applied ethics, especially in the areas of medicine, business, law, public policy and engineering. Professor Alpern's publications include "The Foreign Corrupt Practices Act," *Blackwell's Encyclopedic Dictionary of Business Ethics*, Patricia Werhane, and R. Edward Freeman eds., Blackwell, 1997 & 2005; "What Do We Want Trust to Be? Some Distinctions of Trust," *Journal of Business and Professional Ethics* 16 (1998), translated into Chinese in *Xin Ren Yu Sheng Yi: Zhang Ai, Yu Qiao, Liang, Trust and Business: Barriers and Bridges*, Daryl Koehn, ed., Shanghai, 2003; *The Ethics of Reproductive Technology*, editor, Oxford University Press, 1992; "Moral Responsibility for Engineers," *Business and Professional Ethics Journal* 2 (1983), version in German translation, "Ingenieure als moralische Helden," in Hans Lenk and Gunther Ropohl, eds., *Technik und Ethik*, Reclam, 1987; "Aristotle on the Friendships of Utility and Pleasure," *Journal of the History of Philosophy* 21 (1983).

**Paul F. Camenisch** is Professor of Religious Studies at DePaul University, has taught at DePaul since 1968, where he has served as chair of the Religious Studies Department and as President of the university's Faculty Council. He currently serves as Chair of the College of Liberal Arts and Sciences Faculty Governance Council and as Director of University Academic Program Review. He holds degrees from Centre College of Kentucky, Yale University Divinity School, and the Ph.D. in Religion from Princeton University. He has written one book on professional ethics, has edited another on religious resources for bio–medical ethics, and co–edited one on clerical ethics. He is the author of more than thirty professional/academic articles and book chapters.

**Frida Kerner Furman** is Professor in the Department of Religious Studies, DePaul University. Her academic interests include social ethics, feminist ethics, aging, the body, and religious/cultural identity and diversity. She is the author of *Beyond Yiddishkeit: The Struggle for Jewish Identity in a Reform Synagogue* (State University of New York Press, 1987); *Facing the Mirror: Older Women and Beauty Shop Culture* (Routledge, 1997), which was awarded the 1997 Elli Kangas–Maranda Prize by the American Folklore Society/Women's Section; and *Telling Our Lives: Conversations on Solidarity and Difference* (Roman and Littlefield, 2005, co–authored with Elizabeth A. Kelly and Linda Williamson Nelson).

**Michele Goodwin** is the Director of the Health Law Institute and founder of the Center for the Study of Race and Bioethics. Her primary research interests are tort theory, property relationships in the body, bioethics, and biotechnology. Her scholarship examines patterns of legal distinctions based on the social markers of class, race, gender, and other distinctions. Prior to joining DePaul she was a post–doctoral fellow at Yale University, conducting research on the antebellum politics of sex and law. She was named a Hastie Fellow at the University of Wisconsin Law School, where she earned her LL.M. degree. Professor Goodwin received her B.A. degree from the University of Wisconsin and a J.D. from Boston College. She has been a visiting scholar at the University of California Law School in the Center for the Study of Law and Society and a distinguished visiting professor at Griffith University Law School (Brisbane, Australia). She is also an Affiliated Scholar with the University of Wisconsin Law School. She lectures and researches internationally. England, Austria, France, Ireland, Holland, Switzerland, and Italy are among the countries where she has been invited to presented her research.

Laura P. Hartman is the Associate Vice President for Academic Affairs at DePaul University in Chicago, Illinois, with primary responsibility for academic program development. She is also a Professor in the Management Department, teaching Business Ethics in both the undergraduate and graduate MBA programs and serving on the board of DePaul's Institute for Business and Professional Ethics. Hartman also held the Grainger Chair of Business Ethics at the University of Wisconsin–Madison School of Business. She also served as the Director of the Human Resource Management and Development Program in UW's Executive Education curriculum, and was responsible for the Ethics Program in the School of Business, the Graduate MBA, Executive MBA, and Evening MBA Business Ethics courses. Hartman is the author of numerous articles and several textbooks, including *Perspectives in Business Ethics*. Hartman's most recent research culminated in a book, *Rising Above Sweatshops*, co–edited with Denis Arnold and Rich Wokutch.

Previously, Hartman held the Grainger Chair of Business Ethics at the University of Wisconsin–Madison School of Business. She has also served as an adjunct professor of business law and ethics at Northwestern's Kellogg Graduate School of Management.

Hartman serves on the Board of Directors of DePaul's Institute for Business and Professional Ethics, previously held DePaul's Wicklander Chair in Professional Ethics, and served as chair of the university's Public Service Council. She is past president of the Society of Business Ethics and is co–founder and past co–chair of the Employment and Labor Law Section of the Academy of Legal Studies in Business. In addition, she was co–editor of the section's *Employment and Labor Law Quarterly*, and served as president of the Midwest Academy of Legal Studies in Business for the 1994–1995 term.

Hartman graduated magna cum laude from Tufts University and received her law degree from the University of Chicago Law School.

Ms. Daryl Koehn holds the Cullen Chair in Business Ethics at the University of St. Thomas in Houston. She is the founding Executive Director of the Center of Business Ethics at UST and edits the *Online Journal of Ethics*. Her books include *The Ground of Professional Ethics, Rethinking Feminist Ethics: Local Insights, Global Ethics for Business: and The Nature of Evil*. Her edited volumes include *Corporate Governance: Ethics Across the Board and Trust: Barriers and Bridges*. In additional to scores of journal articles in several languages, Professor Koehn regularly publishes in business newspapers and journals. She is routinely quoted in *The New York Times* and has been interviewed multiple times on National Public Radio. She has been profiled in *Times* and *Life* magazines. She is a past president of the Society for Business Ethics.

**Keith W. Krasemann** is Professor of Philosophy and Religious Studies and Director of the Regional Center for Asian Studies Development Programs at College of DuPage. Professor Krasemann also teaches graduate courses in Ethics and Leadership in DePaul University's School for New Learning and has developed and facilitated programs on ethics and leadership training for businesses. Currently, he has three books in print: *Business Ethics: Problems, Principles, Practical Applications* (Copley Publishing Group, 2001), *Quest for Goodness: An Introduction to Ethics* (Simon & Schuster, 1998), and *Questions for the Soul: An Introduction to Philosophy* (Copley Publishing Group, 1996). He has received awards for his outstanding teaching and humanitarian service and has published numerous articles. Krasemann received a Ph.D. in Comparative Philosophy from Pacific Western University and has both doctorate and masters degrees from Northern Illinois University in Education and Philosophy. He received a second M.A. in Applied Professional Studies at DePaul University and holds a bachelors degree in Philosophy from the University of Wisconsin, Oshkosh. He studied Chinese History and Culture at Beijing University, China. Krasemann completed graduate programs in leadership at Harvard and the University of Chicago.

**Dennis P. McCann** is the Wallace M. Alston Professor of Bible and Religion at Agnes Scott College in Atlanta/Decatur, Georgia, and Executive Director of the Society of Christian Ethics. Before coming to Agnes Scott College in 1999, McCann taught for eighteen years at DePaul University in Chicago. As Professor of Religious Studies at DePaul, he taught mostly undergraduates in the fields of Roman Catholic studies, religious social ethics, and business ethics. In 1992 he was named the first annual holder of the Wicklander Chair in Professional Ethics at DePaul University.

McCann received his STL in theology from the Gregorian University in Rome in 1971, and a Ph.D. in theology from the University of Chicago Divinity School in 1976. His publications include *Christian Realism and Liberation Theology* (Orbis Books, 1981), and *New Experiment in Democracy: The Challenge for American Catholicism* (Sheed and Ward, 1987). Along with Charles R. Strain, he authored *Polity and Praxis: A Program for American Practical Theology* (Winston/Seabury, 1985; reprinted by the University Press of America, 1990) He has served on the Board of Directors of the Society of Christian Ethics Max Stackhouse and Shirley Roels, he edited an anthology of materials for teaching business ethics within an ecumenically Christian perspective, *On Moral Business: Classical and Contemporary Resources for Ethics and Economics* (1995), published by Eerdmans Press. McCann and Patrick D. Miller recently edited *In Search of the Common Good* (2005), published by T and T Clark as part of its "Theology for the Twenty–First Century" series.

McCann has had extensive academic experience in Hong Kong, China, and other countries in east Asia. He also serves as an adjunct professor in the University Dubuque Asian MBA Program, in which he has taught the course in business ethics to MBA students in Singapore (1996), Kuala Lumpur (1997), and Hong Kong (1998). McCann received a Fulbright Fellowship for 2005–06 and will be "Scholar in Residence" at the Hong Kong American Centre at the Chinese University of Hong Kong.

**Steven H. Resnicoff** has been a member of DePaul's faculty since 1988. A graduate of Princeton University (at which he was named a "Woodrow Wilson School Scholar") and Yale Law School, Professor Resnicoff has impressively pursued a wide–ranging scholarly agenda. While he has co–authored three books (including a law school casebook) on negotiable instruments law and published numerous articles and chapters on a variety of other commercial law topics, such as arbitration, bankruptcy, fraudulent transfers, and usury, many of his more recent works focus on business and professional ethics, particularly as they pertain to attorneys and physicians. An ordained rabbi, Resnicoff is a member of the Executive Committee and former Chair of the Association of American Law Schools' Section on Jewish Law and a member of the Executive Committee, and former Chair of the Board of Trustee and Publications Committee, of the Jewish Law Association, an international organization devoted to the promotion of Jewish law studies. Professor Resnicoff has received award from DePaul's College of Law both for his teaching and his scholarship.

**Brother Leo V. Ryan**, CSV, Ph.D., Saint Louis University; LL.D (Hon.) Seton Hall; D.H.L. (Hon.) Illinois Benedictine is Professor of Management–Emeritus, DePaul University. He is a Fellow, St. Edmunds College, Cambridge, a three time Fulbright Professor at Adam Mickiewicz University, Poznan, Poland and the third rotating Wicklander Professor at DePaul. Each Spring since 1999 he has been visiting MBA Professor, Poznan University of Economics teaching HRM and Business Ethics. He is past president, Society for Business Ethics. He is co–author or co–editor of *Human Action in Business* (1996); *Etyka Biznesu* (1997); *From Autarcy to Market–Polish Economics and*

*Politics* (1998); *Students Focus on Ethics* (2000); *Praxiology and Pragmatism* (2002); *Praxiology and Pragmatism* (2002) and *Poland: A Transformational Analysis* (2003). His articles have appeared in numerous publications including: *Business Ethics–European Review, Business Ethics Quarterly, Global Economy Journal, Journal of Emerging Markets, Praxioligca, Polish Review* and chapters in various Polish texts on Business Ethics.

**Jeffrey M. Shaman** has concentrated much of his scholarship in the area of constitutional law and is a nationally recognized authority on judicial ethics. His writings have been widely cited, and he is a frequent lecturer on both topics. Professor Shaman served as senior fellow of the American Judicature Society and as president of the American Civil Liberties Union of Illinois. He is a member of the American Law Institute, the American Society of Legal History, and the U.S. Association of Constitutional Law. Professor Shaman has litigated a number of cases concerning constitutional rights and is the principal author of the Illinois Freedom of Information Act. He has won numerous awards for teaching, scholarship, and service to the community, culminating in his appointment as St. Vincent de Paul Professor of Law.

**H. Peter Steeves** is Associate Professor of Philosophy at DePaul University. His main areas of teaching and research include applied ethics (especially animal/environmental and bioethics), social and political philosophy, philosophy of culture, philosophy of science, and phenomenology. Steeves has taught at Universidad del Zulia, Venezuela and has also been a Senior Fulbright Fellow to Venezuela. He has published more than forty book chapters and journal articles, and his books include *The Things Themselves: Essays in Applied Phenomenology* (SUNY, 2005), *Founding Community: A Phenomenological–Ethical Inquiry* (Kluwer, 1998) and the edited *Animal Others: On Ethics, Ontology, and Animal Life* (SUNY, 1999). His forthcoming work includes the co–authored book *One Hundred Years of Liberalism: The Venezuela that Hugo Chávez Inherited and the Venezuela that Hugo Chávez is Re–Making* and a work on astrobiology, complexity theory, and the origin of life.

**Michael F. Skelley** has been a member of DePaul University's school of New Learning since 1993. He has a master's degree in Biblical Studies (Catholic U., 1979), a doctoral degree in Religious studies (Boston College 1987) and a master's degree in Organization Development (Loyola U. Chicago 1993). Prior to coming to DePaul, he was a faculty member in the Department of Theology at Marquette Univer-

sity. He is the author of the award–winning book *The Liturgy of the World: Karl Rahner's Theology of Worship.*
Skelley's research and teaching focuses on the interrelationships between spiritually and organizational change. He is one of only a handful of faculty members in the U.S. teaching entire courses on spirituality in organizational life. His publications on this topic have included "Creating a Spirituality of Work for Organizational Change" in *New Theology Review: An American Catholic Journal for Ministry* 9 (1996) 59–74 and "Learning Communities: A Spirituality of Work for the Information Age" in *Review for Religious* 57 (1998) 454–471. He was one of the original members of the Institute for Spirituality and Organizational Leadership at Santa Clara University's Leavey School of Business. He is also an active member of the American Academy of Religion and the Academy of Management's Management, Spirituality and Religion group. He is currently at work on a book called *Making Peace with Work: Spirituality in Organizational Life.*

**Patricia H. Werhane** was educated at Northwestern University. Professor Werhane holds the Wicklander Chair of Business Ethics at DePaul University. She is also Director of the Institute for Business and Professional Ethics in the Kellstadt School of Commerce at DePaul University with a joint appointment as the Peter and Adeline Ruffin Professor of Business Ethics and Senior Fellow at of the Olsson Center for Applied Ethics in the Darden School at the University of Virginia. She was formerly the Wirtenberger Professor of Business Ethics at Loyola University Chicago. Professor Werhane graduated from Wellesley College, and received a Ph.D. in philosophy from Northwestern University. She has been a Rockefeller Fellow at Dartmouth, Arthur Andersen Visiting Professor at the University of Cambridge, and Erskine Visiting Fellow at the University of Canterbury (New Zealand). Professor Werhane has published numerous articles and is the author or editor of fifteen books including *Ethical Issues in Business* (with T. Donaldson and Margaret Cording, seventh edition), *Persons, Rights and Corporations, Adam Smith and His Legacy for Modern Capitalism, and Moral Imagination and Managerial Decision–Making* with *Oxford University Press.* Her latest book is *Employment and Employee Rights* (with Tara J. Radin and Norman Bowie) with Blackwell's. She is the founder and former Editor–in–Chief of Business Ethics Quarterly, the journal of the Society for Business Ethics. Professor Werhane is currently a faculty advisor for the newly created Business Roundtable Ethics Institute at the University of Virginia.